ENDORSEMENTS

Joseph Z has written an important book. I especially appreciate the chapter on false prophets. False prophets are a major crisis in the Church. There is a sad tendency among Spirit-filled believers to get excited about a single gift of the Holy Spirit—to the exclusion of all the others. The gift is inevitably taken to extremes, and many have out-of-Bible experiences.

The gift du jour is prophecy. The label "prophetic" is attached to everything, including boat cruises. False prophets sneak in under the smoke screen of this excitement.

Demystifying the prophetic is now urgent. First, because false prophecy is destroying people, and second, because the true gift is powerful and needed. This book by Joseph Z lifts the fog off the invaluable gift of prophecy and true prophets.

Mario Murillo
Mario Murillo Ministries

In these last days, we are seeing biblical prophecies come to pass, as well as numerous prophetic voices coming forth. *Demystifying the Prophetic* is a must-read and a now word that will help you differentiate between the true and the false. This is an excellent tool for anyone wanting to grow in the gift of prophecy! I encourage you to read it again and again!

Sid Roth
It's Supernatural Network

In his new book *Demystifying the Prophetic*, Joseph takes on an important subject with clarity and scripture that has been misused and misunderstood by so many in the body of Christ. A must-read for those wanting to understand the prophetic and its significance in the days we are living in.

Joni Lamb
Daystar Television Network

This book is a gifted and graceful rebuke and revelation to the body of Christ. It's biblical, balanced, and bold. Joseph Z has taken us all on a journey to understand and discern the true Voice of God in our lives. In a day when the prophetic has merged into the streams of witchcraft, this book brings us back to a solid foundation of the gift of prophecy and the true office of a prophet. It's not just another book about the prophetic. It's an end-times guide on how the Church can fully step into the fullness of God. This is a Jesus book, and Jesus is the spirit of prophecy.

Pastor Greg Locke
Senior Pastor Global Vision Bible Church

Acts 13:1 tells us, "In the church that was at Antioch, there were certain prophets and teachers." These two offices spoke to Barnabas and Saul and sent them into their calling by the direction of God. Teachers represent the Word and prophets, the Holy Spirit. We need to bring an understanding of the supernatural direction in the day we are living in. Joseph Z does precisely that in his book *Demystifying the Prophetic*. His scriptural interpretation is accurate, and his understanding of the prophet is clear. You will be blessed and gain a clearer understanding of the present-day prophet's ministry.

Pastor Bob Yandian
Teacher, Author
Bobyandian.com

The prophetic life is the call of every follower of Jesus—to hear His voice as we walk with Him (John 10:27). In this book, Joseph Z shares insightful teachings and inspirational stories to help make the prophetic more accessible in your walk with God. His passion for the truth of God's Word is contagious. Get ready to be equipped and take your faith to the next level!

Dr. Ché Ahn
Senior Leader, Harvest Rock Church, Pasadena, CA
President, Harvest International Ministry
International Chancellor, Wagner University

Whether given to prophetic insights or not, we are all called to understand, discern, and work with the prophetic gifts given to the body of Christ. Joseph Z has written a powerful guidebook to the prophetic, bringing clarity to a key component of our end-time victory. I was riveted by the candor and simple yet deep way he cracked open this previously hush-hush truth.

Religious spirits can affect any of us where there is no revelation from God in an area. This book brings into clear view your prophetic identity and authority and helps you discern both the times and your place in the kingdom. I believe it will get you into position to fulfill the call of the *Ekklesia* to breathe light into the world, speaking the words of God.

I am challenged to chase after, lean in, pursue, and recover all that Jesus meant me to access and walk in after reading *Demystifying the Prophetic*.

Kellie Copeland
Author, Speaker

I can't think of a more important time for this message or a better person to deliver it than Joseph Z. God has imparted both the knowledge and experience of the prophetic to Joseph and the ability to teach it. These are the last days! We all need this book!

Jim Bakker
Christian Television Pioneer
Host, *The Jim Bakker Show*

Demystifying the Prophetic by Joseph Z is a profound and practical guide to nurturing your prophetic gift. With decades of experience discerning and communicating God's voice, he has created a powerful handbook that will equip this next generation of believers. Joseph's unparalleled wisdom and straightforward approach provide an indispensable resource for those seeking to grow and flourish in the realm of the prophetic.

Mike Signorelli
Lead Pastor, V1 Church

This book is a weapon of mass instruction! Joseph Z is arming every believer with artillery and armor to operate in the prophetic realm and take Kingdom territory. This is a once-in-a-generation book!

Joshua Feuerstein
Influencer, Broadcaster

My friend, Joseph Z, is on a heavenly assignment. His is a life and ministry that awakens within others a desire to know God on a more personal and intimate level, a quest to hear from God, and a knowing that God hears us.

Part of Joseph's assignment is his new book, *Demystifying the Prophetic*. What a powerful book! Within the covers of this new ministry resource, all of us can go deeper with God and, as we do, recognize and embrace the prophetic ministry that's alive and active on the earth today.

What I most appreciate about Joseph's new book is the amount of the Word of God interwoven into every chapter. To have an effective prophetic ministry, one must first have a deep and meaningful relationship with the Word of God. I encourage you to read this book and take lots of notes. As you do, I believe you'll be glad you did.

Dean Sikes
Founder, You Matter

Joseph Z is a rare Jesus-obsessed prophetic voice in an hour where so many want the title of Prophet but not the burden of the prophet. The book in your hands is a life message, primer, and the new gold standard for Christ-exalting, local church edifying, and Great Commission completing prophetic ministry. He has paid a costly price in consecration even to have the authority to author such an important book.

What makes Joseph Z rare is his willingness to say what is needed. Not what is popular. This book is theologically tethered to the person and work of Jesus Christ and His Word. Prepare to encounter both encouragement and correction. The Presence of Jesus awaits!

Dr. Malachi A. O'Brien
Forever a full-time prayer and fasting addict
Former Vice President, Southern Baptist Convention
Ambassador, International House of Prayer, Kansas City

Demystifying the Prophetic is a game-changer for the prophetic movement. Bishop Bill Hamon, Cindy Jacobs, and James Goll are true fathers and mothers—pioneers—in the modern prophetic movement; Joseph Z honors this sterling legacy while bringing something fresh to the table. He provides practical and powerful perimeters for prophets and prophetic people to operate in to minister with power, safety, accuracy, and integrity. I always say that the best prophets love the Scriptures more than they love to prophesy; Joseph, I am learning, is such an individual, and as a result, his teaching is sound, and his delivery is trustworthy.

Larry Sparks, MDiv
Publisher, Destiny Image
Author, *Pentecostal Fire*

What a great joy to endorse anything Joseph Z does. I have found him to be a man of integrity who hears from God. His new book, *Demystifying the Prophetic*, is a crucial word to appreciate God's voice for the time we are living. Joseph accentuates our understanding in this key work to better understand the gift of prophecy and the prophet. As Joseph asserts from 1 Corinthians 14, the job of prophecy is to strengthen, encourage, and comfort, and upon occasion to give a corporate word of knowledge.

It is every believer's responsibility to prophesy into our culture. In your hands is a tool to use till the very end. Make use of this beautiful weapon made available in Joseph Z's penetrating book. It's time to prophesy!

Ron McIntosh
President, Ron McIntosh Ministries
Author of *Shift, Quest for Revival,*
The Missing Ingredient, and others

Jesus Himself reveals to us in Matthew 16:13-18 that when we give place to the Voice and Word of our heavenly Father above the report of the world and the reactions of our flesh, the gates of hell cannot prevail. It has never been more critical that the Church moves in a high level of the prophetic. I cannot think of anyone better than Joseph Z to help us. He flows powerfully in the prophetic, believes in prophetic integrity and accountability, and is an excellent teacher and communicator. *Demystifying the Prophetic* is much more than "the prophetic made simple." This is understanding the prophetic from heaven's perspective so we can all move in this gift more powerfully, with a fuller understanding and a renewed sense of awe, responsibility, and integrity. Well done, Joseph. Thank you for this important, needed, and empowering book, my friend!

Robert Hotchkin
Founder, Robert Hotchkin Ministries
Men on the Frontlines
roberthotchkin.com

Joseph Z is a strong prophetic voice in this hour. This book is a right-now message that not only gives language to hearing and understanding the Voice of God, but will mark you and stir your heart to find your mountain and build history with The Great I AM.

Matt Cruz
Evangelist
MattCruz.com

It's rare to find a genuine prophetic leader with the heart of a teacher, and yet this is what Joseph has so eloquently demonstrated in his writing. This book should be an indispensable reference text for anyone with a prophetic calling. By building precept upon precept from the Word of God, bringing clarity to this often misunderstood office, the reader will be taught as a student to accurately discern revelation from God, interpret it, and apply it. This alone is worth reading the book for! Be prepared to have the "mystery" taken out of the prophetic in your life and start understanding with spiritual clarity!

Ashley & Carlie Terradez
Terradez Ministries International Global Church Family

First Corinthians 14 reveals that God desires all of His children to operate in the gift of prophecy. *Demystifying the Prophetic* is a scriptural handbook for the prophetic that brings clarity and understanding concerning this important desire of God's heart. In this book, Joseph shares practical teaching and personal stories that will help any Christian increase their prophetic acumen and become a yielded vessel that God can use to do amazing things. I highly encourage you to read and apply what you learn from this timely book.

Kerrick Butler
Senior Pastor
Faith Christian Center

Whether you're new to prophecy or seeking to deepen your spiritual connection, Joseph's groundbreaking book makes the complex world of prophecy understandable for everyone. Through clear explanations and real-life examples, it takes you on a journey to unlock the secrets of hearing and interpreting the messages of God. If there was ever a time to hear and interpret the Voice of God, it is now! What sets this book apart is its emphasis on applying prophetic insights to the days ahead.

Mondo De La Vega
Author, Host

Welcome to prophet school! These pages are a primer for pastors and saints who want to better understand or experience the prophetic gift in revelation, interpretation, or application.

Douglas Weiss, PhD
Executive Director, Heart to Heart Counseling Center
Co-Host, *Ministry Now* on Daystar

Demystifying the Prophetic is the most thorough, practical, and inspiring teaching on prophecy I have ever encountered. Become a prophecy expert in one read! You will learn the full scope of the prophetic with its proper functions and parameters while at the same time gaining a more earnest desire for the greatest spiritual gift.

Ken Peters
Senior Pastor
Patriot Church

In his book *Demystifying the Prophetic*, Joseph Z removes the mystical from the prophetic. He beautifully weaves a very rich and solid biblical foundation into this book that makes the prophetic ministry palatable spiritually and practically. The subject of the prophetic has been viewed by many in the body of Christ as a weird, spooky, and mystical ministry that is hard to understand. Many in the body of Christ have rejected it due to a lack of clarity and understanding.

Demystifying the Prophetic removes this hindrance by providing a language that communicates this complex and mystical subject in a style that is easy to understand. This book is written in an easy-to-read style that brings much-needed clarity on the operations of the supernatural realm, especially the prophetic. I love how Joseph Z reveals the mysteries of the prophetic ministry/office and helps people recognize it as a responsibility, a job description, and not a hierarchy of power and authority over the body of Christ.

I wholeheartedly recommend *Demystifying the Prophetic* for all those hungry to go deeper into the prophetic or are called to operate in the office of the prophet. Among many books I have read, there has never been one that has had such a quick and profound impact on me like *Demystifying the Prophetic*. Since reading this book, I have started having powerful prophetic dreams and spiritual encounters. This book will challenge your prophetic paradigms, equip you for prophetic ministry, impart a fresh anointing, and fast-track you into a new dimension of prophetic flow.

Charles Karuku
Author, Speaker
President, Unity Revival Movement
UnityMovementUSA.org
Burnsville, Minnesota, USA

Demystifying the Prophetic is one of the most eye-opening books I've ever read. It brings clarity and normality to the prophetic. The revelation and personal stories Joseph Z shares will open your eyes and ignite a passion in your heart to become a voice of God to those around you! This book will stir your spirit and help you understand even more about the prophetic gifting! I highly recommend this book to every believer.

Landon Huie
Pastor, Oasis Church
Eau Claire, Wisconsin, USA

Meeting Joseph Z has been a wonderful and refreshing experience. After 40 years of being in the ministry, finding someone balanced and healthy, who regards the local church and keeps the prophetic real, is a delight. Joseph's journey with God, family, and ministry have been exemplary and a great testimony. This book should help those who are exploring and are intellectual, and looking for understanding in different arenas of the prophetic. The Lord bless you as you read this book and travel in your God-given journey.

Prophet Ed Traut
Propheticlife.com

For far too long, there have been so many questions and concerns that we all have had concerning the prophetic that have just been swept under the rug. If you are hungry for the truth to be revealed, this book is for you. Throughout every page, I have found Joseph Z accurately teach biblical truth that answers all the uncomfortable questions and experiences that I know so many people have had.

Gabe Poirot
Social Media Influencer
Gabe Poirot, YouTube Channel

This is the book you've been waiting for all your life! It's more than a read. It's more than just another book! It's a manual, an invitation, an opportunity, masterfully written from the Father to us all! Joseph takes you on a journey as you turn the pages of each chapter. You won't want to put it down; ultimately, it leaves you wanting more! Get ready for change!

Paul Brady
Senior Pastor
Millennial Church

Demystifying the Prophetic is a compelling and timely book. With all that is happening in our world, we need a correct understanding of prophecy and how to grow this gift and identify the true from the false. Joseph Z does a fantastic job of explaining this biblically and accurately. I truly appreciate Joseph, not only as my close friend but also as a voice to bring a rightsizing to the prophetic. I encourage you to read this book!

Joshua Ercoli
Founder, Souled Out International, Z Ministries Team Pastor

Demystifying the Prophetic is the book that defines Joseph Z's ministry. This isn't just a book for him but a life-calling. I have done ministry with Joseph for more than twenty years, and this calling has been making the supernatural a normal part of the Christian's life. There are many self-proclaimed prophets out there, but Joseph Z is not only the most accurate I have seen personally, but he does it so that it doesn't turn people off from the supernatural. *Demystifying the Prophetic* will be a pillar in Christian literature.

Ryan Edberg
Speaker, Author
Founder, Kingdom Youth Conference

For far too long, the prophetic movement has been misappropriated and thrown out by many churches and Christians alike for its "weirdness." Many have only used the prophetic as an excuse to control and manipulate others. *Demystifying the Prophetic* by Joseph Z is the richest and most complete work I have ever read on the subject of the prophetic. It will help readers understand the beautiful gifts of the Holy Spirit and God's desire for all His sons and daughters to prophesy.

As a pastor, I have seen all sides of the prophetic movement. I have even been hurt by unbiblical words and dreams of prophetic people to the point where it would have been easier to become a "non-prophet" church. However, that is exactly what the enemy would love.

In this personal journey to rediscover the prophetic, God sent us Joseph Z. He has ministered in our church many times. I am so grateful for an incredible prophet who can teach and articulate the Word of God with so much love. In addition, Joseph is very mature, humble, and accurate with his gifting. If you are willing to learn (and unlearn) some things and rightsize wrong ideas and concepts, then *Demystifying the Prophetic* will become your best guide to developing your walk in the prophetic!

Benjamin Diaz
Vida Church

In his book *Demystifying the Prophetic*, Joseph Z—with empowering grace—gives one of the most comprehensive perspectives on the prophetic I have personally encountered. The misguided and misapplied topic of prophecy finally has a voice of reason to confront the unnecessary ambiguity and strangeness the Church has endured. I believe this book will become a staple for governing the prophetic, thus making prophecy normal and respectable once again. Joseph brings clear, straight-to-the-point biblical insight.

As I immersed myself in the message contained herein, I felt the Spirit of the Lord on it for God's people today. I believe you will too!

In Joseph's own words, he aims to "rightsize the prophetic mania." Thanks be to God for giving us someone to help accomplish this through the very resource you now hold in your hands. I bless you, dear reader, as you glean and grow from the wisdom in these pages. The world needs your voice like never before. May these words sharpen your prophetic sight and voice for this generation!

Kent Ward
Senior Leader, Overcomers Church International
Perryville & Bonne Terre, Missouri, USA
Author, Co-Founder of Ward Ministries

A few years ago, I was introduced to Joseph and Heather Z while on a trip to Colorado, but I had no clue what I was about to encounter. Shortly after we began a conversation, Joseph paused and gave me a powerful word from the Lord. This prophetic word proved out over my family, and we are walking in the reality of those words today!

In the flurry of prophetic voices popping up everywhere, let me say that Joseph Z is a true prophet of God. In *Demystifying the Prophetic*, Joseph brings a much-needed balance to the current prophetic climate and challenges us to utilize a better hermeneutic: the art and science of the prophetic in action.

His depth of biblical study and years of experience in prophetic ministry have been poured out on the book's pages, revealing the true workings of the prophetic ministry. You will come away with a better understanding of the unique attributes of the prophetic gifts and be better equipped with tools to rightly divide them.

Kyle Loffelmacher
Publisher, Harrison House

Every few decades, a transformative book emerges, guiding us into a deeper understanding of spiritual gifts. *Demystify the Prophetic* is a pinnacle contribution on the subjects of prophecy and prophetic ministry. With skillful mastery, Joseph imparts fresh wisdom and revelation, enriching our understanding of this vital gift and function. Whether you're new to prophetic ministry or a seasoned veteran, Joseph's insights offer not just clearer accuracy but also a path to greater heights in experiencing the magnificence of the Son of God. I wholeheartedly love this book and am confident it will profoundly impact the body of Christ today and for years to come.

Brad Herman
Former Publisher
Harrison House

SPECIAL MESSAGES

In these last days, there are numerous so-called "prophetic voices" that, like sirens, lure uninformed believers to the rocks of confusion and ruin. Sometimes, it feels like we're living in the "wild-west" prophetically, as many fire off random predictions and prognostications in the city square or on social media. Combine all this with the fact that biblical literacy in the Church is at an all-time low, and we have a perfect storm for confusion and deception. This is unfortunate, especially at a time when we need to be able to hear the Voice of God with clarity and precision.

In this untamed landscape, where everyone does what is right in their own eyes and follows after their frail discernment, we are in danger of losing our moral compass and this generation among the cacophony of divergent voices. We find ourselves in dire need of a steady hand to bring order to the chaos, or else I'm concerned that much of the Church will attempt to excise this perceived extremism by cutting their nose off to spite their face. If we don't right this ship, then many will uncouple themselves from *all things prophetic* and lose out on the riches God has reserved for us. In this turbulent terrain, discernment and discerning leadership become paramount, providing the necessary stability and direction to navigate the uncharted waters of this prophetic wilderness, ensuring that our ears remain attuned to the Voice of God's Holy Spirit.

Demystifying the Prophetic by Joseph Z emerges as a beacon of wisdom within the body of Christ in an age characterized by spiritual uncertainty. Joseph Z invites readers on a voyage to distinguish between genuine prophecy and regrettable forgeries that are all too common. Through his unflinching commitment to scriptural integrity, Joseph Z will help you discern between the prophetic and the pathetic and teach you how to know when God is speaking to His Church. He can do this because he has spent his life honing this gift for such a time as this.

The urgency of this message cannot be overstated. Here, you will learn to examine the multidimensional nature of God's Voice with a comprehensive look at a prophetic spectrum ranging from personal revelation to the grand narrative of eschatology. God is trying to speak to you in more ways than you know. Get ready to hear God's Voice with more clarity than you ever thought possible. You'll need it in this hour!

In a Church rife with excesses and abuses, discernment is more than a virtue; it is an imperative necessity. In spite of the mayhem, there are genuine voices who faithfully and with humility proclaim His Word. Joseph Z is one of these voices, and *Demystifying the Prophetic* is his contribution to the Church.

What you have in your hand is more than just inspiring reading; it's a heavenly summons to hear the Voice of God. It is a must-read for anyone serious about walking in end-time victory. Don't just read it; absorb it and allow it to transform your life.

Bishop Alan Didio
Speaker, Author, Influencer
Senior Pastor, Encounter Today Church
EncounterToday.com

I am thrilled to endorse Joseph Z's latest book, *Demystifying the Prophetic*. In an age when the realm of prophecy is often shrouded in confusion and misinterpretation, this book emerges as a beacon of clarity and guidance. Joseph Z's deep insight and commitment to biblical truth make this work an essential resource for anyone seeking to understand and operate within the prophetic ministry.

In today's world, the prophetic gift is both a blessing and a potential minefield. Many well-meaning individuals are either misunderstanding or, worse yet, misleading others in this vital fivefold ministry. Having known Joseph personally for some time, I have witnessed his unwavering dedication to equipping people with a genuine understanding of what the Bible truly communicates about prophecy. His heart is set on training and empowering individuals to hear from the Holy Spirit and discern authentic prophecy from the counterfeit.

One of the book's standout qualities is its emphasis on discernment. In these times of increased spiritual deception, understanding the difference between true biblical prophecy and falsehood is of utmost importance. *Demystifying the Prophetic* will guide you in distinguishing between angels of light and the doctrines of demons, offering valuable insights to navigate these treacherous waters.

Joseph also delves into hermeneutics, providing biblical understanding of the various types of prophecy. This scholarly approach ensures that readers gain a solid foundation in interpreting prophetic passages accurately and contextually.

In a world where the spirit of antichrist and deception is on the rise, this book serves as a powerful antidote. It will dispel confusion and set you on a path toward spiritual success as you hunger and thirst for righteousness. *Demystifying the Prophetic* is not just a book; it's a transformative resource that will equip you to navigate the prophetic realm with wisdom, discernment, and unwavering faith. Don't miss the opportunity to embark on this enlightening journey toward a deeper understanding of the prophetic ministry.

I am thankful for the ministry of Joseph and Heather Z and I believe this book will set up many for success and help them go deeper in their walk with Jesus in this critical hour.

Pastor Todd Coconato
President, Religious Liberties Coalition
Founder, Remnant News
Dallas, Texas

In today's world there are more voices coming at us than ever. Corrupt communication from the mainstream news, politicians, business executives, the medical community and yes, even the Church. It can be overwhelming. Who do we believe?

In the last few years, the prophetic ministry has seen quite a variety of those who claim to operate in the prophetic. Some call themselves prophets but merely repeat the news of the day, or regurgitate a prophecy someone else gave, and then call it their own. Many a Christian has endured a false prophetic word personally, such as, "This is God's will for you; go to Africa." Some of us remember a popular prophetic word that Jesus was returning in 1988. That one didn't pan out either.

One fact remains true: God IS STILL talking to the prophets. And the basis for all prophecy is rooted in God's Word as Joseph instructs us in this book. That is non-negotiable. We need to pray for those called to the prophetic ministry. Don't be quick to judge when the timeline isn't what you thought it was going to be. I like this statement Joseph makes: "Keep fine-tuning your spiritual ear to hear His Voice. Keep listening for His highest and best purpose for your life. God wants you to live, move, and have your being in Him." Pray before you read this book. Then turn the page and begin to *Demystify the Prophetic!*

Dr. Gene Bailey
Host, *FlashPoint*

DEMYSTIFYING
THE
PROPHETIC

Harrison
House

Shippensburg, PA

Published by Harrison House Publishers
Shippensburg, PA 17257

ISBN 13 TP: 978-1-6803-1885-2

ISBN 13 eBook: 978-1-6803-1886-9

For Worldwide Distribution, Printed in the U.S.A.

1 2 3 4 5 6 7 8 / 28 27 26 25 24

DEMYSTIFYING
THE
PROPHETIC

UNDERSTANDING THE
VOICE OF GOD FOR THE
COMING DAYS OF FIRE

JOSEPH Z

DEDICATION

To my mom, Sherry. Your encounters with the Holy Spirit and the Voice of God are what started me on the journey of walking in the prophetic. Thank you for introducing me to the Word of God and the Spirit-filled life. You stood when others could not or would not. I honor you and love you.

ACKNOWLEDGMENTS

My amazing wife, Heather, and my two adult children, Alison and Daniel. You are my best friends. Thank you for your constant support while writing this book and the many projects like it that you assist me in every day. I love each one of you. You are my world.

Rick Renner, thank you for literally walking through nearly every page and spending many hours editing this manuscript with us. You consistently challenge me to be better in every way. My life has been tremendously impacted by who you are and your obedience to Jesus. I honor you and possess the highest gratitude for the privilege of having you as a dear friend and spiritual father in my life.

Mary Ercoli, without your dedication and hard work my books would not hit the mark they were meant to. Thank you for your diligence and belief in this project. I am honored to work with you.

Kyle Loffelmacher, you are one of God's greatest agents. Your belief and insight have been invaluable. Thank you for believing in me and this project!

CONTENTS

FOREWORDS

efore I write a word of endorsement or a foreword for any book, I first take time to read the manuscript from beginning to end, because I believe that when someone writes an endorsement, it is so important that the person is fully aware of what he or she is endorsing. James 3:1 says that any leader who publicly communicates—and that includes endorsing a message—will be more strictly judged for what he or she has said.

For this reason (and because I believe in Joseph Z's ministry and deeply care about him and his wife), I took extensive time to read every word of this book. I even marked certain passages to discuss with Joseph as he finalized the manuscript before sending it to the publisher to be printed.

In *Demystifying the Prophetic*, I find that Joseph Z has attempted to explain prophetic ministry, which is a difficult task since many aspects of genuine prophetic ministry, although scriptural, are rooted experientially in the spirit realm and are difficult to describe in natural words. In First Corinthians 2:14 (KJV), the apostle Paul wrote, "But the natural man receiveth not the things of the Spirit of God: for they are foolishness unto him: neither can he know them, because they are spiritually discerned." While Joseph seeks to help readers understand various aspects of prophetic ministry, there are simply some facets of this type of ministry that cannot be naturally discerned, or shall we say "demystified."

But Joseph's goal is to help readers more generally understand the prophetic ministry, which is admirable and needed, especially in this day. Thus, in this book, he covers key ingredients about the prophetic—such as, how a prophetic beginning may first surface in a person's life; the specific traits of a prophetic character; the prophetic DNA that may reside in certain families; discerning true versus false prophets; how a true prophetic anointing operates, as opposed to the workings of the occult; and a wide range of other related topics that you will find so interesting.

There are many flavors of prophets, just as there are various flavors of every fivefold ministry gift. I am significantly impressed with Joseph Z's flavor on many levels, but what impresses me most is his love for Jesus, his love for his wife and family, his humility and willingness to submit to those he respects in the Lord, and his rock-solid commitment to the written Word of God.

I personally find it disturbing when any person who claims to be a prophet veers from a focus on the Word of God to primarily focus on personal experiences and personal revelations. While there is room for personal experience and personal revelation in any ministry, when these become the focal point, the ministry usually gravitates toward sensationalism.

However, I do not find this to be the case with Joseph Z. He is well-grounded in the Word; in fact, he is a serious student of it, and he is open to hear from other mature leaders who come alongside him to add insights and to provide adjustments, if, and when needed. This signifies a mark of maturity that is needed in every apostle, prophet, evangelist, pastor, and teacher.

My conclusion is that, after thoroughly reading this book, I can confidently say it is an exhaustive and unique book in a long list of books that have been published in recent years on the subject of prophetic ministry. I find it to be a book worth reading—certainly worthy of your time. But as you read it, remember the words of Paul in First Corinthians 2:14—that such things must be "spiritually discerned."

So as you begin to dive into the pages that are before you, pause and ask the Holy Spirit to open your mind to help you "spiritually discern" what you are about to read in this fascinating book.

Rick Renner
Minister, Author, Broadcaster
Moscow, Russia

Prophets are more diverse than perhaps any other ascension gift ministry. Pastors may differ in the size of their churches and teachers in the reach of their ministries, but they are similar in how they administrate their gifts. Evangelists can be flamboyant like A.A. Allen, dynamic like Reinhardt Bonnke, or statesman like Billy Graham, but in each of these ministries the differences in style dissolve when the time comes to bring the listener to a decision for Christ.

Gather an international group of apostles together and you will be surprised how quickly they understand each other and find common ground, particularly in matters pertaining to church government. None of this is true with the prophetic. One of my mentors, Dr. C. Peter Wagner, told me that conducting a meeting with apostles was easy compared to the chaos he encountered when convening prophets. He said, "It was like herding cats." That is why this book is unique. It addresses a broad spectrum of prophetic styles and expressions. Joseph Z does an especially masterful job of explaining the development of a prophet to those who feel alone or misunderstood as they try to sort out the calling on their lives. Unlike many prophets who simply want to minister the word they have been given, Joseph carries a burden to help mentor and protect the emerging prophets.

The burden of this book is to equip all phases of prophet "for the work of the ministry." In the Old Testament, Samuel conducted schools and traveled in a circuit, fathering the less developed prophets in Israel. Not so with Elijah, who at times challenged his sole apprentice, Elisha, to let him go on alone as he prepared for his departure in a fiery chariot. The Bible does not fault Elijah for his eccentricities. He was fashioned in a unique mold. Both Samuel and Elijah were mightily used of God, but one had the calling to father a company. That is what breathes through this manuscript.

Of particular interest to me were the chapters describing in detail the way Joseph has learned to process prophetic phenomena and not miss prophetic moments. He tells how physical contact or proximity to others would open him up to heightened sensory awareness of what the other person was feeling or circumstances they were going through. He explains the occasions when his own emotions were impacted by what others were experiencing and then goes on to distinguish heavenly encounters from those who arise out of self-induced zeal to experience the supernatural or worse—demonic counterfeits. He navigates through these topics as someone who knows where the rocks are that can sink your ship. I was particularly impressed with his understanding of the role of prophets to institutions, gatekeepers, and groups to set them on course. This will be even more needed as society and institutions are shaken. I was also impressed at the scope of content he covered, all in a way that is highly engaging to read and easy to grasp.

In a word, Joseph is gifted to teach emerging prophets how to develop a prophetic gift and calling. This book found its way into your hands because something in you is drawn to this subject. As Joseph Z says, the last-days Church will encounter an age of shaking and seductive counterfeits to the true prophetic office, but during it all God is raising up a company of authentic prophetic ambassadors, uniquely gifted and prepared to reveal the true nature of Jesus. This book will help you discern your path to becoming a prophetic voice, raised up to bring reformation and awakening in the greatest harvest the world has ever seen.

Dr. Lance Wallnau
CEO Lance Learning Group
Host, *Lance Wallnau Show*

SPECIAL INTRODUCTION

With all its effectiveness and sometimes controversy, prophecy is an amazing gift God gave us and enforced under the New Covenant at the ascension of Jesus. It opens hearts, at times convicts, solves difficult questions, and offers breathtaking glimpses into the spirit realm. As it relates to word of knowledge, more than one person has told me over the years that prophecy let them know that "God saw them." Regardless of how prophecy is perceived, the one thing it truly is meant to do is give *testimony* of Jesus (*see* Revelation 19:10).

A mature spiritual art form is the skillful and tenured use of prophecy as an instrument of life and edification—reading the terrain while employing emotional intelligence in the process. Revelation gifts are at their highest and best when wielded by the selfless for the benefit of those searching.

> *For all who are led by the Spirit of God are sons of God.*
> **—Romans 8:14 ESV**

Over the years, I have served, taught, and practiced the gift of prophecy. While traversing and developing my prophetic gift along this revelatory path, it became routine to encounter unique individuals or highly gifted ones who were in the prophetic spectrum (which we will define and delve into in the pages ahead). Some made prophecy a whimsical thing that didn't carry the power or impact it was designed for, whereas others made the prophetic a complicated function—causing their followers to believe high levels of prophecy were reserved only for an elite few with the supernatural ability to interpret special doctrinal things, as well as special revelation.

Throughout many conferences both in the USA and abroad, prophecy became a major part of my life. At times, we would minister daily in meetings that lasted anywhere from four to twelve hours long. It was not uncommon to hold several weeks of meetings every night until their conclusion. I never had a moment when I woke up to the gift of prophecy, as it has always been a part of my experience going as far back as I can recall. At nine years of age, I have my earliest memory of hearing an audible voice call my name, an encounter that greatly impacted me, which I will expound on in the pages of this book. Personally, experiencing the Voice of God with accompanying revelatory encounters throughout my journey has led to something of great personal value, has been the training and tempering of the prophetic gift and all of the experiences that go along with it.

When the gift of prophecy is wielded by a believer under the unction of the Holy Spirit, a potent force is released; however, as a novelty or misappropriation, the genuine can suffer with the stains or markings of something else. Something off target, or a better definition, is to call it a rogue application of a gift utilized without the unction of the Holy Spirit. Where does this take us? It creates a posture of the inflated self and opens avenues to mislead and cause the recipients to wander.

Like many gifts or unique abilities, a certain amount of negative behavior can accompany it. Due to experiencing several strange and negative things within the prophetic movement, there came a season when I refused to call myself prophetic and avoided the title of prophet. A change came by simply going deeper into the Word of God until the realization came that any gift in the New Testament is designed to serve the body of Christ, which changed everything. One such realization caused me to laugh out loud and declare, "Wow, ministry is about people!"

I wrote this book, *Demystifying the Prophetic*, for you as it is my great desire to celebrate the prophetic, bring order to some of the well-intending wildfires, confront the damaging effects of wrong operation—even deceptive witchcraft, sometimes inappropriately mislabeled prophecy. Of utmost importance is taking the mystical and bizarre out of the prophetic and discovering where the rubber meets the road in your life. You have the Holy Spirit calling you to a greater place in Him, which comes through the Word of God and ultimately, revelation. Legitimate revelation brings real change, and it gets results. A proper understanding of prophecy and how this magnificent gift works through you is a powerful doorway to revelation. We will look at it with a strict foundation on the Word of God. Together as we go through the pages of this book, it is my prayer for you that you catch the heart of the matter. Which is the spirit of prophecy that is the testimony of Jesus.

> ...*Worship God! For the testimony of Jesus is the spirit of prophecy.*
>
> **—Revelation 19:10**

Of the utmost importance is to recognize we are being plunged into the last of the last days. We are at the very end of a biblical timeline. All spiritual gifts especially prophecy deserve a mature and most effective use of their purpose. Now is the time to bypass what is not of God and embrace what is grounded in the Word of God, mixed with faith, and demonstrated with tenure and healthy practice. Now is the time for the prophetic to be utilized at its highest and best, fulfilling its purpose—the testimony of Jesus!

SECTION ONE

THE VOICE OF GOD

One of the main objectives of this book is to demy-stify the prophetic or simply give information and clarity on the topic. For many years we have used a saying in our organization, "Good information brings peace." The need for good information as it relates to prophecy and supernatural encounters is of high necessity. It is my prayer that this is what you will discover while reading *Demystifying the Prophetic*.

God is Spirit, and those who worship Him must worship in spirit and truth.

—John 4:24

CHAPTER ONE

THE VOICE OF GOD FROM THE MOUNTAIN

That the Lord called Samuel. And he answered, "Here I am!" ⁵ So he ran to Eli and said, "Here I am, for you called me." And he said, "I did not call; lie down again." And he went and lay down. ⁶ Then the Lord called yet again, "Samuel!" So Samuel arose and went to Eli, and said, "Here I am, for you called me." He answered, "I did not call, my son; lie down again." ⁷ (Now Samuel did not yet know the Lord, nor was the word of the Lord yet revealed to him.)

—1 Samuel 3:4-7

A t a young age, the topic of prophecy or "the prophetic" was not even in my vocabulary. Nevertheless, these were circumstances that seemed to occur, and due to their normalcy in my young life, I thought this was something everyone must be encountering.

One recurring encounter was a Voice calling my name from a distance. This Voice would seemingly travel with the wind ringing over the treetops where I was and had a distinctly familiar sound. Its cadence was much like an echo, although twice as loud—loud enough to be heard clearly—but in the form of a distant shout. When I say it had a distinctly familiar sound, that is because most of the time, the shout would sound very much like my dad's voice.

This became so frequent that one day, after mistaking this Voice for my dad's, I drove my ATV to find him back at the house. After asking him what he wanted and why he called me, he replied, "I didn't call you." It was very strange, yet I knew never to question my dad. This scenario developed into a regular occurrence.

Just as God called to Moses out of the burning bush, I would learn He was calling out to me. Moses positioned himself to draw close to God and he is described as a friend of God. It was this relationship that positioned him to go from the burning bush to the burning mountain. We should continually seek this place in Him.

GOD DESCENDED UPON THE MOUNTAIN

Now Mount Sinai was completely in smoke, because the Lord descended upon it in fire. Its smoke ascended like the smoke of a furnace, and the whole mountain quaked greatly.

—**Exodus 19:18**

One can only imagine what an entire nation experienced for six days and nights as they watched Mount Sinai burn with a savage fury! Raging fire *engulfed the summit,* intermingled with a brooding dark cloud—God Himself had descended upon the mountain!

Something I have given much thought to over the years is the encounter the children of Israel had at the foot of Sinai. My youth was filled with shocking interactions with the Voice of God, making me wonder what impact it must have had on the Jews!

Considering what they encountered as the Divine, the looming spectacle was only interrupted by the intense and periodic *shaking* of the ground they stood on. Gasps and even shrieks from those awe-struck people would have followed regularly. With each billow of the black cloud mixed with fire, claps of thunder, and quaking, thoughts of their mortality were likely at the forefront of everyone's minds.

Everything witnessed and felt in these unbelievable moments carried a terrifying ambiance for these helpless onlookers: What will happen? Why is this happening? Are we going to die?

Over those six days, the mountain violently burned while veiled (at least partly) by the black darkness of clouds.

THE RAW FIERCE SOUND OF THE SPIRIT!

Great suspense induced by such overwhelming imagery was nearly more than the onlookers could bear. That is until the arrival of the seventh day when the unseen realm gave way to a mighty sound. It tore through the barrier of concealment, suddenly exposing the natural world to the raw, fierce sound of Spirit—it resembled that of thunder, like a roar, an audible blast equaling *countless waterfalls* colliding with rock hundreds of feet below—on the seventh day, God spoke!

THE VOICE OF GOD
TORE INTO THE NATURAL

*Now the glory of the Lord rested on Mount Sinai, and the cloud covered it six days. And **on the seventh day He called to Moses out of the midst of the cloud.***
—**Exodus 24:16**

Those gathered at the mountain's base were suddenly exposed to the incomparable and unrivaled sound of *Spirit* breaking into the natural. Of eternity invading the temporal. Of holiness interrupting corruption. It was Him! It was the *Ancient of Days, The Great I Am*, the *One True Living Creator*.

On this seventh day—He was speaking! His sound was heard, His thoughts revealed, His spoken words perceived by all. It was His Voice—*The Voice of God!*

> *For you have not come to the mountain that may be touched and that burned with fire, and to blackness and darkness and tempest,* [19] *and the sound of a trumpet and the voice of words, so that those who heard it begged that the word should not be spoken to them anymore.* [20] *(For they could not endure what was commanded: "And if so much as a beast touches the mountain, it shall be stoned or shot with an arrow."* [21] *And so terrifying was the sight that Moses said, "I am exceedingly afraid and trembling.")*
>
> **—Hebrews 12:18-21**

Each demonstration of His presence was dramatically evident leading up to that point. Every clap of thunder and quake, all the smoke and fire were only the *opening act* in a dramatic progression until suddenly, His Voice exploded through the veil! What began as a sight never observed by human eyes had now reached its zenith as Yahweh's words erupted from the mountain!

HIS WORDS CARRY POWER!

*I will worship toward Your holy temple, and praise Your name for Your lovingkindness and Your truth; for **You have magnified Your word above all Your name.***

—**Psalm 138:2**

Every time God speaks, causation is in motion! His words from the mountain led up to the forming of the Ten Commandments. Whatever He says is true and induces causation, which is why the *written Word* is so mighty!

Think of it! The one true living God reduced His spoken Word and His will down to *writing* for the good of humankind. The very thought of this is amazing. He gave us His words and will, a direct extraction of His supernatural world, and made it accessible to look at and hold in the natural as the ultimate corporeal point of contact and an unmovable absolute truth. He was giving wisdom, understanding, and the opportunity for the renewing of a carnal mind.

Of the highest use, the Word of God is to be believed entirely, but when it is mixed with faith, there is nothing the Word of God cannot do through you! It is designed to cleanse your mind. Taking it a step beyond when the Word is utilized in prayer, praying it out loud, in faith, induces what I like to call "raw spiritual horsepower!"

Consider that we have the same substance sitting in our laps or on our digital devices, which formed the very foundation of this material world!

GOD'S SPOKEN WORD CREATED THE WORLD

God's words created all things; therefore, this natural world responds to words! Not just any words, the words of the risen Son of God—which we could say is technically *anything in the Bible*. Why? Because Jesus Himself is the Word. The Word made flesh and dwelt with men. That same Word, who ultimately became flesh, was the same Word God used to speak creation into existence.

> *I wisdom dwell with prudence, and find out knowledge of witty inventions. [13] The fear of the Lord is to hate evil: pride, and arrogancy, and the evil way, and the froward mouth, do I hate. [14] Counsel is mine, and sound wisdom: I am understanding; I have strength. [15] By me kings reign, and princes decree justice. [16] By me princes rule, and nobles, even all the judges of the earth. [17] I love them that love me; and those that seek me early shall find me. [18] Riches and honour are with me; yea, durable riches and righteousness. [19] My fruit is better than gold, yea, than fine gold; and my revenue than choice silver. [20] I lead in the way of righteousness, in the midst of the paths of judgment: [21] That I may cause those that love me to inherit substance; and I will fill their treasures. [22] **The Lord possessed me in the beginning of his way, before his works of old.** [23] I was set up from everlasting, from **the beginning,** or ever the earth was. [24] When there were no depths, I was brought forth; when there were no fountains abounding with water. [25] Before the mountains were settled, before the hills was I brought forth: [26] While as yet he had not made the earth, nor the fields, nor the highest part of the dust of the world. [27] When he prepared the heavens, I was there: when he set a compass upon the face of the depth: When he established the clouds above: when he*

strengthened the fountains of the deep: [28] *When he gave to the sea his decree, that the waters should not pass his commandment:* [29] *When he appointed the foundations of the earth:* [30] *Then I was by him, as one brought up with him: and I was daily his delight, rejoicing always before him;* [31] *Rejoicing in the habitable part of his earth; and my delights were with the sons of men.*

—**Proverbs 8:12-31 KJV**

BACK TO THE FIRE AND VOICE ON SINAI

Back to Sinai—when God makes appearances in the Bible in a physical form, it is known as a *theophany* or a form of God. Another example of this is found in Exodus 33, where God hid Moses in the cleft of the rock and passed by. God appeared in a form that Moses could *see*.

The Oxford Dictionary of the Christian Church defines theophany this way: "An appearance of God in visible form, temporary; not necessarily material. Such an appearance is to be contrasted with the *incarnation*, in which there was a permanent union between God and complete manhood (spirit, soul, and body)."

Imagine it! The Hebrews saw the ultimate drama, a moment in history forever marked with intensity and eternal significance.

The Ten Commandments were about to be written in stone by God's own doing. So severe was this time of visitation that all the people gathered, *along with Moses*, and collectively trembled from great fear! Let's look at Hebrews 12 once again.

For you have not come to the mountain that may be touched and that burned with fire, and to blackness and *darkness and tempest, ^{19} and the sound of a trumpet and the voice of words, so that **those who heard it begged that the word should not be spoken to them anymore**. ^{20} (For they could not endure what was commanded: "And if so much as a beast touches the mountain, it shall be stoned or shot with an arrow." ^{21} And **so terrifying was the sight that Moses said, "I am exceedingly afraid and trembling."**)*

—Hebrews 12:18-21

GOD WAS TRYING TO SPEAK TO HIS PEOPLE

Here is the place of awe and reverence for the great Lord of heaven and earth. He is our one true living God. God, in His purest form, is fire. Not just any fire, our God is a consuming fire!

*For our God **is** a consuming fire.*

—Hebrews 12:29

Consuming fire is what God is; and the perception of God from the vantage point of fallen creation and fallen, sinful man is terrifying!

PURE LIGHT COLLIDED UNVEILED SIN!

Let me explain. God is *pure holiness*, and there is no comparison to His purity and magnificence. He is Light, pure light, and there is no trace of darkness in Him. First John 1:5 says, "*God is light* and in Him is no darkness at all."

When pure holiness is confronted by sin, the result is terrifying for sin. However, the pure light is equally repulsed at the sight and exposure of unveiled sin!

THERE WAS NO MEDIATOR

During these days of Moses, there was no complete mediator. Moses acted as one, however in comparison to Jesus, who would become the ultimate mediator between God and man—Moses fulfilled the role of messenger, mouthpiece, and leader. He was also fulfilling the office of a *prophet* to the Hebrews and Egyptians. As tremendous of a leader as Moses was, he was still not the kind of mediator necessary for a real connection between God and man.

What we see in Exodus and the description in Hebrews 12 regarding God invading the natural is simply an image of what happens when pure holiness and fallen humanity come into contact! Fire, thunderbolts, lightning, threats of judgment, earthquakes, and fear! All of this is due to not having a mediator!

WITHOUT A MEDIATOR, HOLINESS KILLS!

In this monumental visitation, He, the great God of heaven, sternly warned Moses that the Hebrews ought not to see Him or even catch a glimpse of Him, or they must all be put to death! Why? Because the Hebrews would see God in His perfect holiness, or as He was, and *from a natural standpoint.* These natural human beings would be exposing God in His perfection to their fallen states. Another way of saying this would be to say their sin (caused by Adam's fall) would have been intolerable for God's pure holiness. This is why the perfect mediator had to come—Jesus. Without the faultless mediator, exposure to God's holiness would be lethal for anyone to look upon Him as He is.

> And when the voice of the trumpet sounded long, and waxed louder and louder, Moses spake, and **God answered him by a voice.** [20] And the Lord came down upon mount Sinai, on the top of the mount: and the Lord called Moses up to the top of the mount; and Moses went up. [21] And the Lord said unto Moses, go down, **charge the people, lest they break through unto the Lord to gaze, and many of them perish.** [22] And let the priests also, which come near to the Lord, sanctify themselves, lest the Lord break forth upon them. [23] And Moses said unto the Lord, the people cannot come up to mount Sinai: for thou chargedst us, saying, set bounds about the mount, and sanctify it. [24] And the Lord said unto him, Away, get thee down, and thou shalt come up, thou, and Aaron with thee: **but let not the priests and the people break through to come up unto the Lord, lest he break forth upon them.**
>
> —Exodus 19:19-24 KJV

The people and the priests at that time could not perceive God's holiness. None of them had proper access to God. Moses was a mediator and prophet but did not possess the means to connect the people to their God truly.

THE TRUE MEDIATOR HAD TO COME

The final Mediator had to manifest, or hearing God's Voice would eventually kill those who heard it! There are two reasons why I believe people could not simply look at God in His actual form.

1. Seeing God from a sinful state without the Mediator would cause a breach of God's holiness (as explained in the section, *Without a Mediator, Holiness Kills*).

This breach of God's holiness would be better described by saying God Himself was violated. In like fashion, this is what happened when sin was found in Lucifer. It induced a transgression against the very essence of God.

This is also why I believe Heaven and Earth will be recreated into the new Heaven and Earth because the stain of Lucifer's sin must be abolished in both places.

2. It would have simply killed those who saw Him.

Likely as a response of holy anger against or as a reaction to sinful flesh, which was forcing itself into contact with His holiness. Whether visually or physically, sinful flesh cannot come into direct contact with God's pure holiness and survive. Remember the story of Uzzah? That is what happened to him when he violated God's holiness.

> *And when they came to Nachon's threshing floor, Uzzah put out his hand to the ark of God and took hold of it, for the oxen stumbled. [7] Then the anger of the Lord was aroused against Uzzah, and God struck him there for his error; and he died there by the ark of God.*
>
> **—2 Samuel 6:6-7**

It was such an intense moment that David was upset at God for striking Uzzah down. However, God was so infringed upon by Uzzah's careless action that God struck him.

PEACE AND GOODWILL BETWEEN GOD AND MAN

Now for the good news! Remember what the angels announced when they appeared to the shepherds?

> *Now there were in the same country shepherds living out in the fields, keeping watch over their flock by night. [9] And behold, an angel of the Lord stood before them, and the glory of the Lord shone around them, and they were greatly afraid. [10] Then the angel said to them, "Do not be afraid, for behold, **I bring you good tidings of great joy which will be to all people.** [11] For there is born to you this day in the city of David a Savior, who is Christ the Lord. [12] And this will be the sign to you: You will find a Babe wrapped in swaddling cloths, lying in a manger."[13] And suddenly there was with the angel a multitude of the heavenly host praising God and saying: [14] "Glory to God in the highest, and **on earth peace, goodwill toward men!"***
>
> **—Luke 2:8-14**

It could be said that the hostility God had toward mankind ended with the death and resurrection of Jesus. Jesus is the *peace on earth and goodwill toward men* spoken of by the angels in Luke 2.

Everyone must repent of their sins, turn to Jesus, ask for forgiveness, and confess Him as Lord to be saved. There is only *one way* to

God the Father: through repentance and the new birth only found in Jesus Christ.

Everyone, no matter how kind and well-intending they are, or how many good deeds they do in this life, without Jesus, they are headed for a *crisis*, an eternity with the devil and his angels in hell and eventually the lake of fire. That is why we often say, "Thank God for Jesus!"

THE GOD KIND OF LIFE

Peace on earth and goodwill toward men came with Jesus. To those who receive Him, there is God's quality of life.

> *I have come that they may have **life**, and that they may have **it more abundantly**.*
>
> **—John 10:10**

Life is the Greek word *zōē* and carries a powerful meaning described in more ways than one. A particular way to describe this kind of life would be to say, *the God quality of life.* Jesus said, "I came that you might have God's kind of life working in your experiences and operations. And that you may have the God quality of life more abundantly!"

WITHOUT JESUS, THERE IS NO PROPER ACCESS TO THE FATHER

My point is this, without Jesus, there is no proper access to the Father. God is still the consuming fire. However, that is not the way we perceive Him. Why? Because Jesus is, for us today, the exact representation of the Father! Philip even asked Jesus to show them the Father. The response Jesus gave is very insightful—Jesus is the physical representation of the Father.

> Philip said to Him, "Lord, show us the Father, and it is sufficient for us." ⁹ Jesus said to him, "Have I been with you so long, and yet you have not known Me, Philip? **He who has seen Me has seen the Father;** so how can you say, 'Show us the Father'?"
>
> —John 14:8-9

If someone took a picture of God, it would be Jesus in the photo!

> Who being the brightness of his glory, and **the express image of his person,** and upholding all things by the word of his power, when he had by himself purged our sins, sat down on the right hand of the Majesty on high.
>
> —Hebrews 1:3 KJV

> In whom the god of this world hath blinded the minds of them which believe not, lest the light of the glorious gospel of **Christ, who is the image of God,** should shine unto them.
>
> —2 Corinthians 4:4 KJV

> Who is the image of the invisible God, the firstborn of every creature.
>
> —Colossians 1:15 KJV

TODAY, THE VOICE OF GOD IS A LOCAL CALL

The Voice of God is the basis for everything in our walk with God, especially how we hear His Voice. When the Lord speaks today, it is a *local call* to you as His child and family.

Jesus made a way for that same consuming fire that will yet shake heaven and earth to live in you! To operate through you—to speak to you right where you are.

> *My sheep hear my voice, and I know them, and they follow me.*
>
> —**John 10:27 KJV**

Prophecy and hearing God as a generation is a must! The days of His roar on the mountain, though not beyond Him to do so again, is not the primary way He has chosen to speak to us. We must learn His Voice, especially as it relates to the prophetic, because society as we know it is entering a time of *insanity and confusion.* As the generations progress, standards and absolutes are free-falling into darkness. This is because the entire world, every living person, is approaching the end of the road—the end of the age is near!

THE DAYS OF NOAH

Things will be *business as usual for the non-discerning,* just like Jesus said regarding the days of Noah and the days of Lot. There will be a perverse and wicked society that will operate, eat, drink, buy, sell, plant, and build *until their complete and irreversible destruction.* Here, we are amid significant numbness and confusion among the masses.

And as it was in the days of Noah, so it will be also in the days of the Son of Man: [27] *They ate, they drank, they married wives, they were given in marriage, until the day that Noah entered the ark, and the flood came and destroyed them all.* [28] *Likewise as it was also in the days of Lot: They ate, they drank, they bought, they sold, they planted, they built;* [29] *but on the day that Lot went out of Sodom it rained fire and brimstone from heaven and destroyed them all.* [30] *Even so will it be in the day when the Son of Man is revealed.*

—Luke 17:26-30

Matthew 24 speaks of this time as the hardening of their hearts or the hearts of many growing cold. However, that Voice that spoke straight out of the consuming fire is alive and dwells in you.

SPIRIT OF PROPHECY

Today, we must understand that the testimony of Jesus is the spirit of prophecy, and we are to operate in it effectively, based on His Word and that same authority. That same power of the Great I AM will manifest through His *body*, His *Ekklesia* (the Church) breaking the haze of confusion and striking hearts and minds with revelation straight from the Creator of all things.

God's Voice legitimately working through a person will empower others with His presence, which is life changing and will demand an explanation. A better way to say it would be that the Voice of God in operation through you will cause *your presence to demand an explanation.*

He's wild, you know. Not like a tame lion.

—C.S. Lewis,
The Lion, the Witch and the Wardrobe
(Chronicles of Narnia)

From the fire of Sinai to the fire upon the heads of the 120 who were in the upper room in Acts 2, your great God has wanted to communicate with you. Now in the days we are living, nothing could be more vital than to hear His Voice. The prophetic and the clarity to listen to, discern, and deliver what the Spirit says to those around you is precious.

> *Worship God! For the testimony of Jesus is the spirit of prophecy.*
>
> **—Revelation 19:10**

Remember, the testimony of Jesus being the spirit of prophecy is realized at a greater level from the understanding that He is the original Voice of God! He was with Him in the beginning and is at His right hand today, and the Holy Spirit is an extension of Jesus. Therefore, when anyone moves in that same unction to both speak for or interpret God's Voice—it must glorify the Son!

CHAPTER TWO

CONVERSATIONS IN HEAVEN

For now we see through a glass, darkly; but then face to face: now I know in part; but then shall I know even as also I am known.

—1 Corinthians 13:12 KJV

M uch like my dramatic encounters as a young person, my wife, Heather, had a life experience that forever changed her. Upon comparing notes, we recognized the story you are about to read was during the same period of time when I was being asked to leave my father's house. Our parallel journeys have been very interesting, to say the least. Only the great God of the universe could have arranged our lives to intersect with such unique paths.

HEATHER'S JOURNEY TO HEAVEN

My wife, Heather, had a legitimate firsthand encounter with the Voice of God. She had suffered a horrible accident which ultimately rendered her lifeless. At that time, Heather had a heaven experience reinforcing the idea of God speaking *heart to heart*. Her visitation to heaven resulted from a gymnastics accident. One day, while she was swinging back and forth on parallel bars, her arms gave out as her feet were on a back swing; this was due to her arms being tired from a previous gymnastic class that day. This situation caused her to fall, striking her forehead on the ground with intense force. Her head violently snapped back from the impact, causing her to break her neck at the C1 vertebrae, the same break that paralyzed Christopher Reeves, the actor who played Superman in the 1970s and '80s.

Heather lay there lifeless for a while and woke up to find herself holding her neck and walking home. She stumbled and wandered down the street, finally making it home to see her mom, who realized something serious had happened and immediately rushed her to the hospital. In the emergency care unit, the doctors ran tests and scans. They discovered that the vertebrae she had broken were linked to what controls *breathing*—the doctors were, in essence, waiting for Heather to die, as there wasn't anything they could do for her.

HEATHER LEFT HER BODY ON THE CAT SCAN TABLE

During those tests, she was brought into a room for a CAT scan, and this is where things took a unique and life-altering turn—Heather began to experience herself leaving her body. She not only sensed herself leaving but found herself looking down at her own body on the CAT scan table. As Heather was staring down at herself in that hospital room, she sensed herself moving and leaving as if being pulled away to somewhere else, to a new location. This transition happened in moments until she finally found herself standing in what she intuitively knew was her *home* in heaven.

Outside, the vegetation was profound in color, with plants and grass that were different, or *better*, as she put it. Heather didn't recognize many of them but said they were rich in appearance, vibrant, and full of life. I have had lengthy conversations with Heather about her time there, and for many years, she never spoke of it publicly. She describes everything she experienced there as "more"; she says it's simply more alive, more vivid. Earth is a dull place in comparison. In heaven, everything is dialed up to an eleven: sounds, feelings, senses, and a deep knowledge of everything happening around you.

One profound moment occurred when she was in her heavenly home and, upon looking outside, was filled with a desire to be there. By "there," she referred to a location out in a large pasture. Desire was met with motion, and she passed through the wall at the speed of thought. Now standing where she had wanted to be, she was met by the Lord.

It was a tremendous experience for her. The Lord spoke to her about her life, things to come, and why she was to go back. The things He told her carried her through another time when she was in dialysis for nearly three years due to hereditary kidney failure. Frequently, the doctors told us that she would likely die without much hope of living. The Lord provided miracle after miracle for us during that time; thankfully, she is healthy today.

THE WAY GOD SPOKE IN HEAVEN

Returning to her time in heaven, there is a point of interest regarding how she and the Lord communicated. It was fascinating for me to learn the way that she and the Lord spoke to each other. Their conversation was thought-to-thought or, as Heather says, heart-to-heart. When the Lord spoke, she knew it; when Heather spoke, the Lord knew it. To hear her tell of this interaction is so amazing!

Her time in heaven ended when the Lord returned her to her body. She inhaled and opened her eyes. During the CAT scan, her body had died and came back to life. When they arrived and examined her neck shortly following the scan, the specialist noticed the break had fused back together! We know that the Lord healed Heather from a broken neck. She left the hospital with a soft collar and fully recovered wonderfully.

WHAT LANGUAGE DID ADAM AND EVE SPEAK?

Adam and Eve walked with the Lord. They were in proximity to Him, there were animals everywhere, and everything they needed was present. So, we might ask this question, "When Adam walked through the Garden alongside the Lord and in the cool of the day, what language did they speak?" This question is fascinating regarding the early days of the Garden of Eden.

Many people would say it was Hebrew or Greek. An argument could be made for many different languages. Truthfully, the Bible doesn't say what language they spoke; we know that they were undoubtedly communicating.

Knowing God and the way His Holy Spirit speaks to us today, it has caused me to ponder if there was any language in the Garden at all. Communication may have been more on a heart-to-heart or even thought-to-thought level. Although there is no way of knowing for sure how they spoke or what language was used in the Garden of Eden, one thing we do know is that the Holy Spirit communicates often on a heart level. That still small voice which is internal and learned through spending time with God and in prayer.

One survey I remember reading stated that 90 percent of every conversation is found in what is not said, based on body language, how the people stand, the emotional place they are speaking from, and the context in which communication is happening.

In the Garden, the language was *knowing*. A distinct communication was exchanged, not simply the black-and-white meaning of a thing, but every nuance, intent, and feeling—full context would've been present to both hear and fully understand. It was how Heather experienced the Voice of God—heart-to-heart, thought-to-thought. Every intent and meaning, with an entire lifetime of context, was known with each internal exchange.

SPOKEN WORDS ARE FALLEN

The fall of man reduced language to *guttural sounds*. These sounds had to be formed into specific words that allowed individuals to relate to one another. Words also became the way humankind released decrees and communicated what they wanted. In a sense, it was a departure from walking with the Lord in the cool of the day, and it elevated carnality and the natural above the spiritual. The natural *guttural sound was now the primary interaction between world residents.*

Today, we don't communicate heart-to-heart or mind-to-mind; "God is Spirit, and those who worship Him must worship in spirit and truth" (John 4:24). Allow me to explain this; Spirit is the realm God lives in. Truth is the correct biblical reality we build on and correct our natural experiences by.

Romans 12:2 says, "And do not be conformed to this world, but be transformed by the renewing of your mind." Renewing your mind by the written Word of God is the process of worshiping the Lord in truth, and Jesus said *My words* are truth. In John 6:63, Jesus also said His words were *spirit*. The takeaway is this: We are to renew our minds with the written Word of God and understand that it is the purest spiritual substance we can grasp in this natural world. By this process of mind renewal with the Word of God and relating to the realm of the unseen by the written Word of God, we will begin to have the eyes of our hearts enlightened.

> *I pray that the eyes of your heart may be enlightened, so that you may know what is the hope of His calling, what are the riches of the glory of His inheritance in the saints.*
> **—Ephesians 1:18 NASB1977**

Eyes of your heart in Ephesians 1:18 is the inner man or the spirits of righteous men made *perfect.*

> *To the general assembly and church of the first-born who are enrolled in heaven, and to God, the Judge of all, and to the spirits of righteous men made perfect.*
> **—Hebrews 12:23 NASB1977**

The eyes of the heart being enlightened is the same arena where the spirits of righteous men are made perfect and reference the realm of the spirit, where your spiritual senses operate. A more precise way of saying this would be, through the Word of God and becoming sensitized through prayer, as well as having a mind renewed to the written Word of God—you will become highly sensitive to the Voice of God.

CLEAR THE MECHANISM

> *My sheep hear My voice, and I know them, and they follow Me.*
> **—John 10:27**

God desires to speak to you as His sheep. After all, they hear His Voice and run away from a stranger. His sheep hear His Voice, heart-to-heart,

Spirit-to-spirit. God will speak to your thought life if you keep the mechanism clear. On this premise, your dreams are impacted, and sensitivity to situations becomes heightened. Your *awareness* of the realm of the Spirit will tune in at a higher level. God desires His people to understand, discern, and accurately hear His Voice.

He wants to communicate with you, just like He did initially with Adam as they walked in the cool of the day together. It is the ultimate form of communication to be heard and know you were understood. God also wants to be heard and understood, this is why He gave us the Bible and His Holy Spirit. With the combination of His Word and Spirit, you will experience a heightened level of clarity regarding the Voice of God.

The Voice of God can speak audibly to you on the rarest occasion or send a messenger angel. However, He primarily speaks to the heart. You hear Him on the inside, like a still, small voice.

CLARITY IS GOD'S NATIVE TONGUE

But you, beloved, building yourselves up on your most holy faith, praying in the Holy Spirit.

—Jude 1:20

One of the highest acts of engagement with the Lord is by speaking in tongues, not just for a moment but for extended periods. An internal fine-tuning begins to happen, and with it, clarity. God is not the author of confusion; therefore, clarity is His native language. Praying in the Spirit brings *clarity* to your mind, will, and emotions. A calming down and great empowerment is released, which engages surrender to the Spirit of the Lord. God longs for you to spend extended time with Him as He greatly desires to be heard and understood!

I thank my God I speak with tongues more than you all.
—**1 Corinthians 14:18**

Paul said, "I thank God I pray in tongues more than you all!" A place of high capacity is developed by praying in the Spirit for an extended time. It renews, builds, and sharpens the gifts within you, especially regarding prophecy. Persecution and a demonic assault have been launched against speaking in tongues for generations. Speaking in tongues is one of the most effective spiritual development tools God gave us, and religion, under the devil's guidance, wants it destroyed, for what it does to you and through you—tongues are a potent force.

> *Though I speak with the tongues of men and of angels, but have not love, I have become sounding brass or a clanging cymbal.*
>
> —**1 Corinthians 13:1**

Much can be said about the necessity of tongues for their many benefits. The statement, the *tongues of men and angels*, alludes to the possibility that when we speak in tongues, angels understand what is being said, and more could cause them to act. Could it be that tongues are a Holy Spirit language that angels understand? They may even hear the Voice of God coming through you, and thus it activates them. Additionally, praying in the Spirit or tongues is a tremendous way to communicate and build a relationship with God. You are exercising your senses to be readily available for the Holy Spirit to speak to and be heard by you. The very foundation of prophecy and hearing God's Voice is developed in the practice of this simple faith gift.

A journey to heaven is unnecessary as you build yourself up by praying in tongues! Tongues are direct communication with the Holy Spirit. When you develop in this arena, you will begin hearing the Voice of God on a tremendous level. Remember, God wants you to hear His Voice even more than you do! He is looking for you to spend time with Him—tongues and reading His Word is the path to growing in discerning and hearing His Voice!

CHAPTER THREE

MULTIDIMENSIONAL GOD

Then I will take away My hand, and you shall see My back; but My face shall not be seen.

—**Exodus 33:23**

M oses had a unique perspective on God and the Spirit realm: so did Daniel the Prophet and John the Revelator. The fascinating point is to consider that God is not only outside of time but also outside our dimension!

Seeing things from God's eternal perspective is caught in glimpses. His eternal vantages are sometimes shared with us in fragments and by His Spirit. Our tremendous challenge is working through the realization that spiritual revelatory moments must be *ascertained* while living in our natural capacity, leaving a vast arena open for clarity and misunderstanding. However, there is a measurable way of sharpening perception, which we will explore together!

THE SCOPE OF GOD'S VANTAGE POINT

Let's broaden this understanding; imagine, if you would, that one day represents a generation or roughly 80 years. Now let's take those same 80 years and imagine that they represent one day. If one day represented 80 years of history, each day would be filled with significant historical milestones. For example, World War II ended only last night on this timeline! The Civil War was fought two days ago, and the 13 American colonies declared independence last week!

If we were to go even farther back on this imaginary scale, Jesus was born in Bethlehem about 25 days ago. Moses led the children of Israel out of Egypt about 20 days before that—additionally, the oldest written works of the Near East were penned roughly a few months back!

On this unique and *imaginary timeline*, if we were to go back to the beginning of recorded history, then the entirety of human history as we know it would have begun just under a year ago—what a perspective to consider!

I remember reading a similar exercise in university many years ago. It struck me with a fascination about the power of time. What if we could grasp all history in such a manner? While considering this, an even greater thought came to me. The mighty God of heaven far supersedes such a picture. His ability ventures far beyond our most creative ideas for grasping time and history.

GOD SUPERSEDES TIME AND HISTORY

Moments of revelation are better understood when we look at the Greek word for "revelation": *apokalupsis*, which means *an uncovering* or *a revealing*. A term used to describe an entire book of the Bible. The Revelation of Jesus Christ—a book that ultimately reveals Jesus. When an opening of the veil separating our natural world and the realm of the spirit encounters a momentary split, it is then that a revelation, an unveiling of something, may glimmer through.

This glimmer is where prophecy begins to operate in its various facets, by a revelatory or unveiled glimpse where our knowledge or natural senses experience information from the realm of the spirit. It requires the cooperation of knowing in part (natural)—with prophecy (faith or the spiritual part of you) to operate in a healthy prophetic way. First Corinthians 13:9 offers us insight into this.

> *For we know in part and we prophesy in part.*
> —1 Corinthians 13:9

In this verse, you see two things. Knowing and prophesying—each in part. The simplicity of this scripture is something we should greatly consider. We can see in part, know in part, and have prophetic experiences in part. Our worldview and preconceived notions often set the framework to which we embrace what God is saying. Expanding your grasp on hearing Him is necessary, which begins by adjusting the scope of how we see the Lord. Expansion is required to receive all He has for us regarding His Voice and revelatory experiences.

OUR INFINITE GOD

God operates by an infinite ability, allowing Him to be actively present in each moment with you. In hindsight, He sees far beyond a summary of events—instead, He knows the end from the beginning. He is ever-present. When grappling with issues of time, distance, and space, it is helpful to use an *illustration*, such as the simple imaginary model we just used to process history. With that same lens, imagine now if we were to turn it forward to the future—there would be much to discover! This is what the Word of God does for us, and this is partly what prophecy does.

To clarify, consider another simple illustration. If reality and time as we know it was presented as a parade, in which you could only see what your eyes and ears were able to perceive directly in front of you or as far to the left and the right as your vision allowed. From this position, you may be able to see what is coming next, but only one moment and line of sight at a time. To go beyond that line of sight would require educated speculation at best.

The living God doesn't see things in that same way. He knows the end from the beginning and has a vantage point outside our plane of reality. God doesn't see a parade moment by moment as it travels by. He sees things (for the purposes of this analogy) from above. He is simultaneously seeing the entire parade from the beginning to the end.

The parade is simple imagery but offers an easy way to grasp how God views time. Taking it closer to how He sees, imagine God seeing our reality outside this known dimension of time. He would see things with a unique perspective! He is, after all, omnipresent, which also translates to time and dimensions. What does this mean? The Lord sees everything in heaven and earth without the limitations of linear time.

It is profound to discover that prophecy is one of the ways God speaks from outside our known space and directly into this one. Prophecy is a unique communication between God and mankind.

Consider what Chuck Missler writes about space to further shed light on this concept:

> Space is not simply an empty vacuum. Isaiah 64:1 says it can be torn; Psalm 102 says it can be worn out like a garment; Hebrews 12:26, Haggai 2:6, and Isaiah 13:13 say it can be shaken; in 2 Peter 3:12, it can be "burnt up"; in Revelation 6:14, "it split apart like a scroll." Hebrews 1:12 says it can be "rolled up like a mantle." What is meant by "rolled up"? Let's think that through: in order for space to be rolled up, there must be some dimension in which it's thin. (If it's not thin, you can't roll it up.) Also, if it can be

rolled up, it can be bent. If it can be bent, there must be some direction toward which it can be bent. The whole idea of being rolled up implies thinness and an additional dimension in which to roll it up, which begins to indicate that space has more than three dimensions, which we now know today from particle physics. But the Scripture has said all along that we have additional, spatial dimensions. Nachmonides, a Hebrew sage of the twelfth century, concluded from studying Genesis, chapter 1, that the universe has ten dimensions. Four of those are directly "knowable," and six of them are "not knowable" (in his vocabulary). Particle physicists in the 21st century now believe that the universe has ten dimensions but only four of them are directly measurable.[1]

EZEKIEL'S INTERDIMENSIONAL WHEEL

Flashes of interdimensional prophetic moments are possibly caught in Scripture. In the account of Ezekiel's *wheel within a wheel*, we see what is possibly a vision, or his eyes were opened to a multidimensional scenario.

> *Now as I looked at the living creatures, behold, a wheel was on the earth beside each living creature with its four faces.* [16] *The appearance of the wheels and their workings was like the color of beryl, and all four had the same likeness.* ***The appearance of their workings was, as it were, a wheel in the middle of a wheel.***
>
> **—Ezekiel 1:15-16**

Ezekiel's vision of the wheel within a wheel has biblical understanding as to what it means in context; but additionally, we might be getting a glimpse at a form of an extradimensional kind of revealing—or an encounter with different dimensions being exposed at the same time as angelic beings operate in other planes or higher dimensional realities than mankind.

In his revelatory encounter, Ezekiel was attempting to describe what he saw and, considering the possibility that he is prophetically viewing a multidimensional scenario, takes the strange vision or sight and makes it understandable—at least offering some kind of clarity as to why Ezekiel saw such a strange manifestation.

Let's briefly examine another interesting part of the vision or literal sight Ezekiel experienced. There are some commentators who could suggest that he was seeing the throne of God from underneath, that his position would suggest it was appearing above him. An interesting point to consider is the reference to the wings of these entities being joined together.

> Their **wings were joined** one to another; they turned not
> when they went; they went every one straight forward.
> —**Ezekiel 1:9 KJV**

The scene showing the entities with wings together or touching carries the meaning in Hebrew that they were *fused together* or *joined.* The King James Version uses the word "joined." This gives the image that they were like one or all mingled together. It's interesting to realize that it is possible that John also saw these same creatures in the book of Revelation.

> And before the throne there was a sea of glass like unto
> crystal: and in the midst of the throne, and round about
> the throne, were **four beasts** full of eyes before and behind.

⁷ And the first beast was like a lion, and the second beast like a calf, and the third beast had a face as a man, and the fourth beast was like a flying eagle. ⁸ And the four beasts had each of them six wings about him; and they were full of eyes within: and they rest not day and night, saying, Holy, holy, holy, Lord God Almighty, which was, and is, and is to come. ⁹ And when those beasts give glory and honor and thanks to him that sat on the throne, who liveth for ever and ever.

—Revelation 4:6-9 KJV

In the book of Revelation, we see these same types of living creatures that Ezekiel saw; it is in the realm of possibility that these are the same creatures. Only in Revelation it may be a different dimensional vantage point, not all having a dimensional blending in play. John could have been seeing the exact same creatures—only *as they really were*—not fused together in a multidimensional way. He was looking at the Throne of God directly in front of him.

Considering that spiritual beings are not bound to one dimension helps us better understand why things can be so unique when supernatural manifestations occur.

Ezekiel was a physical man viewing and experiencing multidimensional supernatural beings. Again, it could be why his vision is described in such a difficult-to-understand way.

When it comes to God's viewpoint of space and time, an interesting insight is found in the narrative when Moses asked the Lord to show him His Glory. Moses being in the cleft of the rock was given a response by the Lord as to how He would answer this request.

*Then I will take away My hand, and you shall see My **back**; but My face shall not be seen.*

—Exodus 33:23

God was saying to Moses, "No one can see My face and live, but I will show you My back."

In Exodus 33:23, the word "back" is a very interesting word. Here is why Moses is known for writing the Bible's first five books. The only issue is that many scholars say that is an impossibility. How would he write Genesis 1, for example? He wasn't there, so they assume there is a form of oral tradition passed down telling the creation narrative, and Moses recorded it.

But in the light of Exodus 33, and when we consider that God is multidimensional as He alone is the Master of all creation, including time itself, this narrative takes on a very interesting possibility.

God's use of the word "back" is the Hebrew word *'âchôr*. It means *behind, backward; also (as facing north) the West: after (-ward), back (part, -side, -ward), hereafter, (be-) hind (-er part), time to come, without.* It indicates direction, such as before, behind, or backward. It also can temporally refer to the future. Because this word refers to direction and potentially something previous, it is not a far leap to consider this is what God meant when He said, "You shall see My back." It would have been impossible for anyone to see the beginning of creation unless God showed it to them, therefore God may very well have been showing Moses His great works from the very beginning, such as the creation of the world and the fall of man.[2]

When Moses saw the glory of the Lord and the back (*'âchôr*) of God, the first thing he may have seen was darkness, a formless void, and darkness upon the face of the deep. Moses then would have witnessed the Spirit of God moving upon the face of the deep, and while looking into the darkness, Moses heard the powerful words of God, "Let there be light!"

And the earth was without form, and void; and darkness was upon the face of the deep. And the Spirit of God moved upon the face of the waters. ³ Then God said, Let there be light: and there was light.

—Genesis 1:2-3 KJV

Moses later would write the words, *In the beginning.*

However, this is not all that was conveyed in this story, and the word "back" (*'âchôr*)—for that word can also temporally refer to the future. Is it possible that God, in the exact moment of showing Moses His back, both locationally and in former works of old, also took Moses to a future time. To a mountain which would have been in the future and was likely north of where he was seeing the Glory of the Lord. In the moment of being shown the Glory of God, is it possible that Moses saw both the beginning and was transported through time and space to the Mount of Transfiguration?

And, behold, there talked with him two men, which were Moses and Elias.

—Luke 9:30 KJV

And there appeared unto them Elias with Moses: and they were talking with Jesus.

—Mark 9:4 KJV

And, behold, there appeared unto them Moses and Elias talking with him.

—Matthew 17:3 KJV

That is an interesting thought, for sure! It is open for speculation, but could it be that God may have introduced Moses to Jesus in person! It is not a proven fact, but it is interesting to consider. You be the judge and discern it for yourself.

God is multidimensional, and relating to Him as a Spirit is powerful. Through the prophetic, God can show His people things that have happened and even things that have yet to take place. Remember, God rules outside of time. He sees the end from the beginning and knowing Him more by His Holy Spirit can make His secrets available to you—even if they are outside time and space.

CHAPTER FOUR

THE PROPHETIC SPECTRUM
THE FOUR TYPES
OF PROPHECY

Formerly in Israel, when a man went to inquire of God,
he spoke thus: "Come, let us go to the seer"; for he who is
now called a prophet was formerly called a seer.

—1 Samuel 9:9

There are four *fundamental* types of prophecy; these may not be the only ways prophecy works in believers, but it is a good foundation for understanding its operation. Prophecy is also not limited to the office of the prophet. Many who move in the *gift of prophecy* can be highly developed in the gift and mistakenly labeled as a prophet. Before we go into the four types of prophecy, let us briefly answer the question: *what is the difference between the gift of prophecy and the office of the prophet?*

The answer is both simple and crucially profound! The office of the prophet requires a unique combination of gifts. But, truthfully, most don't know how to define a prophet. As a result, we end up with ideas based on hearsay and current pop tradition in the Church.

To simplify the issue, here is a basic understanding of what creates a distinction between the gift of prophecy and the office of the prophet—*responsibility.*

Yes, responsibility is the difference between the two. Prophets will move in a powerful gift of prophecy and should be highly developed in the prophetic spectrum. However, any believer can desire the gift of prophecy and display a tremendous manifestation of many aspects of prophecy.

PAUL WAS THEIR APOSTLE

Allow me to clarify by using the apostle Paul as an example.

> *Am I not an apostle? Am I not free? Have I not seen Jesus Christ our Lord? Are you not my work in the Lord?* [2] ***If I am not an apostle to others, yet doubtless I am to you.*** *For you are the seal of my apostleship in the Lord.*
>
> **—1 Corinthians 9:1-2**

Paul begins by saying, "Am I not an apostle?" Meaning, yes, he was a real, bona fide apostle appointed by God. He even mentions one of the signs of an apostle, that he had seen the Lord. Then Paul pivots and makes a very revealing statement. "*If I am not an apostle to others, yet doubtless I am to you.*" Here Paul gave us a significant insight. First, he was an actual apostle, then he adds, "If I am not an apostle to others."

The implication here is that Paul was saying although he is an apostle, he isn't an apostle to everyone! He then says, "*Yet doubtless I am to you.*" Paul was their apostle! This scripture means apostles have jurisdiction or are responsible for a segment of the body of Christ.

If this is true for apostles, the same principle can also apply to the rest of the fivefold ministry, specifically to prophets. To clarify this point, we must go to the Word of God.

*And He Himself gave some to be apostles, some prophets, some evangelists, and some pastors and teachers, [12] **for the equipping of the saints** for the work of ministry, **for the edifying of the body of Christ.***

—Ephesians 4:11-12

In the passage in Ephesians 4:11-12, we can see that Jesus gave some to be apostles and some to be prophets; and this goes for the remainder of the five governmental gifts. The main point of interest here is the job description: *equipping* the saints and *edifying* the body of Christ. Based on these two scriptures, each fivefold ministry has a jurisdiction and a job description.

An even better way of stating this might be that fivefold ministers are *not called to everyone* but to those to whom they are assigned. In their jurisdiction and assigned position within the body of Christ, they are to equip and edify the saints and body of Christ. When a truly anointed fivefold ministry is in its grace lane and the proper location of those they are assigned to and positioned, they are a blessing to the body of believers.

A PROPHET'S JURISDICTION

A prophet's jurisdiction applies to the office of the prophet. Prophets have a responsibility to those who recognize them as a prophet because God graced them for that segment of the body. In some cases, the prophet is also assigned to impact culture even outside the Church body. Daniel the Prophet operated that way, as did John the Baptist, along with other prophets throughout the Scriptures.

PROPHECY CAN WORK
THROUGH EVERY BELIEVER

Now this brings us to the point of understanding how the prophetic operates through both a prophet and a believer developing the gift of prophecy. It might be shocking to realize that a believer who eagerly desires the gift of prophecy and exercises it regularly can grow in it to the point they have a stronger gift, specifically in the word of knowledge, than many who walk in the office of the prophet. Let me give you an example from the Bible.

First Corinthians 14 is the best example of how prophecy is to function. You will notice this isn't about prophets; this is talking about believers in a local church body.

> But he who prophesies speaks **edification** and **exhortation** and **comfort** to men.
>
> —1 Corinthians 14:3

Classically, edification, exhortation, and comfort are taught as the only three ways prophecy should be used in the routine operation of the Church. Although it is a correct biblical position, it still needs to be completed. Indeed, it is a trustworthy foundation when solely operating in the three areas named in 1 Corinthians 14:3. However, there is one more! A fourth operation that is most vital and convincing is a *glaring word of knowledge.*

GLARING WORD OF KNOWLEDGE BY ALL

> *For to one is given the word of wisdom through the Spirit, to another the **word of knowledge** through the same Spirit.*
>
> —1 Corinthians 12:8

Word of knowledge is a revelation about a situation whether in the past, present, or future. A word that reveals facts about a person, place, or thing. The Holy Spirit can give information about something that would not be possible to know in the natural. Information that is given directly to us by the Holy Spirit.

Operating in the biblical words of knowledge has corporate implications. Not only is the word of knowledge for the individual, for the prophet, but it is also available for the corporate body of believers in the local church! The corporate word of knowledge is an area in which every believer can develop and even develop past someone standing in the office of the prophet.

> *But **if all prophesy**, and an unbeliever or an uninformed person comes in, he is convinced by all, he is convicted by all.*
>
> —1 Corinthians 14:24

Convinced by *all*, convicted by *all*—what does this mean? *All* is a reference to everyone in the Church! Meaning any Spirit-filled believer can develop in the *prophetic spectrum*, and specifically in word of knowledge so clearly that what they say or prophesy has the clarity and potential to cut straight to the very hidden truth of two classes of individuals—those who are unbelievers or uninformed.

What do these two labels mean? One is self-explanatory, they are unbelievers, and they are unsaved. Yet, through a glaring encounter with the word of knowledge spoken over them by all church members, they are convinced and convicted. This is undoubtedly a powerful evangelistic mechanism!

Next, the corporate word of knowledge impacts the uninformed person. How? In the same manner as the unbeliever. An uninformed person by the very nature of the label "uniformed," means one who has no prior understanding in regard to what is happening in the type of church they are walking into. In this case, the church of Corinth. "Uninformed" would likely refer to the person who is not familiar with a Spirit-filled culture, or speaking in tongues, as well as prophecy. The unbeliever however, is one who simply has not come to the saving knowledge of Jesus Christ. One encounter with this level of word of knowledge revealing the very secrets of their heart by *all* would challenge their belief system.

> *For you see your calling, brethren, that not many wise according to the flesh, not many mighty, not many noble, are called.* [27] *But God has chosen the foolish things of the world to put to shame the wise, and God has chosen the weak things of the world to put to shame the things which are mighty;* [28] *and the base things of the world and the things which are despised God has chosen, and the things which are not, to bring to nothing the things that are,* [29] *that no flesh should glory in His presence.*
>
> **—1 Corinthians 1:26-29**

What a powerful and largely neglected aspect of the prophetic, yet it is like the Lord, who delights in "using the foolish things to shame the wise and weak things to shame the strong!" Wouldn't it be just like God to utilize such a mighty flow of the prophetic through the average person in the Church, rendering the arguments of both the uninformed and unbeliever null and void? But how is this possible?

Aren't prophets the ones who are supposed to prophesy? Well, prophets do prophesy, but God would also use His body of believers in a magnificent way for two reasons.

1. *The Holy Spirit resides in all New Testament believers:* We are no longer under the Old Covenant but living under the new one with better promises. As a result, each believer can be filled with the Holy Spirit and has full access to every spiritual gift. Thus, they can prophesy to any level they develop, such as the word of knowledge.

2. *Desire:* The Word of God tells us to "eagerly desire" spiritual gifts, *especially* that we might prophesy. A more straightforward way of saying it would be that all believers can develop a very clear prophetic ability through desire and practicing the gift of prophecy.

As stated at the beginning of this chapter, the office of the prophet, like all the other fivefold governmental offices, is based on *responsibility*. Yes, an accompanying gift goes along with it, such as a prophet will always move in at least one of the four types of prophecy (which we will learn about as we go further in this chapter).

RESPONSIBILITY BACKED UP BY GIFTING

Ephesians 4:12 states, "For the equipping of the saints for the work of ministry, for the edifying of the body of Christ."

The office of the prophet is not solely based on gifting. It is more than simply prophesying; it is an individual with a prophetic gift called by God with a *responsibility* to the body of Christ and every office gift listed in Ephesians 4 should develop their giftings—especially the prophet! By responsibility I am specifically referring to Ephesians 4:12 where it defines the responsibility of fivefold ministry. "For the equipping of the saints for the work of ministry, for the edifying of the body of Christ." Each fivefold ministry office has this common responsibility: Equipping and edifying the saints. Prophets certainly hold this responsibility. A person who prophesies may do so effectively but this does not place them in the office gift. Responsibility does—and again, it is the responsibility of a prophet to equip and edify the saints.

> *Having then gifts differing according to the grace that is given to us, let us use them: if prophecy, let us prophesy in proportion to our faith.*
>
> **—Romans 12:6**

It is refreshing to think that every person in the body of Christ can grow in the prophetic. However, this does not make them a prophet; it simply means they have an invitation to develop in prophecy as the Bible prescribes. This understanding takes the mystical part of the office of the prophet away when you recognize it as a *job description*, not some hierarchy of power and authority over the body of Christ.

GOVERNING MINISTRY OFFICE— NOT A HIERARCHY

Prophets should be teachers of the Word of God, at least on a fundamental level, accompanied by training in the prophetic, training through a demonstration of how prophecy works by giving words of knowledge, foretelling events, and specific words for individuals and the global body of Christ.

Prophets are also called to edify and strengthen the brethren through the prophetic in a public setting. Often at the end of the meetings, when

I finish teaching, a time of prophetic ministry will flow from me. This is common for prophetic ministers and prophets, as described in the following verse:

> *Now Judas and Silas, themselves being prophets also, exhorted and strengthened the brethren with many words.*
>
> **—Acts 15:32**

Interestingly enough, this sets a precedent for prophetic team ministry. Prophets often find each other and even, at times, work as a company.

THE PROPHETIC SPECTRUM

In a moment you will see the four types of prophecy listed. These are by no means complete, as the Word of God contains a variety of ways God speaks and works through His people. These four you are about to see are simply guidelines and create a spectrum, or a way of understanding how someone's prophetic gift operates.

MAJORS AND MINORS

Universities use the terminology major and minor to describe what study pathways someone is taking. The term *major* describes the main thrust of what they will be studying and gaining a degree in. The term *minor* simply represents the lesser emphasized of the two, but still, an avenue that will be learned and utilized only to the preference of the first.

When considering the office of the prophet, there is also a unique and robust gift of prophecy that works through the prophet. Although every member of the body of Christ can prophesy, the office gift carries a weightier authority, most often packaged with a major and a minor gift on the prophetic spectrum. This is not to say that prophets cannot move in all four functions on the prophetic spectrum; however, it is *typical* to observe prophets functioning with a major and a minor.

Over the years and through observing many prophets, I have recognized diversities of expression in how their gifting operates through them. For example, one prophet may work in the word of knowledge as their major. Upon sensing a flow of the Spirit moving on them, their automatic response is an activated word of knowledge. That would be a major gift.

Whenever the Spirit comes upon them, they have a go-to gifting that begins to operate. Yet they will occasionally experience a vision; maybe it's an intuitive one or a full-out movie trailer-style vision. Regardless, it happens less often than the word of knowledge. Visions would then be recognized as their minor prophetic gift. This is simply an example of majors and minors.

> *Every good gift and every perfect gift is from above, and comes down from the Father of lights, with whom there is no variation or shadow of turning.*
>
> **—James 1:17**

All gifts have been given by Jesus to the Church for empowerment. The Word of God reveals four different types of prophecy or four different types of prophets. Identification is based on the gifting they use *most often*. A prophet can have a major gift while still touching on their minor gifts, meaning it is possible to have one major gift of operation, or the gifting utilized most comfortably, and still operate in all four of them.

At least the first two (*roeh* and *nabi*) of the four types of prophecy are listed in the following scripture reference.

> *Formerly in Israel, when a man went to inquire of God, he spoke thus: "Come, let us go to the* **seer**"; *for he who is now called a* **prophet** *was formerly called a seer.*
>
> **—1 Samuel 9:9**

In the following scripture, three out of the four are listed.

> *Now the acts of David the king, first and last, behold, they are written in the book of Samuel the* **seer**, *and in the book of Nathan the* **prophet**, *and in the book of Gad the* **seer**.
>
> **—1 Chronicles 29:29**

Following are the *four basic operations on the prophetic spectrum* identified by their Hebrew words:

Roeh
Visionary. Seer.

Nabi
Mouthpiece—Proclaimer; Declarer;
Forth teller; Herald. Nabi
literally means "to bubble up."

Chazah
To gaze at, mentally perceive,
or supernatural sight by
visions and dreams.

Chozeh
A Beholder: one who leans forward
peering into the distance.

1. Roeh – The Visionary Seer Mobilizer Prophet

The basic meaning is a *visionary* or a *seer* prophet, such as in 1 Samuel 9:9 and 1 Chronicles 29:29. Not only do these types of prophets supernaturally see outside themselves, but they also possess visionary leadership qualities and are anointed to accomplish the impossible.

Roeh is a gift that also casts vision and has the ability to *"mobilize the troops."* In practical application, this gift can reside in a prophet or any fivefold ministry. When in action, *Roeh* will lead crusades, events large or small, and often is the gifting in motion behind many of the impossible events the body of Christ does to gather people for a cause.

Roeh additionally functions through marketplace leaders in the political arena and beyond. Sadly, like so many gifts, they can be used for man's glory rather than the Lord's.

2. Nabi (nah-vee): The Proclaiming Prophet

First Chronicles 29:29 says, "Now the acts of David the king, first and last, behold, they are written in the book of Samuel the **seer,** and in the book of Nathan the **prophet,** and in the book of Gad the **seer.**" This gifting is to be a mouthpiece, one who declares, a forth teller, a messenger, or a herald. One of the aspects of this gift is "to bubble up." It is the most commonly used of the four. It manifests as an inspirational preaching gift. When people use the words "I feel inspired," they might be operating in the *nabi* spectrum.

3. Chazah: The Gazing Prophet

This gift functions through supernatural sight through visions, dreams, and mental perception, and it also means *to gaze at.*

Word of knowledge, dreams, and intuitive visions are all part of the *chazah* spectrum.

*As for me, **I shall behold** Thy face in righteousness; I will be satisfied with Thy likeness when I awake.*

—Psalm 17:15 NASB1977

*You are wearied in the multitude of your counsels; let now the astrologers, the **stargazers**, And the monthly prognosticators stand up and save you from what shall come upon you.*

—Isaiah 47:13

*Your prophets have **seen** for you false and deceptive visions; they have not uncovered your iniquity, to bring back your captives, but have envisioned for you false prophecies and delusions.*

—Lamentations 2:14

*Son of man, look, the house of Israel is saying, "The **vision** that he sees is for many days from now, and he prophesies of times far off."*

—Ezekiel 12:27

*The burden which the prophet Habakkuk **saw**.*

—Habakkuk 1:1

*For the idols speak delusion; the diviners **envision** lies and tell false dreams; they comfort in vain. Therefore, the people wend their way like sheep; they are in trouble because there is no shepherd.*

—Zechariah 10:2

GAZING

When you see a word such as "gazing", it might come across as something mystical. However, it is not when understood in a biblical scope and within the confines of its Hebrew definition. The actual definition of the word *chazah* means *to gaze*. It is understandable to comprehend words of knowledge, visions, dreams, and even intuitive visions, which is simply the Holy Spirit using your mental imagery to speak to you.

However, gazing is an interesting topic that needs explanation and a clearer biblical reference. An excellent example of gazing in Scripture is found with the prophet Elisha. In 2 Kings 8, the prophet had an encounter with a messenger for the king, an officer by the name of Hazael.

Hazael came to see Elisha on behalf of the king. His request was to find out if the king was going to live or die. But amid this communication, a unique thing happened. Elisha, while he was speaking, began to stare right at Hazael.

The moment became uncomfortable to the point of embarrassment for Hazael. One commentator says Elisha's gaze caused Hazael to blush from embarrassment due to the implied awkwardness of the prophet's gaze. As strange an encounter as this was, it continued until the moment was broken, with the prophet bursting into tears. Why tears? Elisha was gazing through Hazael into a vision of this man's future. A horrible future filled with unspeakable acts of wickedness that Elisha had just lived out in a snapshot through gazing. The prophet was caught in a moment when he gazed into this man's future.

As you are about to read, the scripture makes it sound at the first observation that Elisha was saying, "Go tell him he will live even though he is really going to die." So it would seem as though Elisha was being deceitful. But what was happening was the prophet knew Hazael would kill the king.

Elisha said, "*Yes, you will recover from your sickness,*" which would have been an accurate word for the king. However, the king would still die at the hand of the very officer and messenger Elisha was speaking to—Hazael.

> *And Elisha said to him, "Go, say to him, 'You shall certainly recover.' However, the Lord has shown me that he will really die."* [11] **Then he set his countenance in a stare until he was ashamed; and the man of God wept.** [12] *And Hazael said, "Why is my lord weeping?" He answered, "Because I know the evil that you will do to the children of Israel: Their strongholds you will set on fire, and their young men you will kill with the sword; and you will dash their children and rip open their women with child."*
>
> —2 Kings 8:10-12

> *Then he departed from Elisha, and came to his master, who said to him, "What did Elisha say to you?" And he answered, "He told me you would surely recover."* [15] *But it happened on the next day that he took a thick cloth and dipped it in water, and spread it over his face so that he died; and Hazael reigned in his place.*
>
> —2 Kings 8:14-15

Gazing is interesting, as it comes to prophets who operate in this spectrum at unique times. Gazing is something I experience when ministering. This is why many times, when looking at someone, I won't look at their face. Instead, I often will look at their shoulder or a wall or something like it off to the side. Why? Because looking at a blank space makes gazing more straightforward with less business or traffic, which I describe as emotional, supernatural, or informational data. A sensing that comes forth when in proximity to people, events, or picking up conversations about a person, place, or thing. I will go into more detail on what traffic is in Chapter Thirteen.

Crystal Ball

I suspect that the perversion and prostitution of this part of the prophetic spectrum can be seen when wizards, occultists, fortune tellers, and other demonic operators utilize neutral objects such as crystal balls. Not because the crystal ball itself has unique properties, but it may also be that they are simply perverting and attempting to hijack or copy the way God's gifts operate. After all the devil is not an originator, he is a thief and a deceiver, this is what he does through his demonic operators.

KEEP IT SIMPLE AND IN THE BIBLE

As a vital part of the prophetic spectrum, *chazah* is a mighty flow God has given to the prophetic. It is more common when ministering to individuals prophetically, mainly in the word of knowledge. Much like all the gifts of the Spirit, we as believers are to stand firmly on the Word of God when operating in any gift, especially the revelatory gifts in the prophetic.

4. *Chozeh* (Hebrew): A Beholder; one who leans forward, peering into the distance.

Chozeh involves seeing things involving the future. On this prophetic spectrum are figures such as Daniel and John the Revelator. Seeing in this capacity involves visions and trances. *Chozeh* also tends *to stress the visionary or perceptive aspects of a prophet's experiences.*

*It is doubtless not profitable for me to boast. I will come to visions and revelations of the Lord: ² I know a man in Christ who fourteen years ago—**whether in the body I do not know, or whether out of the body I do not know,** God knows—such a one was caught up to the third heaven. ³ And I know such a man—**whether in the body or out of the body I do not know,** God knows—⁴ how he was caught up into Paradise and heard inexpressible words, which it is not lawful for a man to utter.*

—2 Corinthians 12:1-4

OUT OF BODY EXPERIENCE

When Paul was taken to heaven, he said, "Whether I was in the body or out of the body I don't know," pointing to the *chozeh* spectrum in prophecy. It could simply be that God snapped Paul up, which had nothing to do with prophecy. It is the terminology in or out of the body that Paul didn't know, which is indicative of a *chozeh* encounter. However, it must be said that prophecy is not a paint-by-numbers science; it is an experiential encounter that is difficult to quantify by natural means. Thus, Paul's statement, *I don't know.* Sometimes, that is the most theologically astute thing an honest person can say.

The following scriptures show variations of the Hebrew word *chozeh* as it applies *to leaning into the future and seeing things to come.*

*Son of man, look, the house of Israel is saying, "The **vision** that he **sees** is for many days from now, and he **prophesies** of times far off."*

—Ezekiel 12:27

*Seventy weeks are determined for your people and for your holy city, to finish the transgression, to make an end of sins, to make reconciliation for iniquity, to bring in everlasting righteousness, to seal up **vision** and prophecy, and to anoint the Most Holy.*

—Daniel 9:24

*Now I have come to make you understand what will happen to your people in the latter days, for the **vision** refers to many days yet to come.*

—Daniel 10:14

*As for me, I will **see** Your face in righteousness; I shall be satisfied when I awake in Your likeness.*

—Psalm 17:15

You are wearied in the multitude of your counsels; let now the astrologers, the stargazers, and the monthly prognosticators stand up and save you from what shall come upon you.

—Isaiah 47:13

The vision of Isaiah the son of Amoz, which he saw concerning Judah and Jerusalem in the days of Uzziah, Jotham, Ahaz, and Hezekiah, kings of Judah.

—Isaiah 1:1

*Your prophets have **seen** for you false and deceptive visions; they have not uncovered your iniquity, to bring back your captives, but have envisioned for you false prophecies and delusions.*

—Lamentations 2:14

*The burden which the prophet Habakkuk **saw**.*

—Habakkuk 1:1

THE BOOK OF REVELATION

*The **Revelation** of Jesus Christ, which God gave Him to show His servants—things which must shortly take place. And He sent and signified it by His angel to His servant John, ² who bore witness to the word of God, and to the testimony of Jesus Christ, to all things that he saw.*

—Revelation 1:1-2

John's New Testament encounter on the island of Patmos is among the dynamic equivalents between Hebrew and Greek concerning the *chozeh* spectrum.

In Revelation 1:1, we see the word *apokálupsis*, which is the basis for the word *apocalypse*. Pop culture has used this term to define the end of the world. However, that is not the proper understanding of this word. It means an *unveiling, an uncovering, a disclosure of what was concealed.* John experienced a vision or an unveiling of the future.

Chozeh is likely the least-operated gifting used in the arena of the prophetic spectrum. It mainly works through the office of the prophet and points to things to come.

However, it can apply to any believer should the Spirit choose to open up an encounter for a purpose. Those who have gone to heaven and come back to speak about it may have left their bodies or stepped into this realm of prophetic function.

One thing that can be trusted is that the Lord is not the author of confusion! He desires that you walk in the fullness of what He has for you, and many are experiencing non-biblical experiences that the Holy Spirit is not inducing. We will get into more of that in the pages ahead, but remember that the highest and best thing in our relationship with God is to know Jesus through His written Word—the Bible. We live in a time when celebrating normal prophetic function is necessary, or deception is at the door. You do not have to attempt to move in any of the operations of the prophetic, pray in the Spirit, read your Bible, or get to know God! The gifts will find you!

CHAPTER FIVE

PROPHETIC DNA–

WITCHCRAFT OR LEGITIMATE?

*Then Amos answered and said to Amaziah: "I was no prophet, **nor was I a son of a prophet**, but I was a sheep-breeder and a tender of sycamore fruit. *[15]* Then the Lord took me as I followed the flock, and the Lord said to me, 'Go, prophesy to My people Israel.'"*

—Amos 7:14-15

Ever since I was young, it was common to hear my grandmother and mom talking about a vision, a dream, or some unique encounter with the Holy Spirit, which involved Him speaking to them, revealing revelatory information. It was not uncommon for my mom to see a vision of an event only to see it manifest a short while later.

In our family lineage, there are several prophetic people who are able to see and say or have dreams which come to pass. A few of my cousins, aunts, and uncles are on the prophetic spectrum. Families carry certain traits; among the many abilities seen in my family's lineage is the prophetic.

This leads me to a fascinating point of interest. A statement made by the prophet Amos, *I am not the son of a prophet nor am I a prophet.*

His point has more than one vantage to it, one being this was possibly a reference to being a member of a prophetic community called the School of the Prophets, known as "the sons of the prophets." It also poses a question, which we are going to consider.

Is there a connection between supernatural gifts and your biological or genetic makeup? Do supernatural gifts get passed down in families? It is an interesting thing to consider. Does your family's background have a thread of gifting tracing through your DNA and genetic makeup? Purpose and family calling might have a greater significance than many would consider. Biblical precedent would suggest that people such as Timothy, whose grandmother and mother had faith; that faith was passed down to Timothy "genetically" (*see* 2 Timothy 1:5). Additionally we see that Philip, the evangelist who indeed moved in the realm of supernatural faith, also passed that faith down to his daughters who prophesied. His daughters were the recipients of Philip's faith and it manifested as the gift of prophecy (*see* Acts 21:9). A very interesting thing to note is that oftentimes families of faith pass down their faith, causing similar gifts of the Spirit to operate in members of their lineage.

HEARING GOD FROM MY YOUTH

That the Lord called Samuel. And he answered, "Here I am!" [5] *So he ran to Eli and said, "Here I am, for you called me." And he said, "I did not call; lie down again." And he went and lay down.* [6] *Then the Lord called yet again, "Samuel!" So Samuel arose and went to Eli, and said, "Here I am, for you called me." He answered, "I did not call, my son; lie down again."* [7] *(Now Samuel did not yet know the Lord, nor was the word of the Lord yet revealed to him.)*

—1 Samuel 3:4-7

I would like to go deeper into the story about my personal experience with the Voice of God as a boy, which I briefly mentioned in Chapter One. I am inclined to believe gifts can be something certain people are simply born with.

Early in my life, an encounter marked the beginning of hearing God's Voice. I was nine and heard a Voice over the trees and on the wind. Like an echo on the wind, only distinctly clear. This experience was a point of contact to wake up the gift of prophecy in me. I discovered an attraction to quietness. Being far removed from everything awakened my creativity and caused my imagination to grow. These times of recreational solitude were very enjoyable, and they produced an internal, peace-laden stillness. Off-roading on my ATV (all-terrain vehicle), hunting, and building tree houses were some of the happiest times in my young life.

Duke, my dog, and I would often hike through the vast property, stalking grouse near the banks of the broad river, which ran miles alongside the property. It was during these times that a unique thing would happen. I seldom mentioned it because there was never an easy way to explain the experience.

A VOICE CALLED MY NAME

Yet, over time it seemed to occur more frequently. The experiences weren't startling, but they certainly piqued my curiosity: a voice calling my name from a distance, seemingly traveling with the wind over the treetops with a distinctly familiar sound. Much like an echo, although twice as loud—loud enough to be heard clearly—but in the form of a distant shout. Most of the time, the shout would sound very much like the voice of my dad.

One day, after mistaking this Voice for my dad's, I drove my ATV to find him back at the house. After asking him what he wanted and why he called me, he replied, "I didn't call you."

His response was somewhat confusing but I learned from an early age that I shouldn't question my dad.

Another time, after once again finding my dad—thinking his voice had been summoning me—he admitted something that I will never forget.

He asked me, "Did you hear someone call your name?"

"Yes."

"Did it sound like I was calling you?"

"Yes," I replied again.

Smiling, he said, "I know. I have had that happen to me as well."

That was the last time we directly spoke of it. I didn't know what to do with this mystery, nor did I understand my dad's response to it. As a result, it was left as a strange family understanding and treated like no big deal.

This experience was a point of contact to wake up the gift of prophecy in me.

NORMALCY BIAS

Psychology uses the term *normalcy bias*. Something strange and out of place occurs, but everyone subconsciously ignores it and goes on with life as usual. This was the case regarding this situation and my family. If it ever did come up in the slightest reference, it was wry and a little humorous, then dismissed as quickly as it came up. After this conversation with my dad, it happened again, but this time it was frightening.

A DIFFERENT VOICE

I stepped off my ATV and began looking over a half-mile-long field. It was one of those moments meant for me to enjoy the peace and stillness that ignited creativity and imagination. Duke and I positioned about a football field length from the tree line behind us.

The stillness was beautiful but was starkly broken by the shout of my name. Once again, in the distance, but out over the open field in front of us. After listening for a moment, I called back, "Yeah? —What?!"

Silence. My attention turned to Duke for a moment, but then the voice came again, "Joe!"

Now it was closer—a *lot closer!* Standing beside the ATV, I called back again, "What?"

Again, there was no sound, no voice calling. Then Duke's hair began to rise. As the hair on the nape of his neck bristled and stood tall all along his back, his demeanor changed into an intent stare.

Suddenly, I heard the same voice, yet it was no longer a shout and no longer from far away—it was slightly above a whisper and within arm's reach.

Duke flinched, laid his ears back, and ran away as fast as possible, which was not a *typical* response—he was a courageous dog!

BEYOND VOICES

Even beyond just hearing voices, I had other strange experiences as a boy. Unique moments would periodically happen, but they never seemed out of the ordinary to me because they were familiar.

For example, one day, while watching TV, I "zoned out," for lack of a better term. This makes me laugh writing it because anyone with children will say, "Yeah, we see that all the time!"

However, this was different.

Not long before this day, my dad had taken me to see *Rocky III* in the theater. So there I was, laying on the floor with my hands supporting my face, subconsciously watching TV and simultaneously daydreaming about the third Rocky. Then I saw a snippet of a movie trailer for the next film. I saw a big Russian guy and read the title, *Rocky IV*.

I thought this new movie looked pretty cool, so I told my family about the trailer I'd *seen*. In a matter-of-fact tone, I conveyed, "Rocky is going to fight a Russian in the next Rocky movie, *Rocky IV*." Not knowing the plot, just a straightforward theme from the images I had seen, I continued, "Apollo Creed will have to train him again because his old trainer, Mickey, died."

I don't remember who, but one of my family members said, "Umm, *Rocky III* just came out. You don't know who he is fighting in the next movie or even if there will *be* another movie."

It hadn't even occurred to me that I couldn't have known if there were plans to make another movie, as *Rocky III* was still in theaters. A new trailer for *Rocky IV* couldn't possibly have existed yet!

Yet while I was watching TV, my imagination had transformed from a simple daydream into a moment of watchable information in the form of a short movie trailer that no one else in the room witnessed. It wasn't necessarily spiritual or spooky; it was just information in the context of something I was *thinking about*.

Interestingly, this hadn't even been a big deal because it seemed normal. It was like a sharp picture in my mind, only like I was viewing it on the outside. I thought I had seen it on the TV. It's hard to recall how

I responded then in the face of my family's disbelief. I know this experience was a supernatural prediction shown to me a couple of years before any news or movie preview for that film.

This situation stands out in my memory because both family and kids at school just shrugged it off when I said, "Rocky will be fighting a Russian." Yet I knew with my heart that it was true. Sure enough, a couple of years later, Rocky fought a Russian in *Rocky IV*.

This moment wasn't something *I made happen*, and the many moments like it afterward never came with a warning either. The relevance of these events became enlightening to a degree; they showed me that regardless of whether people believed what I said or not, my experiences were real.

Still, after these episodes and not being understood, I hid most of these encounters in my heart. It was a significant discovery that information would sometimes come to me when I was very relaxed and thinking about something specific.

The information was most often related to what I was thinking about. It would come in different ways, such as seeing it or having an intuitive "knowing" about it in the present, past, or future tense, as though someone had told me the information.

As time went on, I learned that there are certain times when I look at someone or something long enough, and information will begin to come to me about them, often in an emotional way. This experience gave me a heightened sense of empathy, which caused me to be somewhat introverted, especially when meeting new people.

A RADIO ANTENNA

My close friends would never have thought of me as an introvert. However, it was because of knowing them and no longer experiencing what I now call *traffic*—the feelings or impressions I would get from people. The closer I got with people, the less I *"felt"* things from them.

It was not easy to walk around like a radio antenna! I remember going to the funeral of a lovely aunt of mine who had died of cancer. At her burial, we were all gathered around her casket, and there was a reading of her journal entries during her last days.

As they read it, I suddenly felt like I was in her room with her as she wrote in her journal, experiencing all her pain and hopelessness. There was no way for me to process what was happening. The sensation of tormenting sorrow caused me to weep violently, which was not common in our family, and it must have embarrassed my dad. I was overcome because I was directly experiencing her feelings, and I couldn't avoid it.

It was a horrible thing to feel at that age—someone dying—and the darkness that entered my mind and heart was unbearable. The imagery of her torment was in full color inside of me—to the point that it was as if I was actually in the room. I could see her looking around her room at times, finding no one to bring relief. All I could do was sob.

One of my cousins approached me after the service and said, "Wow, that really hit you hard, huh?" Being that we were just kids, there wasn't a way of articulating what was happening to me. So, she just hugged me and said, "It will be okay." The weird thing is that during this experience, I felt like a bystander. It wasn't that the scenario was so sad; it was that I ran into the traffic of her emotions and memories through hearing her journal being read.

My response to that season of random encounters was to head back to the woods, back to farming, back to hunting with Duke, and do my very best just to enjoy peace and creativity. However, these encounters were only the beginning. The Voice of God impacted my life then, and the journey continues to this day.

Before the age of ten, I had already encountered several supernatural experiences. Some were unique and relatively harmless; others were uneasy and even terrifying. But as time went on, I discovered it was mainly due to the gifting God had placed inside me from birth that I experienced these things. There was no way to grasp what was happening to me as a young boy, as much of what I encountered seemed normal. Such as hearing my name called outside over the trees as if carried by the wind, to a sense of empathy toward people and circumstances happening in my proximity. There were moments of seeing events or people in my *mind's eye* only to see those same events or circumstances in all reality a day or two later!

Some nights I experienced dreams, only to have them come true. They came true in type, or on occasion, very close to how I dreamt it a day or two before the event.

HOW PSYCHICS ARE MADE

That recurring voice which I mentioned earlier, there was a different voice. It was not the voice of God, it was a demonic voice present for deception. That voice was so clear and had been speaking directly to me that it would have been easy to begin communicating or dialoguing with it!

The Holy Spirit revealed to me one day that this is how many people, who do not know the Lord, are led down the wrong path. They are approached by a voice, a vision, an apparition, and not being born again, nor having any biblical foundation, they wrongly engage with it. They give permission through that engagement for the said entity or voice to communicate with them by responding to it and may even go as far as allowing the voice to channel through them.

The reason the enemy comes to deceive is for *access*. He needs human beings to allow demonic operation to flow through them. It is my suspicion that this *access* is the foundation of many who are deceived into believing they are "psychic." Sometimes those who have an inclination and curiosity for the supernatural can easily fall for the counterfeit. Unsaved families who are gifted, or sensitive to the realm of the spiritual world can be drawn away by false, deceptive encounters, ultimately producing a perversion of the legitimate. For every counterfeit, there must be a legitimate one, and let me make this point really clear that there are a lot of fake psychics out there, tricksters— there are also real ones who move in a demonic spirit of divination (*see* the slave girl who prophesied about Paul and Silas in Acts 16:16-19).

BORN WITH GIFTS

Going back to the words of Amos, "I am not the son of a prophet nor am I a prophet." There may be a connection between supernatural gifts and your genetic makeup or your DNA—your family's makeup.

In my case, I have experienced prophetic things since I can remember. Way before encountering the salvation of Jesus! Consider that some people being born with gifts is not out of the ordinary.

For example, we can observe families that have skills unique to them, such as a family of musicians. Have you ever seen a family where it would seem every member of the household plays an instrument or sings? How about a medical family made up of nurses, doctors, and professionals who assist in caring for people? Or teachers; I come from a family with many teachers, and our family has common traits due to that part of our makeup. Some families are better wired for specific abilities and gifts: technicians, construction, pilots, and service members. You might be considering what gifts or common traits run through your lineage.

SPIRITUAL DNA

Prophecy is a spiritual gifting that operates by faith but can also be passed down through families. Prophetic unction, dreams, visions, or sensitivity to the things of the unseen realm can be a gift some are born with because they are in a household of faith.

There is a perversion of this. As even in those who are not born again, there can be a sensitivity to spiritual things. If a relationship with Jesus has not happened, but rather, their only encounter is through demonic activity, deception is the result. Such encounters may engage a spiritually sensitive person, and a pathway may be created which leads to psychic activity, mystics, or those who walk in a clairvoyance that they believe is simply within them—sadly, they could be right! It is an unction or spiritual sensitivity that is recognized by both the light and darkness. A territory war will take place over such an individual. This is why preaching the gospel is vital! However, we must recognize that although there are counterfeits, there will also be those who are real. This applies to the light and dark side of things.

Issues arise when a person with a genuine experience has the ability, maybe a gift, to prophesy or sense things before they happen. These people may have had encounters with dreams, visions, visitations from entities, or familiar spirits claiming to be lost ones.

DELIVERANCE IS NEEDED

It might be startling to realize that *unbelievers can have gifts in their DNA*, and when brought into a spiritual environment, they *act out*. What would be the highest and best experience for them would be a discerning body of believers leading them to salvation and the baptism in the Holy Spirit. They may need deliverance to remove demonic influence and deception relating to deceptive spiritual encounters that may have impacted their life.

It is crucial to determine whether an individual is walking in a demonically induced operation or has a spiritual sensitivity they were born with that is functioning through their soulish arena, devoid of all anointing—or is it both? As said at the beginning of this chapter, Timothy had the gift of faith, which was passed down through his family line.

> When I call to remembrance the genuine faith that is in you, which dwelt first in your grandmother Lois and your mother Eunice, and I am persuaded is in you also.
>
> —2 Timothy 1:5

You can see Timothy carrying the family calling and gifts passed down from his mother and grandmother.

> And when we had finished our voyage from Tyre, we came to Ptolemais, greeted the brethren, and stayed with them one day. ⁸ On the next day we who were Paul's companions departed and came to Caesarea, and entered the house of Philip the evangelist, who was one of the seven, and stayed with him. ⁹ **Now this man had four virgin daughters who prophesied.** ¹⁰ And as we stayed many days, a certain prophet named Agabus came down from Judea.
>
> —Acts 21:7-10

Again, with the example of Philip's daughters, we see that spiritual gifts can run in families. He had four daughters who prophesied! These examples are how pure and legitimate spiritual operation should be passed down through families.

GIFTS MISHANDLED IN THE CHURCH

When new believers who are new to practicing the spiritual gifts arise in a local church, it can scare those in leadership who do not possess a doctrinal makeup for the prophetic or may have never been around it. As a result, the "new to gifts" individual may be cast out by rejection and mishandling by the Church. Many who have come to the Church for training, acceptance, or understanding might become outcasts due to lack of proper biblical understanding.

In our ministry, we desire to rescue the outcasts, or gifted yet misunderstood individuals, train them in the Word of God, and turn them *from an outcast into a broadcast for Jesus!*

WHAT SPIRIT IS DRIVING THE GIFT

Again, remember, a person with a tremendous ability to sing can sound just as good in a club as they can on stage at a church. The difference is which spirit is powering the gift.

Someone born on the prophetic spectrum, may find that they have an interesting, even acute spiritual awareness.

In our modern church culture, there seems to be a greater sympathy, even curiosity, to venture into areas of revelation that are not biblically on point. Or worse, doctrines originated in Eastern religions are being embraced by segments of the body of Christ, and this fallacy should be exposed for the sake of believers to have a proper encounter with the Holy Spirit.

Those who have had gifts from birth often need to be discipled more than others; without discipling, they can fall prey to wrong understanding and operation. These people must learn what the Bible says about such things, including the proper operation. Your life may have such gifts, and it is vital that you develop the gifts God gave you for the glory of Jesus and your fellow brothers and sisters. You count. Your life matters: a high act of worship to the Lord is when we surrender all we are and have to Him!

CHAPTER SIX

ENCOUNTERS WITH THE SPIRIT

*Come up here, and I will show you things which must
take place after this.*

—Revelation 4:1

Prophetic people have many encounters while learning the Voice of God. Encounters must always be leveled with the Word of God; yet along the journey, prophetic people may find unique things transpire.

My life has been filled with many—like a magnet. It would seem prophetic people draw in supernatural moments. Without the placement of the written Word of God firmly in their lives, experiences can pull *called people* away from their highest purpose. However, when you are set firmly on the Word of God and have experiences and encounters, they won't lead you astray because your heart will be clear and filled with the goodness of God.

Lovers of the truth can have intense encounters, and it will be a place of obedience and peace. Consider John the Revelator. He certainly had some intense encounters in the book of Revelation! What he encountered turned out to be a profound blessing as it became what we know today as *Revelation* or the last book of the Bible.

The Word of God had become something I couldn't do without. An intense hunger took hold of me for it. One summer, while living in northern Minnesota, I decided to dedicate myself to the Bible and prayer. A series of interesting things began to take place!

MY NAME ON A WHITE STONE

One day, when I was 15, I was walking by a lake when the Holy Spirit spoke to me. The impression in my heart said, "Take off your shoes and wade out into the lake." I stopped momentarily and thought, *Did I just hear this right? Take off my shoes and walk out into that cold lake?*

After not hearing anything else, I thought, *Okay, I'll do it.* Off came my shoes, and after rolling up my jeans as far as I could, I waded into the lake. I was knee-deep when my feet stopped. Let me tell you, the journey was cold, and I felt odd.

I stood there for a minute or two without knowing what else to do. Suddenly, I felt a gentle pull in my heart to turn to the right and walk a little more. Then, the sense to stop brought me to a halt. Again, as if speaking to me, that same sense said, "Look down and pick up the first stone you find."

It was difficult to see into the water, but I did what I sensed I was supposed to do. Reaching down into that chilly water, I located a small stone. Standing upright with the stone in hand, I noticed that the stone was white, unlike the other rocks in the area. I stood there for a moment and examined this marble-sized, white stone.

To my astonishment, it had natural grooves on its exterior, which were very dark gray. As I inspected the rock, it didn't take long to identify that these nearly black lines looked like letters, which spelled the word *Joe*.

I had discovered a rock in the water onto which nature had carved *my name!* It was shocking, so I stood on the shore, my gaze fixed on this surreal, little white stone. At that moment, I felt an overwhelming sense that the Lord had called me and would always be with me.

ENCOUNTERS

My primary purpose in sharing some of the stories in this chapter is to show that laying hold of the Word of God and realizing your identity and authority in Jesus will bring order to any supernatural chaos in your life.

The latter half of that summer erupted with wild, supernatural encounters. That is the best way I can explain them—everything from wild, scary things, to confronting witches and casting demons out of people.

The environment of the conference center in Northern Minnesota where we were was known for supernatural encounters. Of course, this attracted many people from all around the world, people who had a hunger to have these supernatural experiences.

During these meetings, people were consistently healed of sickness and set free from depression. Many individuals who dealt with dark spiritual issues were also engaged.

DEALING WITH WITCHCRAFT

There was one encounter that I will never forget. I was attending a Christian camp. A friend and I were in a room to the side of the camp's central meeting place when no services were happening. As we were inside praying, a lady walked in, praying strangely and loudly. It made the two of us feel very uncomfortable.

She approached us and said, "I'm going to lay hands on you." I immediately responded with a polite, "No, thank you."

However, she proceeded to lay hands on Matt, and he sat still as she spoke loudly over him in a creepy language. It was not a Holy Spirit encounter at all! When she had finished, she burst into laughter and exited the room.

My friend looked at me and said, "I don't feel well." So, I said, "Let's get you up to your place."

As we walked, he said, "I felt something come over me while that lady spoke to me."

When we arrived at his house, he went to the restroom and became sick. Shortly after, his wife came out holding a baby. Suddenly, chaos flooded the scene: the baby vomited on the floor and started screaming, the lights went out, and their stereo popped on, blaring, without any logical reason for doing so.

I immediately ran to find help, but as I did, something came over me, and I began to feel nauseous and upset. People around me asked if I was okay, but I couldn't reply due to feeling ill.

This next part sounds even more strange, but it is true. One young lady went into my friend's house to pray for his family, and when she walked through the door, she fell and passed out! This wild experience continued until a different and seasoned minister friend caught wind of what was happening, went into the house, and spoke the Word of God over it. Suddenly, it all stopped.

I got up off the sidewalk outside and found my way to a bed. Laying there, I felt hatred and anger pressing me to a degree I had never experienced before. Finally, I opened my mouth and said, "The victory is the Lord's, and I resist this, in Jesus' name!"

Everything I was feeling swirling around me—the anger, hatred, and sickness—left instantly! I got up as if nothing happened other than feeling very dehydrated and weak.

The friend who had those demonic hands laid on him was rushed to the emergency room. I went to see him with a couple of guys, and I will never forget that as we were walking along the street, a person shouted, "*Jesus Christ,*" from across the street while glaring at me. My friend's dad said, "Nope! Sorry, just one of His followers!"

We got to the hospital room, where my friend was in bed receiving IV fluids. My friend said, "I had something come over me like darkness." We prayed for him, and he got better.

This experience impacted me greatly, and I decided I would never be a victim of something like that again. So, I began to read the Word of God even more and it put steel inside me! I can remember thinking, *There is nothing like this Book!* The more I read it, the stronger and more secure I became.

Not long after this, the same lady was standing in the back of one of the meetings. This was a time of ministry when I was involved in praying over people. This lady came toward me, and I felt strength and authority rise inside me as she approached.

She was only a few steps from me, and she raised her hand as if to reach out and touch me. On the inside, I rose and lunged at her in faith and power. I laid my hand on her and commanded whatever was working through her to leave. She fell like a dead person and just lay there.

CALLING ON ANGELS

Various people who struggled with demonic issues would come to the prayer room at the camp. I would pray for them, and demons would come out screaming. One young girl, who had been part of occult practices, had a voice speak through her, saying it would kill her and me. I was young and didn't know what to do, but there I was.

She wildly manifested demons and attacked me. Wow, she was strong! Her voice even changed. As she tried to harm both herself and me, I commanded the evil spirits to leave. However, this only made her behave more violently.

I read in the Word of God that angels obey the voice of the covenant—God's Voice working through me. A better way of saying it was that I prayed the Word of God out loud. After this and not knowing what else to do, I called on angels for assistance. Immediately, she was pinned to the floor like a starfish. It looked like someone had tackled her and thrown her to the floor in a velcro suit! She was stuck to the floor and couldn't move. I said, "Thanks, angels!" It wasn't long before that girl was completely set free.

Another time, a young lady and I were riding in the backseat of a car moving fast down the highway. Along the way, she manifested a demonic voice and said, "I need air." After rolling down her window, she lunged out the opening and almost got all the way out!

Her hair was blowing hard in the wind, and I went out that window nearly as quickly as she had. I grabbed hold of the back of her belt but could not stop her hands from striking the ground at highway speed. It was awful. I was working hard not to let her arms and head hit the ground. It all happened so fast, but I was able to pull her back through the window. After arriving at our destination, we cast that destructive spirit out of her!

These types of experiences were routine throughout the second half of that summer of my 15th year.

A SUPERNATURAL KNOWING

One thing has always been present in my life, even from the time I was a young boy—supernatural knowing. Like the *Rocky IV* story, sometimes I would say what I *knew*, but as time went on, it seemed better to me to keep those experiences to myself.

This *knowing* wasn't just regarding facts or events. Ever since those teen years, I had a heightened form of empathy that was nearly too much to bear at times. This heightened sensitivity to what others were feeling could make it uncomfortable to even look people in the eyes because of what I would feel, which caused me to develop an introverted personality. My nature is to be very outgoing and social, so when I was around people who were close—friends or family—I didn't have the same sense of empathy, so I was extroverted. Close friends mostly knew me that way.

This sense of empathy was often magnified by looking at or being near others. The sense of what they felt was not necessarily an emotional, moment-to-moment tracking of their every feeling but rather a revelation of a deeper, more permanent part of their identity.

A *knowing* would rise inside me that conveyed whether a person was sweet, depressed, angry, perverted, or something else. For example, if a person was not to be trusted, I would experience a sense of distrust or a feeling that the person was working an angle or being manipulative.

There were other times I would sense the good in people who displayed terrible behaviors. In those cases, when I saw their obvious potential, I'd overlook the bad and only act according to the good I sensed in them.

Friends have asked me (regarding different people), "Don't you know who this person is or what they are like?" There hasn't always been a good answer because my sense of the true nature of a specific person might override the apparent negatives. Even when these individuals behave negatively toward me, my response is most often to let it roll off my back.

Why? Because potential and good reside in certain people and are trying to get out. I discovered that if I stay in my anointing, show mercy, and call to the good in those individuals—based on that sense of empathy—they have a real chance at winning! The Lord has brought many people into my path for this purpose. Through the simple belief—of even just one person—of the good in them, He has brought them to a higher realization of their identity in Jesus.

There has been another side to this empathy. Sometimes the people who are the most adored and loved by many are the ones for whom I carry a sense of repulsion. False humility is a hard thing for me to be around. If someone is a little arrogant or even rude but remains true to their inner self, although they may not be pleasant, at least they are being authentic.

These supernatural encounters, and my empathic sensitivity, were part of a bigger picture that needed to be refined in my life. The Word of God and the Holy Spirit are the best Teachers! However, I discovered that there are avenues of development that can move you into your lane even faster.

GRAVEYARD ENCOUNTER

I encountered two voices that tried to speak to me at a young age. One was the Voice of God, and the other brought fear and uncertainty. I discovered that this was the voice of darkness that took the form of a spirit and was allowed to operate in the members of my family and on our property. The working of that spirit was a regular occurrence, and it was intimidating. However, at the age of 16, I put a stop to that fearful voice.

I was home following the summer of the supernatural experiences I previously wrote about and began to seek God. I had been leading people to the knowledge of Jesus at my school, even praying over people who received healing. One night, while I was praying, I took a significant turn.

Being prompted by the Holy Spirit at around midnight, I felt the urge to go to my paternal grandfather's grave. I felt little hesitation in my heart, even though it was a peculiar thing to be prompted to do. However, I recognized it as the same prompting that led to my discovery of the white stone. That had turned out well, so I obeyed!

The sense I had was that the Holy Spirit was instructing me to go to the cemetery to cut off every curse over my life so that it could no longer influence me or affect my future family. I was to draw a line by making a declaration that would stop the progress of any evil thing that had ever happened in my family history.

My heart thought, *Who am I to disagree with this prompting?* So, I responded, "Yes, Sir," got into the car and pulled into the country cemetery within a half hour, arriving somewhere between twelve-thirty and one o'clock in the morning.

It was completely dark. There was no light except the soft glow of the moon filtering through the trees. Usually, the black-as-ink darkness would have stopped me from proceeding, especially in a creepy cemetery. But this night, the Spirit of God came upon me with peace and authority.

Without hesitation, I shut off my car's headlights and confidently made my way to my grandfather's grave, weaving in and out among the tombstones, with only that faint light of the moon to guide me.

Finally, I stood in front of my grandfather's headstone. Poised in silence for a few minutes, a boldness for my legacy and future family rose inside me, accompanied by righteous and indignant anger. Rather than fear—being in an eerie graveyard barely one lumen above pitch black—I felt an attitude of aggression against the things that had held my lineage bound.

I passionately declared that every curse was broken: "As for me and my house, we will serve the Lord! In the name of Jesus, no physical or spiritual curse will follow me from this day forward!" I boldly drew a line in the spirit realm. I made many such declarations for what seemed like a half-hour, first to the Lord, then to the kingdom of darkness, as I informed it that this was now my legacy and that Jesus would be glorified through my family after me.

I did this with a heart of love and respect for everyone before me who had simply lived in all the light they had. However, it was imperative that I cut off anything and everything that was ungodly from the past behavior of any of those from whom I was descended. I rejected abuse, sexual wickedness, addiction, witchcraft, violence, etc.

This was the point in my life where all the negative spiritual *traffic* instantly ceased. The intense things I had heard as a boy were permanently silenced. From that moment forward, the only voice I developed a sensitivity to hearing was the Voice of the Holy Spirit. Other things attempted to knock on my door, but Jesus and the Word of God answered.

About a week after the cemetery experience, I walked into a youth meeting held at the church I attended. This particular evening, I arrived late, and when I walked in the door, a young lady saw me and instantly manifested demons. She went into convulsions and fell to the floor. *Whoa*, I thought, *what's happening?* Yet it was obvious to me that it was full-tilt demonic.

Now it's important to understand that this was a *seeker-friendly* church. The culture was, "Let's play music, play games, and maybe do a drama or puppet show to reach people for Jesus."

A demonic manifestation was not the norm and was a radically new experience for this crowd. The young people responded by crying and panicking, not knowing at all what to do when a demon manifested. Some of the kids ran away while others encircled the girl, trying to calm her down. It was chaos!

Yet the Spirit of the Lord came upon me with an overwhelming sense of peace. I walked over to her and calmly said, "You come out of her, in Jesus' name."

She replied, "The voices saw you; they told me not to talk to you!"

"Okay, I don't care about the voices," I replied. "They can go now, in Jesus' name." With all the demonic theatrics you can imagine, she told me the names of two entities that were speaking through her.

"I couldn't care less what their names are," I said. "Now leave!"

In one final attempt to stay, these demonic voices piped up through the young lady with gnarly voices, saying, "We saw you in the grave-yard—we were there! We know you, and we know what you were doing!" They laughed and mocked me.

This really got my attention! Holy anger came upon me, and I snapped back, "Who cares where you were and what you've seen? Now get out of her, and leave this place!"

The girl sat up and turned her attention to my friend, who was not in the Word, and like so many of the others, had just come for a "seeker-friendly" meeting.

With a mocking demeanor, she said, "He doesn't believe. He is afraid." So, I sent him out of the room.

Then I said, "I believe in Jesus, and you are beaten. Now get out of here, and I don't want to hear another word from you." In that instant, the girl went limp, and fell back to the ground, and the two demons left.

After she had recovered, she explained to me that she was a young witch who was part of a coven that came to disrupt the service. After our encounter, she abruptly left.

I thought it was thrilling that the kingdom of darkness had been impacted by what the Spirit of God led me to do a week earlier. It was confirmation to me that my offensive attack against the darkness in my family had worked!

ENCOUNTER AT A CHURCH GATHERING

Not long after experiencing this demonic manifestation at the church, my mom hosted a church gathering at her house. At these parties, we would set an enormous stack of wood and brush on fire. Everyone would drink hot cider, hang out together, play football, and simply enjoy one another's company.

As I was walking around at the party, I came to the front of the house and saw that same girl standing there. However, this time she was not alone. A man in a long black coat stood with her.

He stared at me for a while until I said, "May I help you two?" I don't even know how they found my place or even knew about the bonfire. I assumed it was through asking around where I lived, but no one in my circle knew who these two people were.

She gestured to the man next to her and said, "This is my warlock."

I simply replied, "Hello, warlock. Do you two want some apple cider or something?" He remained silent, so I said, "I'm going to head over by the fire again. Have fun!" I had been in the Word and broken so much stuff off my life that this was a non-issue to me.

I continued to walk and mingle at the party a bit, and then I went back into the house. When I walked in, I found the two of them inside. He wanted to speak to me about power.

I said, "Yeah, you want to know about that? What would you like me to teach you?"

He said, "I can curse people."

"Great!" I replied. "Because Jesus in me breaks every curse." I literally treated him as though the topic of conversation was boring. This was the first time I understood that the kingdom of darkness is nothing unless you allow it to be something. I could tell that my complete lack of concern annoyed him.

Time passed, and I went back into the house again. They followed me into the kitchen, and I noticed they were both bleeding down their arms.

"What happened?" I asked them. "Did you fall down or something?" Then I realized they were cutting themselves to get a pretty good blood flow. They began to lick and drink it the best they could.

"Gross!" I really don't know if this was the right thing to say or not. Remember, this girl already had demons come out of her at the church, and instead of staying to get help, she had bolted and returned to her nasty setting.

I responded by grabbing the warlock's shoulder, and threw him out the front door. As they were both standing in the front driveway, I said, "If you came here for help, I'm your guy. If you came here to continue this kind of stuff, and want to continue, then I'm going to knock you out."

I gave him an ultimatum to either knock off that behavior or get knocked to the ground. They were trying to curse me, so I told them, "Your curses have no power and are laughable. What kind of person tries to obey their spiritual force by drinking blood? Only a total loser would do that. You and the devil are total losers. If you want a life, I have it for you. But if you're going to push the issue, I will smack you right in the mouth and throw you out of here." They abruptly turned and left. I never saw them again.

Now I'm not saying I handled the situation exactly right. Please remember, I was young. However, I was learning how to walk in boldness and to deny the kingdom of darkness's influence over my life in any way.

THE DISCOVERY OF AUTHORITY

It is a profound thing to me that there is such significance in cutting off spiritual things. What I did at the graveyard shook the kingdom of darkness enough to send agents to my church and home to confront me!

I learned that my authority in Jesus is based on what He did. However, it is my enforcement of what He did that releases His power in this world. I realized that not only had I stopped the negative encounters from when I was much younger, but even more importantly, knowing Jesus through His Word gave me authority over anything that might stand in front of me.

Walking in the authority of the name of Jesus became my way of life. Many people are unwilling to *"give up to go up."* What I mean is that they are not willing to follow Jesus, no matter the cost. When you truly surrender all to Him, you enter a position of absolute authority.

In Matthew 16:24-25, Jesus says, "If anyone desires to come after Me, let him deny himself, and take up his cross, and follow Me. For whoever desires to save his life will lose it, but whoever loses his life for My sake will find it."

This is what *"giving up to go up"* means: if you lose your life by exchanging it for the life of Jesus, you will actually gain everything you never knew you wanted! There is a higher way to live, and it is found in the truth of the Gospel. When you discover it, it will make you bold!

SECTION TWO

NAVIGATING AND INTERPRETING THE SPIRIT REALM

CHAPTER SEVEN

THE MAP
AND THE TERRITORY

For we know in part and we prophesy in part.
—1 Corinthians 13:9

I n 1931, scientist, author, and mathematician Alfred Korzybski—
who came from a family of mathematicians—presented a paper on
General Semantics. In his presentation, he introduced and popular-
ized the idea that *the map is not the territory.* In his presentation came
the point of interest regarding the statement, *The map of reality is not
reality.*[3]

He stated that even the best maps are imperfect. That's because
they are reductions of what they represent. If a map were to describe
the territory with perfect fidelity, it would no longer be a reduction and
thus would no longer be helpful to us. A map can also be a snapshot
of a point in time, representing something that no longer exists. This
concept is vital to remember as we think through problems and make
better decisions. In other words, *the description of the thing is not the
thing itself. The model is not reality. The abstraction is not the abstracted.*
This idea has enormous practical consequences. The conclusion was
that when maps and terrain differ—follow the terrain.

A SENSORY COMPASS

If you were to use the same principle of the map and the territory, it becomes a helpful point of reference when discussing prophetic encounters and navigating them. The map is not the territory—the map is the map. Another point of constructive thought we could utilize regarding the idea of map and territory is to say your *prophetic imagery*, encounter, or future prediction is not the actual event. It is an interpretive glimpse through a glass dimly to be grasped by faith. Knowing and prophesying, *in part*, sit at your feet as a *sensory compass* that the Word of God must adjust.

REAL-WORLD APPLICATION

When dealing with the areas of prophecy, the experiences are very subjective. Your emotions, environment, doctrinal norms, upbringing, and where you come from all influence your prophetic worldview. I like something my good friend Rick Renner says, "How you view the news kind of depends on what part of the world you are watching from."

This saying has merit regarding the topic at hand also. How you view prophecy or prophesying is affected by what part of the Church you herald from. Everyone's sensory compass is engaged when a prophetic moment finds you through a dream, a word of knowledge spoken over you, or various experiences.

A sensory compass is a word picture explaining what happens to most individuals and is a person's mechanism to determine what God is saying. What is crucial is the proper understanding attached to that compass. Is the process surrendered to the Word of God, or is the process a subjective experience based on the norms and values of the individual? It is the individual who decides.

Many who navigate the waters of supernatural encounters do so with their wits and reasoning. This process is not necessarily bad unless it is detached from God's Word and disciplined prayer life.

Without the proper foundation and connection to God, error and misguided steps are waiting at the door. That sensory compass must be placed within an appropriate scope to define what is happening for real-world application, which comes first and foremost through the written Word of God. It also comes through tenured leaders with a track record in such areas.

> *It is the Spirit who gives life; the flesh profits nothing. The words that I speak to you are spirit, and they are life.*
> —John 6:63

Of great importance is the recognition that no one has everything perfected, yet we are to pursue clarity and sharpen our walk of faith constantly. The Spirit is perfect, and we are to continuously place ourselves in the Word of God to walk in that perfection accurately. Many interpret God and prophetic happenings through their process and go by gut instinct.

INTERPRETING PROPHETIC HAPPENINGS

Heuristic

Heuristic is a term used to describe how many interpret prophetic happenings. By definition, heuristic is any approach to problem-solving, learning, or discovery that employs a practical method not guaranteed to be optimal or perfect but sufficient for the immediate goals. Where finding an optimal solution is impossible or impractical, heuristic methods can be used to speed up the process of finding a satisfactory solution.

Heuristics can be mental shortcuts that ease the cognitive load of making a decision. Examples of this method include using a *rule of thumb, an educated guess, an intuitive judgment, stereotyping, profiling, experimenting, trial and error, or common sense.*

To operate in this capacity is acceptable when a heart is full of the Word of God and faith because God has chosen to work with us and through His saints, through you!

> *For it seemed good to the Holy Spirit, and to us, to lay upon you no greater burden than these necessary things.*
>
> —Acts 15:28

It seemed good to the Holy Spirit, and to us, this is a true statement that divulges God's partnership with His people, the body of Christ. First John 4:17 says, "Love has been perfected among us in this: that we may have boldness in the day of judgment; *because as He is, so are we in this world.*" The "we" in that verse points directly to the body of Christ.

Together with the Lord, we are, after all, part of the Great Commission. Our partnership with the Lord places the "CO" into the mission. He has chosen to work through us and along with us as "co-laborers with Him." There is much to be said regarding the mystery— "Christ in us the hope of glory."

> *The spirit of man is the candle of the Lord, searching all the inward parts of the belly.*
>
> —**Proverbs 20:27 KJV**

Interpreting prophetic happenings and experiences purely by your natural senses, gut feeling, and emotions has a place, but not in comparison to the Word of God and a person who has trained their senses to discern and operate God's way. So often, when prophetic moments happen, that sensory compass is all many rely on—that is a mistake.

Therefore, a purely heuristic approach to following God's Voice leads to error. A heuristic process works when people exercise their senses to discern good and evil, which means their five senses.

> *But solid food belongs to those who are of full age, that is, those who by reason of use have their senses exercised to discern both good and evil.*
>
> **—Hebrews 5:14**

Another way of saying this is *by reason of* practice! The practice we execute is two things:

1. Bringing our emotions and all other natural senses under the authority of the Word and prayer. Romans 12:2 says, "And do not be conformed to this world, but be transformed by the renewing of your mind, that you may prove what is that good and acceptable and perfect will of God." Renewing your mind to the Word of God is how you transform and is the foundational place to bring your emotions, training, and discipline.

2. We must practice the gift given to us, or it will not grow. We not only desire the gifts, but we must practice them. Stretch out in faith by serving those around you with your gifting. By doing so, you develop a gift of prophecy in yourself—desiring and practicing it!

Prophetic utterances, words given, or predictive declarations regarding an event or that point out a specific date, time, or season must have an anchor to revisit constantly. That anchor is the Word of God. Anything outside of that is a pathway headed for error.

Do not despise prophecies.

—1 Thessalonians 5:20

Now in no way do we need to be sarcastic or critical in spirit when addressing negatives such as strange utterances, outlandish predictive declarations, and the like, which we may see in the prophetic. However, what does offer value is not to criticize but instead to introduce a constructive way to build a solid foundation for those coming after us in the prophetic.

RIGHTSIZING THE PROPHETIC MANIA

I greatly desire to build you up regarding this topic, as the prophetic has taken a lot of heat and criticism due to seasons of inaccurate declarations, strange prophetic teaching, sensational tales, non-biblical activity, and the like.

A thinking person knows when something is not correct. However, there comes a point when the suspension of logic and reason will no longer hold back the hard and necessary questions that rightly deserve answers. Let me give you an example in the area of prediction.

Imagine if a Babe Ruth figure stood at the plate to bat in a baseball game, not just any game, the final time up to bat in the World Series. Imagine, for a moment, the baseball player standing at the plate and pointing into the stands exactly where he will hit the ball in that epic last game. The crowd would go ballistic with excitement as he pointed to make his prediction, especially if he played it up and stood there momentarily, just pointing and staring. It would undoubtedly create anticipation and wonder.

Now imagine that right after this player finished pointing and gazing into that direction with his thousand-yard stare, the pitch is thrown, and the predictor swings hard, *Smack!* Only it doesn't hit the bat. Instead, the ball smacks into the catcher's mitt. "Strike one!" cries the umpire. It would be disheartening, especially after the pointing and staring, but acceptable as they have two more opportunities.

The second pitch is hurled toward the batter, and again he swings with all his might, *Crack!* This time there is contact, and the ball is a solid line drive directly out of bounds and labeled by the umpire as a foul ball. *Okay, okay,* the audience would think. *That didn't go as expected, but there is still one more try!*

The pitcher again winds up and throws a fastball right down the center of the plate—it's perfect! Dramatically there's a connection! Crack goes the baseball from a direct impact with the bat. Suddenly, everyone notices that the ball goes in the same direction the batter pointed! What a rush! Everyone would be holding their breath as that ball is lifted high into the air and coasts toward the location predicted!

There is an abrupt interruption as the ball begins to come down, falling faster and faster still in the general direction predicted by the batter. Then, finally, a fielder comes out of seemingly nowhere and manages to catch up with the ball that is heading over the back wall, where, to everyone's amazement, the fielder leaps higher and higher, stepping on the wall as he jumps to reach with all his might and catches the ball!

"You're out!" shouts the umpire. But, wow, imagine the disappointment to the fans who would have anticipated seeing if the batter's prediction came true!

YOU CANNOT WIN
LAST YEAR'S WORLD SERIES

Lance Wallnau made a powerful statement: "You cannot predict who will win last year's World Series!" A humorous and simple metaphor explaining the need to adjust prophecies that missed the mark.

Take a moment with me and imagine now that the story doesn't end there. Imagine that the batter looks at the fans and the rest of the team, including an earshot of the opposing team, shouting not to worry because he didn't miss it. Regardless of what the umpire just said and the game rules, he hit that ball, which will still be a victory for his team. What would you think or say? It might seem odd, or you might even feel embarrassed for the batter.

What if after the World Series ended, the losing team threw a celebration for their victory and the whole world watched the batter make a public announcement saying, "You all need to celebrate and party it up!" Although it may look like they lost, in all actuality, his prediction of hitting the ball would still come to pass. Not next season, but this year!

People would be astonished at such a bold and brazen remark. Questions would arise, such as, *Is the batter, okay? Is he mentally doing well?* There would be a tsunami of responses as to why that is impossible!

Not only that, imagine if the batter rebuked others for not believing what he was saying! That they needed to line up with what his prediction was to see it come to pass.

It just wouldn't make any sense! Yet this type of scenario has taken place in the prophetic community. So, it leaves us with the questions: What do we do about it? How should we respond? The answer is that we should consistently teach and train proper protocol and biblical foundation regarding such things.

For future generations to reach the highest and best in the prophetic, we must offer them the best information and biblical foundation we can. No more sweeping issues under the rug or metaphorical jargon. We need something we can count on. A powerful foundation will unlock the mightiest prophetic experiences any generation has experienced! Returning to the original thought about how to deal with different maps and terrains, we must hold the Word of God above all, practice the things we have learned, remain in the Spirit, and read the terrain!

ENAMORED WITH PROPHETS

Many believers today are caught up in this same kind of scenario related to the prophetic. Unfortunately, prophets and their prophecies so enamor them that they forget to keep their brain intact and execute due diligence.

They fall into the wandering loop of voices, projected by attempting to adjust a missed word to fit the present circumstances. A loop of voices is something many good-hearted and sincere people have wandered into. They will shoehorn past prophecies to fit into today's events. They force the previous missed word into the reality of what took place. It is a temptation for every person operating in a revelatory way to keep the image of a flawless track record.

However, God allows us all to know *in part*, prophesy *in part*, and see through a glass dimly. Why? So that we, as New Testament believers, will rely on Him and the body of Christ. God loves it when His body depends on one another. Humility is a high currency with God. Humility is a mighty prophetic force effective in longevity and spiritual warfare.

THE POWER OF HUMILITY

But He gives more grace. Therefore He says: "God resists the proud, but gives grace to the humble."

—James 4:6

What should we do next regarding words missed? Let truth have its day! Be honest, be humble. Somewhere along the way, many in a revelatory persuasion decided humility was not part of the package.

Humility reads that terrain of what was prophesied versus what actually came to pass. Humility admits that it *knows in part and prophesies in part.* From a lens of knowing in part, seeing through a glass dimly while not forsaking steps of faith with the Spirit of God, humility squares up the declared words and what the terrain is saying in real-time.

At this moment, you should do something vital. As a believer and prophetic person, you must engage your mind, wisdom, and the Word of God. His entire sum of tools will go from available to active and invaluable when surrendering to the Word of God and in great peace—*read the terrain.*

USE REASON

Reading the terrain means don't disengage your brain!

Significant issues and terrain that must be navigated are those who narcissistic, pseudo-prophetic voices have damaged.

Let us draw near with a true heart in full assurance of faith, having our hearts sprinkled from an evil conscience and our bodies washed with pure water.

—**Hebrews 10:22**

Many fall to misguided parts of navigation because they have a guilty conscience or a damaged sense of what is right and what is wrong. This is something we will deal with in the pages ahead. Some who cannot navigate are confused by a steady diet of the world's system and information. Others have fallen prey to those who manufacture prophecies for their benefit. Not having their own trained discernment makes these hearers likely candidates to have their fledgling emotions and untrained discernment taken advantage of.

We will also be dealing with the issue of *false prophets* and *false prophecy* very clearly in the coming chapters—it is a legitimate issue that Jesus Himself warned us about in Matthew 24. It is my prayer to see you and many in this generation experience and become clear-eyed, clear-minded prophetic voices that raise the banner of healthy gifts that bring glory to Jesus Christ!

NEVER FOLLOW A SECOND LIEUTENANT

In WWII, Heather and I each had grandparents who served. One of the things they told us was that when going into battle, never follow a second lieutenant, as they had a very short life expectancy. Why? Because all their training was in book form, they were often straight from the military academy or had just emerged from their place of preparation, having zero field experience. So, when the bombs began falling, they were less competent than a seasoned veteran.

God places great value on veterans, those who have continued with Him for a long time. You must know who you are following when it comes to supernatural guidance. Knowing a person's track record is vital in understanding what God is saying in any situation. Who is influencing you will make a significant impact on where you are heading and in the manner you will arrive there.

God desires you to follow the people to whom He assigned you. Your tribal alignment carries far more significance than simply what is essential for you as an individual. Your location, associations, and what you're hearing will impact your loved ones. Many will not reach their potential or have the proper alignment without you! Think about that momentarily; many are waiting for you to be in the right place at the right time!

NEW TIMES, SAME HOLY SPIRIT

There are various reasons why people cannot read the terrain, both in their own hearing of the Voice of God and when receiving from voices who prophesy. I have discovered that the things of God are simple, but they require dedication and consistency. *A dedicated, disciplined follower of Jesus Christ* is what a disciple is. You can only be a devoted follower of Jesus Christ if you are a follower of the words of Jesus, meaning you should be an avid reader of the Word of God.

If we take the concept of discipleship and widen the scope to make it applicable to spiritual gifts, we might say we should train and practice the gifts based on the foundation of the Word of God.

Every generation has new opportunities to experience a *newly packaged* version of the good and the bad. However, we can take refuge in knowing that Jesus is Lord. He will always lead you into triumph. Even if you have had negative experiences with hearing the Voice of God or with unhealthy prophetic ministry, there is always tomorrow. Because there have been counterfeit experiences, it only says it is time to encounter the real! The highest way to grow in this arena begins with ongoing healthy teaching but ends with a disciplined physical and spiritual life. A disciplined spiritual life means you will have a foundation to grow.

NAVIGATING THE DESIRE TO PROPHESY

Prophecy, like other spiritual gifts, has a function in many ways, the same, yet very different in at least one way—*desire*. We are told to desire spiritual gifts, but especially that we might prophesy!

> *Pursue love, and desire spiritual gifts, but especially that you may prophesy.*
>
> —**1 Corinthians 14:1**

From this passage of scripture, we can see that desiring gifts is part of activating the gift of prophecy in your life. You must desire and pursue spiritual gifts to experience them activating in your life, which involves practicing them and acting on them in faith. It is much like Peter, who walked on the water with Jesus. He first stepped out of the boat, then took one step at a time until he made it to Jesus. Someone might say, "Yeah, but Peter sank!" True, but just before he sank—*Peter walked on water!* Desire led him to the childlike faith that caused him to walk on the water.

It's essential to recognize that faith in the Son of God is faith. Jesus is who Peter was walking toward and who he believed in. Gifts operate similarly to this unique story. You must get out of the boat, keep your eyes on Jesus, and trust that your feet will stand solid even as you *step out* to move in a gift, much like Peter stepped out and solidly planted his feet on the water.

Let's focus on the word "desire" by looking at it in Greek.

The word "desire" in Greek is *zēloō*, where we get the word "zealous," which means "to have strong affection toward or ardently devoted to something"—an even better way of saying it would be to vigorously or eagerly pursue a thing!

That is not all the scripture is letting us know in this instance. Desire is a foundational place regarding the activation of spiritual gifts. But if we take it a step further, that verse goes beyond desire and uses the word "especially" regarding "to prophesy."

The word, "especially" in Greek, is *mallon,* meaning *more, to a greater extent, or a higher degree.*

Based on this meaning, we are to pursue love and desire or have strong affection and be ardent in devotion to the gifts like an artist is passionate and committed to his craft, so should you be toward the gifts of the Spirit!

Then it adds the word "especially," to which you could say it this way: above all the gifts you desire—pursue the ability to prophesy with ardent devotion, zeal, and strong affection! What a thing to say about the gift of prophecy!

ARE YOU TRAINED OR UNTRAINED

Intense training is required to use a tool or weapon skillfully. For example, a significant difference exists between a person who throws a punch and a person trained in hand-to-hand combat. Several things are different, such as effectiveness, accuracy, and dominance. One, the person who may be capable of throwing a punch can hit someone or something, but they will only do as much as they can muster. The other, the trained individual, has developed their abilities through reason of practice and use and can now execute their training in a moment. There is a difference between effectiveness and gracefulness, which is why some people like to watch martial arts films because of the form and grace of a master.

Seeing someone fight like a couple of drunken uncles at a barbeque might be exciting and even attract a crowd; however, what brings in a global audience is seeing two highly trained and qualified contenders step into the ring. These are the best of the best. Whether it is the symphony, ballet, the Olympics, or any other extraordinary, practiced ability—everyone enjoys watching skill!

Wouldn't it bring glory to the Lord if we trained the gifts of the Spirit in the body of Christ, much like Olympic athletes train their talents? What a powerful experience both the Church and the world would encounter. Many prophetic people would operate with accuracy and possess legitimate humility and power by knowing how to wield their gift like an artist who is confident, humble, emotionally intelligent, and delivering results!

The prophetic needs clear-eyed, clear-minded masters, comfortable in their skin, highly trained, trustworthy, thick-skinned, intelligent, and loving warriors who bring the Word of God with high accuracy and results for the body of Christ. And it all begins with training.

TRUE NORTH

Most individuals misled or taken off track by some misinterpreted prophetic experience or understanding are usually those who follow an inaccurate sensory compass that doesn't apply. I remember my grandfather giving me a compass as a young boy for the annual deer hunting season, which my family gathers for each fall. It was my first time doing so, and he equipped me with that compass assuming I knew how to work it! Many of my uncles and family members are skilled outdoors people. They are a lot of fun to be around, and I suppose, although I was young, they figured I would be just fine navigating what seemed to me to be the deep woods.

After a long time of walking, I found myself deep into the forest and far away from all the others. At this point, the realization struck me; I had no idea where I was! That's when the words of my grandfather came back to me, "Use this, Joe, and you will find your way out." I must chuckle because I should have asked, "How?" My basic action plan was to lick my thumb and stick it in the air to see which way I should go while looking at the compass.

While wandering around feeling a little, or maybe a lot, lost, my lightning-fast mind realized if I remembered where north was, I could figure out the rest. What a good-working compass should do is point its user to true north. Once I determined true north, it was easier for me to navigate the terrain back to the general area I needed to be. Ultimately, it all worked out, not in the perfect return location, but close enough to get me to my point of origin.

Using a compass is like operating in the prophetic, hearing God, and moving in spiritual gifts. You are off to the right start if you can determine true north. What comes next is learning your compass. Someone highly trained in utilizing a compass or instruments of navigation can go anywhere, through any terrain, in just about any condition.

SHARPENED CLARITY

Navigation requires sharpened clarity as well. We find a prescription for this in the Word of God. With this in mind, let's look at Hebrews 5:14, which states the formula for walking in higher clarity.

But solid food belongs to those who are of full age, that is, those who by reason of use have their senses exercised to discern both good and evil.

—**Hebrews 5:14**

Maturity is what this is talking about. One sign of spiritual maturity is exercising your senses, referencing your natural physical impulses, emotions, and persuasions. Your five senses are significant players in this. Notice it says through "reason of use" their senses are exercised, which means a disciplined practice of putting what you see, smell, taste, touch, and hear under the truth of the Word of God.

Another way of saying this would be that the more you walk by faith and not by your natural persuasion, the greater the level of discernment you will carry. A discernment that will recognize good from evil. We must walk spiritually with discernment that cuts between good and evil in razor-like accuracy.

Training and teaching can accomplish this, and so can copious amounts of time in prayer and the Word of God. However, there is much to be said when it comes to training. The Word of God and prayer will give you raw gifting experiences, yet missing things will come faster and with less hardship if learned through a veteran, and this is where the tenured leadership comes in to further edify and equip the believer.

PROPHETIC VOLTAGE AND DISCERNMENT

If a prophetic person is not training, not walking in the Word of God, and not submitting to the fivefold ministry to some level, offense or hardship enters their life. This issue can derail or destroy a prophetic person if left unchecked and not dealt with.

Prophetic people have a different voltage in them, as well as in their emotions. Prophets move in a powerful flow of prophecy; they are like lightning rods for everything sensory. They can also be odd because they sometimes deal in a different space with feeling, hearing, and sensing things both seen and unseen. Prophetic people, in general, can have some of these same traits, and the more time they spend in the prophetic spectrum via prayer, the more they become sensitized to the moving of the Holy Spirit through the gift of prophecy.

CHAPTER EIGHT

A BETTER HERMENEUTIC

REVELATION, INTERPRETATION, APPLICATION

*So that you may learn from us the meaning of the saying,
"Do not go beyond what is written." Then you will not be
puffed up in being a follower of one of us over against the
other.*

—1 Corinthians 4:6 NIV

I have often experienced someone deliver a truly inspired word from the Lord. The power of God could be *felt* as the word was delivered. It was emotional, intense, and filled with expectation—however, there were times when what they powerfully predicted didn't come to pass.

In other moments there have been prophetic words declared to people about their life only to realize what was shared was very off and unhelpful. Or prophetic words given for a specific season of time only to see the season come and go without fulfillment. Does this mean the words are not accurate? Does it mean the person is false? Does it mean that prophecy is not for today?

Not at all! Many times, it is simply missing the process of *revelation, interpretation, and application.*

Legitimate moments of prophetic power put on display are wonderful! They build up the recipients and infuse believers with encouragement and faith.

In my younger years, being exposed to accurate and power-filled prophetic moments led many other listeners and me to believe that when these words were released, God Himself said them.

Moments like these can be marked with distinct words: such and such will happen on this day and time, or surely a particular event will occur. I am forever grateful for these types of prophetic words being in my life; as a young believer, they were a source of strength. As one friend once said, when explaining their encounter with prophetic ministry, *they felt that God saw them.*

NOT HITTING THE MARK

Again, the harder issue is when the same type of word given *doesn't hit the mark*; especially when the details given do not happen. Disappointment or even confusion can result from such experiences, even leading to disillusionment with spiritual gifts.

Hearers of such words may be able to roll past a one-time hazy prediction, yet when this type of thing repeats itself, it begins to cause a lack of confidence in the gifts of the Spirit—resulting in some throwing out all experiences with the prophetic—which is an error.

Others begin embracing anything (*accurate or not*) thrown at them. After all, their thought is, that God is speaking, and we must believe it even if we don't understand it.

What the prophetic voice heard and delivered was likely from the Spirit of the Lord speaking to them. Still, their ability to properly communicate the revelation was lost or altered from the original intent God wanted to communicate.

LOSING THE MEANING IN TRANSLATION

Losing the meaning in translation is a serious issue. Again, it doesn't mean the source message was inaccurate. It may simply mean that the heart of the message was lost while relaying it.

It makes me think of the game of telephone, or whisper down the lane, that we played in elementary school. The class sat in a circle and the teacher whispered a sentence to the student beside her, then that student whispered what he heard to the student seated beside him, and she passed along what she heard, and so on around the circle. After the initial whispered message was passed through a dozen or more students, the last one wrote down what they heard, and the teacher read it aloud. The message was always very different from the intent and meaning of the teacher's original whispered sentence.

In the same way the original intent and meaning were lost in the passing of whispers, so can the prophetic words be altered or even unrecognizable, missing the original intent of what the Holy Spirit was conveying.

THE BIAS LENS

A better way to describe it would be to say most ministers are taught in a specific avenue of thinking and, therefore, will only view revelatory things through the lens of their own bias. An issue that can cause a limiting effect on what they can actually see. Regardless of what they see or sense, there is a doctrinal lens also. Many prophesy their doctrine if you listen closely. However, if you can discern the biased lens, doctrinal cloud, or opinions any given speaker may be including, it will help you go much farther in prophetic understanding.

TAKE THE HEART OF A WORD

Interpretation is the responsibility of the person releasing a word and the responsibility of a person receiving a prophetic word. We must recognize that prophecy is not always released in a laboratory environment with perfect conditions and accuracy.

This has led me to approach receiving words in a more discerning way. Regarding dreams, words, or visions and receiving a prophecy, I believe in taking *the heart* of what is being said—not always picking apart the specific details.

Even when I release prophetic words to others, about 60 to 80 percent of what I sense or see I don't share with a person. This is due to not having a strong interpretation as to what I'm seeing and why I'm seeing it. What I find most helpful is to share the heart of the word, not all kinds of details, unless led to do so by the Holy Spirit.

SPECULATION INTRODUCES CONFUSION

Speculating when receiving or releasing a prophecy can bring confusion. I aim to release the word in a way that reveals the heart of the matter at hand. Symbolically "pulling a bunny out of a hat" by sharing details for the wow factor should never be the goal of prophecy. True prophetic ministry is to get the heart of an issue across to the recipients because God is a "heart God."

God's great desire is for you to catch what He is saying on a heart level more than intellectually grasp every point being stated. It's the equivalent of hearing someone talk to whom you have only spoken with once or twice as opposed to those you spend time with regularly. The closer the relationship, the more likely it is to know the heart and nuances of a conversation. They would catch the meaning and heart of a conversation much better than the passing one.

YOU CAN'T SAY THE RIGHT THING TO THE WRONG PEOPLE

We have a saying that *you can't say the right thing to the wrong people; likewise, you can never seem to say the wrong thing to the right people.* This is because the right people will know your heart. They know your intentions and motives even if you don't explain yourself perfectly. This is the same when you become more acquainted with how the Spirit of the Lord works through others and you!

REVELATION INTERPRETATION APPLICATION

Where there is no revelation, the people cast off restraint;
but happy is he who keeps the law.
—Proverbs 29:18

Accurate truth is found in a biblical process I like to call *revelation, interpretation,* and *application.* As we have said, hearing God is like *a science* but there is no perfect formula. There is only growth, development, childlike faith, common sense, and, above all else, the Bible.

Most of the issues we have experienced surrounding prophecy result from immature prophecies falling on the ears of immature listeners. This is typically a result of a lack of good teaching on the subject. Let me explain. For decades my wife and I have taught around the world and held many training conferences on the subject of prophecy.

Throughout our time doing so, we have developed a biblical process we label *Revelation, Interpretation, and Application.*

These three points are a result of 1 Thessalonians 5:23 (KJV), which says, "And the very God of peace sanctify you wholly; and I pray God your whole *spirit* and *soul* and *body* be preserved blameless unto the coming of our Lord Jesus Christ." The Word of God lists for us the three parts that make up a person: spirit, soul, body.

SPIRIT, SOUL, AND BODY

> *Now may the God of peace Himself sanctify you completely; and may your whole **spirit**, **soul**, and **body** be preserved blameless at the coming of our Lord Jesus Christ.*
>
> **—1 Thessalonians 5:23**

The spirit is the God part of us. The place where we are connected to God the Father through Christ Jesus. Where we possess the God-breathed life that causes us to exist; this is also the place where we are born again. John 3:5 says you must be born of water and spirit. When you are born again, your spirit is made perfect!

*To the general assembly and church of the firstborn who are registered in heaven, to God the Judge of all, **to the spirits of just men made perfect**.*

—Hebrews 12:23

The soul is made up of your mind, will, and emotions.

*And do not be conformed to this world, but be transformed by the **renewing of your mind**, that you may prove what is that good and acceptable and perfect will of God.*

—Romans 12:2

The mind is the area of decision and belief. The soul is like a valve that opens to you what you already possess in the spirit realm and allows it into the natural world.

The natural is your body's arena. It is made up of what you can sense, literally through your five senses. You receive from the realm of the spirit by exercising these senses to discern good and evil.

*But strong meat belongeth to them that are of full age, even those who by reason of use have their **senses exercised to discern** both good and evil.*

—Hebrews 5:14 KJV

These *senses exercised to discern* are in reference to your five senses: seeing, smelling, hearing, touching, and tasting. The point is that the natural ability to navigate life must regularly become subject to a renewed soul with a revelation from the spirit. In a daily disciplined way, we are to read our Bibles and pray.

Let's make the connection. Here we have three major areas that make up a human being. In each arena, we find an applicable equivalent to the process of *revelation, interpretation, and application*.

SPIRIT - REVELATION
SOUL - INTERPRETATION
BODY - APPLICATION

*It is the Spirit who gives life; the flesh profits nothing. **The***
***words that I speak to you are spirit**, and they are life.*
—John 6:63

John 6:63 says *"the words I say to you are spirit"*; the purest form of spirit you can encounter are the words Jesus speaks.

Now we must realize that Jesus is the Word made flesh. He brought the Spirit into full manifestation by becoming flesh. When discussing prophecy, we recognize Jesus is the highest example we have. Prophecy ultimately is all about Jesus.

The testimony of Jesus is the spirit of prophecy.
—Revelation 19:10

Jesus is the ultimate example of *revelation, interpretation, and application*. He not only became flesh; He fulfilled His purpose. Jesus was with the Father when He formed creation (*see* Proverbs 8). John 1:1 says, *"In the beginning was the Word, and the Word was with God, and the Word was God."*

The Greek word for "was with" is *pros*, meaning *face to face*. The Father and the Son looked into one another's faces for eternity past. This represents the spirit realm. Jesus was spoken about and prophesied into existence for much of the Old Testament, until finally, the very words that God spoke about Him in Genesis, and that were carried along by the prophets throughout history, were fulfilled through Mary.

When Jesus was born, it was a birth of the many prophetic words, beginning with God the Father, and spoken out through the prophets by the unction of the Holy Spirit until the Word was made flesh!

REVELATION
SPIRIT - REVELATION
SOUL - INTERPRETATION
BODY - APPLICATION

A *revelation* is a realization of what exists in the realm of the spirit. Jesus walking this earth as a blameless Man began as a revelation. The revelation was interpreted and believed until the fullness of time had come for application, the virgin birth.

Revelation is revealed knowledge to your spirit man! It is that moment you sense something. You have an impression and maybe it's to bless someone; it could be a dream you've had, and it sticks with you throughout the day. While standing in worship, God's presence floods you with a sense, a pull to do something.

A revelation is a Holy Spirit moment when you strongly or subtly believe God has spoken to you. Revelation is usually the fun part of walking out the prophetic process. I like to call it the "Mufasa moment," with shivers, much like the hyenas experienced in the movie *The Lion King*, each time they said "Mufasa."

It may involve intense emotion. Sometimes a revelation is you receiving a powerful prophetic word from a prophet. It is that wow moment that is so strong your five senses can become overwhelmed by what is happening internally and externally. These moments are so impacting and emotionally overwhelming that many who have these encounters are left with the impression that this must be from God!

REVELATION NEEDS SCRIPTURE

These experiences are wonderful and very life-giving! However, they can also come with long-term issues. When times like these happen, through a prophetic word or in various supernatural encounters, what begins as a legitimate revelation or experiential encounter can result in individuals who go off and do something presumptuously without giving it another thought—as there is no process for measurable longevity to the experience.

If it were not for a very intense and rock-solid foundation in my own life, there would have been many devastating consequences to the long-term effects of certain words and encounters I had received. This is true for so many, especially in the younger generation. Many go by feeling, where the Word of God is not the standard. Some launch into something they are unsure about, saying, "It must be God, so here I go!" Examples of this would be people who have received prophetic words about marriage to a specific person and married them only to endure damaging results.

A friend of ours once told my wife, Heather, and me a story that had happened to her in her younger years. Someone had given her a prophetic word that she was to marry a specific individual. So, wanting to obey the Voice of God, she began dating this person and, as time went on, found nothing compatible or even remotely good about the picture.

Thankfully, she broke it off but felt guilty for disobeying "the Voice of God." We were able to explain to her that that she wasn't disobeying the Lord as that word was not from God; it was someone's manipulation under the guise of prophecy, in an attempt to get her to marry someone they thought she should marry. This type of thing sadly happens more often than it should. People in organizations or positions share prophetic words with those who don't know any better, and these innocent ones can get worked over by a manipulative angle.

This is horrible and should never be allowed in the body of Christ, but it is. It is a serious thing to mess with people who are legitimately and even desperately trying to hear God or are newly following His Voice.

The good news is that God is always speaking, and even if someone is misled but remains in faith, the Holy Spirit will always lead them out. He always provides a way of escape.

Dear reader, please remember God loves you; and if you are looking to get out of a difficult situation, remember God wants you free more than you do!

A REVELATION ALONE IS NOT ENOUGH

A revelation alone isn't good enough. Most people stop at a revelation because, as we alluded to earlier in the section "Speculation Introduces Confusion," experiencing some form of a revelation typically feels good! The "wow factor" and sensing the supernatural are in full throttle, opening the hearts and minds of individuals wanting to please the Lord. When these experiences happen, the results, most often, can be incredible.

However, many people wander around the body of Christ, going from revelation to revelation, experience to experience, yet never with any form of measurable application that moves them forward in life.

DISCIPLINE MUST BE APPLIED TO YOUR REVELATION

Many are either undisciplined, untrained, or unwilling to develop their senses to hit the mark, which is why God spoke to them through a revelatory encounter in the first place.

Let me repeat this point. A revelation is a wonderful thing: words of knowledge given to you or you to others. Dreams, visions, impressions, that feeling of fire, and goosebumps that come over you in the presence of God are wonderful. However, God's highest and best for you is to walk in all of it rightly.

This means a healthy process is in order. I desire for you to translate your revelatory encounters from mere experience into a fruitful journey. God gave us the ability to have these glory-filled experiences so that we might be encouraged and continue onward.

> He is a **double-minded man**, unstable in all his ways.
>
> —James 1:8

> For if anyone is a hearer of the word and not a doer, he is like a man observing his natural face in a mirror; 24 for he observes himself, goes away, and immediately forgets what kind of man he was.
>
> —James 1:23-24

A final thought about a revelation. The book of James speaks of a double-minded man who looks into a mirror. When he walks away, he forgets what he looks like. This is like a person in a meeting, in a worship encounter, receiving a prophecy, having a vision, or another supernatural experience and upon leaving the revelatory moment, they let go of the revelation.

These moments of revelation are spiritual encounters, much like the man who sees himself in the mirror. At that moment, what you see or sense is perfect. When you comprehend something in the spirit realm, it is perfect. However, when stepping away from the encounter, what can happen is *forgetting* what was happening in the spiritual moment.

Remember, the supernatural moment is *perfect*. It is a glimpse from the realm of the spirit. It makes sense to your inner man. It is as if everything now lines up—even for a split moment. An alteration begins the moment you step away from that glimpse. Stepping back into natural logic, natural function, and the carnality of what you know, something from the revelatory experience can be lost in translation. What can take place then is inaccurate, fill-in-the-blank moments that significantly alter the proper interpretation of the revelatory moment. A revelation must be cultivated by faith, through prayer and the Word of God.

INTERPRETATION
SPIRIT - REVELATION
SOUL - INTERPRETATION
BODY - APPLICATION

For it seemed good to the Holy Spirit, and to us…
—**Acts 15:28**

Interpretation is the process of extracting the heart, intent, and meaning of what God said. You find this in Acts 15:28, "For it seemed good to the Holy Spirit, and to us." Here is an interpretation of what they believed God was saying to them by the Holy Spirit.

This is a healthy approach to hearing God. An interpretation is best walked out by a renewed mind to the Word of God, in addition to having godly counsel around you. "It seemed good to the Holy Spirit, *and to us*." *To us*, refers to godly counsel. When godly counsel surrounds you, it produces greater clarity to find the heart of what the Spirit is saying.

MISINTERPRETING A REVELATION

Often while speaking, I will humorously use an example of someone who misappropriated the revelation they heard. Imagine a man standing in worship during church on Sunday. They are all caught up in the Lord's presence when he is suddenly impressed by the words "Africa" and "Money!" He begins to envision the beautiful people of indigenous regions of Africa. He gets himself all worked up with the idea of Africa until he convinces himself that this is God telling him to move to Africa!

The man promptly replies, "Yes, Lord, your servant hears you!" Immediately leaving the church service before worship is over, he proceeds to clear out all his bank accounts, sell off everything he has, and pour everything into a move to Africa.

Sometime later, all his resources are spent, and he is broke now living in Africa. At this moment he cries out to God in frustration, and to his surprise, God answers him, "I wanted you to write a check to a missionary in Africa! He was the guest speaker that Sunday, but you ran out of the church, sold everything, and moved to Africa!"

A little far-fetched, but I'm sure a person in this position would find favor from the Lord to get out of the predicament. However, the point is that it is important to interpret the heart and intent of the word properly. Our hypothetical missionary could have rested on that revelation until peace came for what to do next. In this case, it would have been confirmation that he was to support the visiting missionary.

Weak Interpretation

The reason people miss it or get upset is due to weak interpretation. Revelation knowledge transferred from the realm of the Spirit to your soul can become fuzzy or even lost in translation. This is not because revelatory experiences and the prophetic aren't legitimate. It is the vessel, the recipient of a revelation, which, upon communicating what they received, can fail in properly relaying information. This is where the discipline of *good interpretation* comes into play.

Good Interpretation

Interpretation is a weighty subject. Remember when Jesus asked the disciples in Matthew 16:15, "Who do people say that I am?" Some said *Elijah*, some said *John the Baptist*, and others *a prophet*. Jesus then asked the question that needs to be answered by every person who has ever lived and will ever live. "Who do *you* say that I am?" The disciples must have been looking at one another, not quite sure what to say, maybe some even having the urge to say who they thought He was, but Peter said, "You are the Christ, the Son of the Living God." Jesus said, "Man has not revealed this to you, but this was revealed to you by the Spirit of God" (Matthew 16:16-17).

REVEALED BY THE SPIRIT

Revealed by the Spirit of God—that is what a revelation is—something revealed to you by the Spirit of God. Each of those disciples had a

A BETTER HERMENEUTIC

revelation, and their hearts were with Jesus because of the revelation. Nathaniel approached him, and Jesus prophesied to him, saying, "I saw you before you came here" (*see* John 1:48). This blew Nathaniel's mind! He followed Him from that revelation.

The woman at the well said, "*I perceive that You are a prophet*" (*see* John 4:19). She told the town about a man who *told her everything she ever did* (*see* John 4:29). Jesus had just told her who He was, the revelation was clear, and her takeaway and interpretation were, *Come see a man who told me everything I ever did!*

Peter is the one who had a revelation and interpreted it rightly, then spoke it out—which was the application. He responded to Jesus' question with accuracy.

APPLICATION
SPIRIT - REVELATION
SOUL - INTERPRETATION
NATURAL/BODY - APPLICATION

Application is where we act in faith on what we hear. This often is simple once you have clarified your interpretation of what you had a revelation about.

Many years ago, I worked for a specialty aircraft company. After being with them for some time, I attended a prophetic meeting and was given a word that confirmed something God had been speaking to me.

It was, *You are to step out, move, and go into the ministry full-time.* I knew what the word meant, where I was to be, and how to do it. So,

155

the following week, I went to the HR office and put in my resignation from employment. They were sad to see me go. Shortly following this decision, I couldn't sleep. Nothing felt right, sweat would break out on my face, and this great sense of uncertainty would rush over me. To the point that I questioned the decision I made to quit my job. I went back to HR and said I was not sure about this, and they offered me my position back as they liked my work and value to the company.

After thinking it over, I decided to stay in faith and leave the job.

Now the prophecy was confirmed. Everything about it aligned with what the Lord had already spoken to me. The writing was on the wall. But why this conflict? Was it the devil trying to stop me? Was it cold feet? A lack of faith? None of those things were the case.

The revelation was undeniable, and another prophet confirmed my interpretation. My wife and I were in agreement. So, pressing on, I left the job, moved to another city, and began my ministry journey. It was a tough decision for us financially, but we knew we heard God—other than the zero-peace part!

A month went by, and we were struggling to make ends meet but standing on the word from God. A friend I worked with at the company called me one day and said, "You will never believe it. The company just announced another entity is purchasing them, and as a result, there are huge layoffs." This friend, who was in the same department I was in, continued, "The company gave us all a tremendous severance pay for the next several months to find new jobs or until they can bring us back!"

My heart sank in my chest. Now it was clear that the revelation and interpretation were correct, but the timing was off. The Holy Spirit was trying to inform me to wait a little longer and that He was getting my transition to ministry paid for. If only I had heeded the application of *peace*.

Many years have gone by since that costly misapplication. The word was right, and so was the interpretation. The Application was a costly mistake. Heather and I still reference that time when walking out current words we know the Lord is saying to us. Waiting is good when it's God.

THE NECESSARY ATTRIBUTE OF PEACE

Application has several attributes to its execution. Peace is the greatest one when dealing with a word for yourself. Application carries a different function when ministering a word to someone else. It may be as simple as basic courtesy or people skills.

People skills are essential when sharing a revelation. I believe that application is often overridden by crazy behavior, such as shaking or jerking one's body while delivering a word to someone. Wild emotional behavior can sometimes wrongly solidify a revelatory moment or word being released. All because of induced high emotion.

This may be in the form of thrashing hands and heads, or shaking, or wild shouting as they deliver the word. For me, most often (and there are exceptions), the more dramatic—the less clear and impacting the word is. In some instances, outward manifestations are the result of a learned behavior. Several prophetic voices have developed a non-original and uninspired mode of operation. This is based on their education by empirical observation and what they saw others do and taking it as their own. As a result, many are sadly operating as a cheap copy of a great original. Refreshing are those who symbolically go to the top of the mountain and receive their own word from the Lord. A genuinely inspired voice just hits differently.

NEW TRADITIONS ABOUT PROPHECY

When prophetic words are released, well-meaning voices often employ their trusty go-to statements. These include but are not limited to "put it on the shelf and see what happens," "God will never tell you something you didn't already know yourself," and "Prophecy is only comforting, exhorting, and encouraging." Statements of this sort are very present in the Church; although they often are correct, they may also be incomplete. For example, although we have the Holy Spirit as our Guide, and He is leading us, and His sheep know His Voice, there is a place in the prophetic that can tell a person something they didn't already know.

In 2 Kings 5, this was the case regarding Naaman, who wanted to be washed of his leprosy and parked his chariot outside of Elisha's house. The prophet did not come out to see Naaman but sent his messenger with instruction that he should dip in the Jordan seven times.

This insulted Naaman, but he eventually did it. Now if a prophecy only confirms what the Lord has already told a person, then why didn't the commander say, "Ah, yes, just as I knew I was to do!" This is because there are times when prophecy is to help you get *unstuck* from a situation where you cannot hear God due to the stress and noise of the present issue you might be facing.

Additionally, there is a miracle impartation at times also packaged into genuine prophetic words. They speak out the will of God concerning a matter, and they also induce faith and action on the part of the hearer. In Naaman's case, he begrudgingly took the prophet at his word and received his healing. Naaman's direction to dunk in the river was not something he already knew about!

The point is this: The application should come through peace and discerning the timing when you know you have interpreted a word accurately.

And so we have the prophetic word confirmed, which you do well to heed as a light that shines in a dark place, until the day dawns and the morning star rises in your hearts; knowing this first, that no prophecy of Scripture is of any private interpretation, for prophecy never came by the will of man, but holy men of God spoke as they were moved by the Holy Spirit.

—2 Peter 1:19-21

A BETTER HERMENEUTIC

Prophecies can miss the highest and best mark or even fail at times because the person delivering the word doesn't do a good job or those receiving prophetic information have very little understanding. Often what is needed is good information that will assist in extracting the heart of what the Spirit is saying. Therefore, regarding prophecy, we need a better *hermeneutic.*

What do I mean by hermeneutic? In biblical studies, it is referred to as the science of the methods of *exegesis.* Whereas *exegesis* is usually the act of explaining a text, hermeneutics is the science or art by which exegetical procedures are devised.

Hermeneutics—the Art and Science of Interpretation

Hermeneutics, in general terms, is the art and science of interpretation. Although most commonly associated with biblical interpretation, it's a method of analysis through which we uncover the interpretation of a text within its context. Further, hermeneutics involves studying principles of interpretation, its theory, and methods for all forms of communication, nonverbal and verbal. It poses the question, what did the writer/speaker mean?

PROPHECY WILL NEVER BE AN EXACT SCIENCE

As prophetic individuals, it would be wise to take note of and employ a hermeneutically motivated approach to their revelatory experiences. This will result in a more significant percentage of encounters that arrive at satisfying conclusions. Using a general hermeneutic in prophetic encounters will assist in walking out words that may have otherwise caused harm, pain, or confusion. Prophecy will never be an exact science. Still, with a healthy process, the Word of God can help us navigate experiences and produce the highest and best result.

In your life, utilizing a faith-filled analysis of a prophetic word can be a place of safety and comfort rather than needing to justify and spiritualize a seemingly missed word. It is also a contingency process to insulate you from manipulation or well-intended but misguided prophetic ministry.

As we have already addressed, one of the main issues with prophecy is its patchy track record on a large scale. Damage has occurred from an undisciplined form of prophetic words that are frequently released. The issue at hand is it fosters trust in the "popcorn prophetic word culture" that can resemble more of a "checking the horoscope behavior" than a reliance on the Word of God and the Holy Spirit. Due to a lack of a good understanding of prophecy, mystical ideas or personalized superstition can become part of the experience. The reason some deliver a prophecy in a forced and odd way is a result of experiencing the real thing and they attempt to manufacture what they experienced—only without actually having a word from God or the

Holy Spirit guiding them. The real thing has power and dramatically impacts people, leading them to Jesus and glorifying Him.

When an awe-inspiring, predictive prophecy or word of knowledge comes to pass in short order, the power in these prophetic moments can be breathtaking. I recall being in meetings when a man of God I followed for many years stood up and declared there was a dentist in the city where we were holding meetings. This dentist was going to commit suicide. There was an attorney God wanted to use to reach out to this dentist. Within weeks of this word, a local dentist sadly took his own life. Someone we knew in the area was conversing with a person about this dentist when the other person admitted he knew he was supposed to reach out to the dentist but was unable to do so.

Because of the word given at a meeting only days previous, the individual we knew asked this person he was talking to, "If you don't mind me asking, what do you do for a living?" He responded, "I am an attorney." These kinds of moments will make a believer out of you! It's the legitimate that causes the counterfeit, motivated by a desire to replicate an encounter. Those who are not satisfied with the Word of God may desire to wow others with prophecy, but they are headed for disappointment, both for themselves and others.

IF YOU DO THE DIFFICULT, GOD WILL DO THE IMPOSSIBLE!

"If you do the difficult, God will do the impossible," I often say this because it requires a specific type of discipline to remain satisfied with the Word of God and remain the same in moments of incredible breakthroughs. By remaining the same, it matters more to you that you are doing what God desires than what you desire. What I am really describing is a person who is not moved by their emotions, rather they

DEMYSTIFYING THE PROPHETIC

are moved by the Word of God and the faith they have developed. It is difficult to overcome carnal emotions, but if you do the difficult and place them under the Word of God you will be empowered to see God do the impossible!

JUST BECAUSE YOU CAN DOESN'T MEAN YOU SHOULD

Remember the story of Jesus, where after having an amazing miracle service, decided soon after to move on to another city? Common sense, and even a business sense, would say, "Don't leave town. You just hit it big here! We should stay here and hold meetings and events until the full potential is realized!" Not Jesus. He was busy about the Father's business.

This applies to the prophetic in many ways. Obedience and doing what you are supposed to do is vital. Just because you can, does not always mean you should, and the desire to outdo the last experience is why some prophetic individuals feel the need for daily "fortune cookie" prophetic words. Now it's not wrong to do this, but it must be the Holy Spirit causing you to do it.

PROPHECY NEEDS A BETTER HERMENEUTIC

The art and science of interpretation are needed in prophecy more than ever today. We need to take a scriptural approach and arrive at better conclusions. Let me give you an example. For two years leading up to a recent election, the Lord had given me two different dreams involving the outcome.

In each of these dreams, I saw myself waking up from sleep the day after the election, and the president had lost. It also came to me that it would involve technology and an algorithm. I announced this at my public meetings and on my live broadcasts. Some people gave me pushback.

Others said, "Impossible because so many have declared him the winner." I responded, "Yes if all things are equal, he wins by a land-slide! However, my sense is that it will not be equal. It would be a controversy, and he would not be in office." When it played out exactly how the Lord showed me, many people said, "Joseph, you still missed it because he did indeed win."

Then more predictions began to come forward about January. At that time, many were predicting he would still win through various means. On January 6, I was on my broadcast and said, "I see a day of tears." That is what unfolded. Others said the president would be rein-stated in March, then spring, and kept making these claims. A lot has unfolded since that time. Why do I bring this up? To point something out—both points of view were correct!

The interpretation of these things was incorrect and led to over-reaching and prophetic echo chambers. Where groups of prophetic people were all saying the same thing, not considering anything outside the closed environment they were in, like a chamber that only reflected what each other was saying. The truth is what they saw regarding a win was most likely correct. What was not correct was the interpreta-tion that he would not be in office that January.

Now history is still unfolding, and there are yet to come many sur-prises, both in hindsight and regarding how it will all play out, yet I can confidently say that because we had a good hermeneutic regarding prophecy, it helped me not fall into an echo chamber.

As we walk through the chapters ahead, it also needs to be said that the prophets could still be right! Only it would be an unfolding of a fuller interpretation. Who will say their words are incorrect for another future election cycle involving that president or another? The prophets can still be right in several ways. The key is to stay humble, sensitive, and obedient to the Holy Spirit.

CHAPTER NINE

TWO PROPHECIES, ONE KING

But the natural man does not receive the things of the
Spirit of God, for they are foolishness to him; nor can he
know them, because they are spiritually discerned.

—1 Corinthians 2:14

Vantages are interesting to consider, especially when it comes to the topic of contradictory prophetic words manifesting from two or more different sources.

I have experienced contradictory prophecies on a *minor scale* compared to what we will see in this chapter. In my case, the ones giving the prophetic words *knew in part* and *prophesied in part*. Yet it was my responsibility to discern and interpret the words. From a position of faith and patience, it is possible to realize that *the heart of the word* may be ascertained, even if the delivery was unclear.

Let's look at a fascinating example from Scripture.

PROPHETIC VANTAGE POINTS

In the Word of God, we come across what at first seems like a contradiction. The countering prophetic words were prophesied by two of the most recognized figures in Scripture—Ezekiel and Jeremiah. Both prophets released a prophetic utterance about the same king, yet they seemingly contradict one another.

These two senior prophets uttered two differing words about one situation—and it's in the Bible! What happens when two prophets say two opposite things? We can learn a powerful lesson from examining this narrative.

KING ZEDEKIAH

The two prophecies revolved around a king named Zedekiah, who was consequently the last king of Judah. *Zedekiah was king when Jerusalem and the temple were destroyed by Babylon in 586 BC.* An event that coincided with the majority of the people being carried off into exile.

Zedekiah's story is told in 2 Kings 24–25, 2 Chronicles 36, and the book of Jeremiah. Babylon was looming to invade, and because of this, a tipping point was coming for King Zedekiah. Would the king overcome? Would he be defeated? What did God have to say about the matter?

EZEKIEL AND JEREMIAH'S CONFLICTING PROPHETIC WORDS

Ezekiel and Jeremiah were contemporaries, and each received the word of the Lord. Their words were clear regarding the fate of King Zedekiah as it related to the looming threat of Babylon. It may be a surprise to you to learn that these two prophecies regarding the fate of Zedekiah differ. Though they were clear on his fate, the prophetic words are contrary to what would happen to lead to his ultimate end—the prophecies didn't match.

> *My net also will I spread upon him, and he shall be taken in my snare: and I will bring him to Babylon to the land of the Chaldeans; **yet shall he not see it**, though he shall die there.*
>
> —Ezekiel 12:13 KJV

In Ezekiel 12:13, the prophet Ezekiel declared by the word of the Lord stating that "Zedekiah would not see Babylon." Ezekiel accurately prophesied regarding King Zedekiah and the events that would befall him, yet prophesied *Zedekiah would not see Babylon.*

Now let's compare Ezekiel's prophetic word with Jeremiah's prophecy about the same event describing the fate of Zedekiah.

> *And thou shalt not escape out of his hand, but shalt surely be taken, and delivered into his hand; **and thine eyes shall behold the eyes of the king of Babylon**, and he shall speak with thee mouth to mouth, and thou shalt go to Babylon.*
>
> —Jeremiah 34:3 KJV

HISTORIAN JOSEPHUS REJECTED THESE PROPHECIES

Jeremiah declared that Zedekiah would see the king of Babylon and then die inside Babylon! Someone or both must be wrong when comparing these two prophecies at face value. Early Jewish historian Josephus saw these exact two prophecies as so *inconsistent* with one another that he refused to believe either of them!

For a deeper look at Ezekiel 12:13,[4] we see the phrase *my net;* meaning that though Zedekiah escaped out of the city, the Chaldeans would overtake him and carry him to Babylon. In a scenario that had no conflict with either prophetic word, only Jeremiah predicted that his (Zedekiah's) "eyes should see the eyes of the king of Babylon," and when prophesying about the same instance, Ezekiel foretold that he (Zedekiah) should not see Babylon, though he should die there.

To reiterate, historian Josephus struggled with the difference to the point of a comment in his work *The Antiquities of the Jews.*[5] He thought the two prophecies were so *inconsistent* with each other that he did not believe them!

Another reference to Josephus' issue with the two prophecies is found in *The Antiquities of the Jews:*

> But when these prophetic reports came to king Zedekiah, he did not believe their prophecies, for the reason following: It happened that the two prophets agreed with one another in what they said as in all other things, that the city should be taken, and Zedekiah himself should be taken captive; but *Ezekiel disagreed with [Jeremiah], and said that Zedekiah should not see Babylon, while Jeremiah said to him, that the king of Babylon should carry him away thither in bonds.*[6]

ANSWERING THIS PROPHETIC ENIGMA

If left here, this would be a difficult moment for biblical prophecy, showing that two of the main prophets of the Old Testament conflicted with one another according to their predictions. However, we discover an answer upon reading further and examining the event from a larger scope.

> *And the army of the Chaldees pursued after the king, and overtook him in the plains of Jericho: and all his army were scattered from him.* [6] *So they took the king and* **brought him up to the king of Babylon** *to Riblah; and they gave judgment upon him.* [7] *And they slew the sons of Zedekiah before his eyes,* **and put out the eyes of Zedekiah,** *and bound him with fetters of brass, and carried him to Babylon.*
>
> —2 Kings 25:5-7

These two supposed conflicting prophecies are made clear by examining the scripture in 2 Kings 25:5-7. The Chaldeans captured Zedekiah and took him to the king of Babylon, who was in Riblah. Zedekiah saw him eye to eye as prophesied by Jeremiah. His captors proceeded to kill his sons, then put out his eyes. Which would fulfill the prophecy of Ezekiel, who predicted Zedekiah would not see Babylon.

BOTH PROPHECIES WERE FULFILLED!

By putting both prophecies together from the vantage point of 2 Kings 25:5-7, we see that they coincide in a remarkable way! Both prophecies were *fulfilled,* and the enigma of Ezekiel explained when Zedekiah was brought to Nebuchadnezzar at Riblah, where he had his eyes put out, and was then carried to Babylon, where he died.

Much can be learned from this narrative in how we view prophecy. Sometimes it is a matter of perspective or vantage point and having the full context of a matter. Time and context can draw out the complete reality of what was said.

If we were to approach these two words in the same way Josephus did, anyone would be hard-pressed to oppose the same conclusion Josephus arrived at. However, with just a little more scriptural digging, a missing piece surfaces—adding clarity to both prophecies.

Each prophetic word depicted a bad ending for the king. They each held a different but matching part of the narrative. Interestingly, if one prophecy had been read independently of the other, they each would have lined up with 2 Kings 25:7, and there may have been no conflict in interpretation by Josephus or anyone else.

THE TAKEAWAY

The same is true for the prophetic today. Don't become confused or frustrated when prophecy doesn't seem to line up exactly as your expectations demand. Instead, find the *heart of the matter* and apply faith and patience, as in some cases, like King Zedekiah's prophecies, there may be a complete interpretation.

The conclusion is this; when all the facts are present, the information becomes clear. Within this gruesome story is a lesson on gathering all the data and coming away with the heart of a matter and its complete interpretation.

A PERSONAL EXPERIENCE WITH
CONTRADICTORY PROPHECIES

As I stated at the beginning of the chapter, I encountered conflicting prophetic words. As you will see, this type of thing also happens in word of knowledge, not just predictive prophecy.

Heather and I were newly married, and I was leading worship for a week of prophetic meetings. There were several speakers, each taking a different night of the week. These speakers would often minister prophetically to the audience at the end of their messages.

One of the speakers turned their attention to me on a particular night and began to prophesy these words, "You have thought that you were called to ministry, my son, but it is not so. You are called to business and politics; there you will make great wealth! This will be for you to finance the work of ministries." The word was powerful and from a very tenured, credible voice.

I remember thinking, *If this is You, Lord, I am listening and will place my faith in what was said to me!* Amazingly, it was the following night when a different speaker was present.

The two speakers had not met, and the former speaker was not even in the particular meeting. After teaching a powerful message, the second speaker turned their attention to me, much like the previous speaker had done on the previous night. A prophetic word once again came forward. Only this time, the revelatory information shared was the exact opposite of what was prophesied to me just one night earlier, "My son, you have thought you would enter into business and politics, that you would be a supporter of ministry, but I say unto you this is not to be! You have a Nazarite anointing on your life, and you shall be separated unto the ministry!"

You can imagine my confusion! It was such an issue that one of the leaders (who happened to be running for governor of the state I was in at the time) pulled me and the leaders of the meeting aside for a discussion, saying that these two words were quite contrary, how do we reconcile this?

No one had a great answer. So, I did what I often did at that time in my life; I prayed and sought the Lord about it. After pondering and praying, an answer came to me from the Holy Spirit—it was very revealing. When the answer came, it was in the form of a strong sense which rose in my heart, saying, "Both were right!"

Each time the thought came about these (seemingly) conflicted words, that sense from the Holy Spirit was imprinted on my heart again, saying, "Both were right." This really helped me, as both words had information that was exactly true and has played out in various ways in my life to this date.

CLARITY IS ALWAYS BEST

However, clarity would have been better right out of the gate than confusion. Looking back at that experience offers insight for a better understanding. What I can now see regarding those two opposing words is that both were right and that the missing piece was better interpretation and delivery of the words by the speakers. What each prophetic voice shared with me was undoubtedly revelatory and in the same territory, topically. They were picking up something very important. They amazingly tapped into correct scenarios—each had a right revelation that something was changing in my life. However, their interpretations were different. It would have been better to say "there is a change happening in your life" and not step into territory they had not fully seen. Admitting that they only saw change, not the specifics that followed. It is vital to move in a place of honesty and not

go beyond what is actually being seen for the purpose of sensationalizing the moment.

SANHEDRIN MISINTERPRETED A PROPHECY!

Another instance and a bit more technical is found in extra-biblical
history involving the altering of the legal power of the Sanhedrin.
Upon a change of government and a shift of rulers, laws were changed,
which caused a crisis in how the Sanhedrin interpreted Scripture! To
them, the Word of God had been broken!

Here is what I'm referring to regarding scriptural promises. You will
see that they are prophesying about Jesus and His millennial reign.
However, the way the prophetic word from Scripture was interpreted
led the leaders of the day to believe the prophecy was broken.

> *For unto us a child is born, unto us a son is given: and
> the government shall be upon his shoulder: and his name
> shall be called Wonderful, Counsellor, The mighty God,
> The everlasting Father, The Prince of Peace. [7] Of the
> increase of his government and peace there shall be no
> end, upon the throne of David, and upon his kingdom, to
> order it, and to establish it with judgment and with justice
> from henceforth even forever. The zeal of the Lord of hosts
> will perform this.*
>
> **—Isaiah 9:6-7 KJV**

> *The **scepter** shall not depart from Judah, nor a lawgiver
> from between his feet, until **Shiloh** come; and unto him
> shall the gathering of the people be.*
>
> **—Genesis 49:10 KJV**

The term *scepter* refers to the tribal identity and right to apply the Mosaic Laws and the authority to enforce them. The Sanhedrin adjudicated capital offenses. They could make judgments regarding legal cases, even when the nation was in Babylonian captivity between 606 and 537 BC. They could continue with their own tribal identity and retain the ability to withhold their own rule of law by their very own judges.

Shiloh is a term held by early rabbis and Talmudic authority, meaning Messiah.[7]

HISTORY DIFFERED FROM THEIR INTERPRETATION

At the end of the reign of Herod the Great over the Jewish people, somewhere between AD 6-7, King Herod the Great's son Archelaus was dethroned and sent away to Vienna, a city in Gaul. Being the second son of Herod the Great left an interesting position, even vulnerability, in the kingdom, as Herod murdered many of the other members of his household—including his older son Antipater. Herod the Great's death had come before this moment, around 4 BC, when Archelaus was placed over Judea. After Archelaus was widely rejected, he was removed in the same time frame, somewhere between AD 6-7.

A procurator from Rome named Caponius replaced Archelaus—this is where the collision with the Sanhedrin's perception of the prophetic word entered the scene.

SANHEDRIN'S LEGAL AUTHORITY REMOVED

The Roman policy was immediately enforced upon Caponius being placed into power, eliminating the Sanhedrin's ability to preside over their legal cases. These new restrictions, suddenly enforced on the Sanhedrin, created an outcry! When the members of the Sanhedrin found they were deprived of their ability to judge *who had a right to life and who should be condemned to death*, they placed sackcloth on themselves and ashes upon their heads.

IT SEEMED TO THEM PROPHECY AND SCRIPTURE WERE BROKEN

They believed the Word of God and the prophecy spoken in Scripture had been broken and failed! Truthfully, if they had interpreted the Word accurately, they would have discovered the prophecy was completely accurate. It was their interpretation of the prediction that was off!

THE PROPHECY WAS ACCURATE

Know therefore and understand, that from the going forth of the command to restore and build Jerusalem until Messiah the Prince, there shall be seven weeks and sixty-two weeks; the street shall be built again, and the wall, even in troublesome times.

—Daniel 9:25

The scepter had been removed from the land of Judah, but *Shiloh* had come! While the Sanhedrin wept throughout Jerusalem, a Boy, the Son of a carpenter, was living in Nazareth. He would present Himself as the Messiah, the King, on the day predicted by Gabriel to Daniel, the prophet, five centuries beforehand.[8]

INTERPRETING AGABUS

The New Testament prophet Agabus was accurate in his predictions and was known as a prophet. He associated with Philip's daughters, who prophesied and encountered the apostle Paul one day. His word was accurate, with a minor exception.

> And when he was come unto us, he took Paul's girdle, and bound his own hands and feet, and said, *Thus saith the Holy Ghost, **So shall the Jews at Jerusalem bind the man that owneth this girdle***, and shall deliver him into the hands of the Gentiles.
>
> **—Acts 21:11 KJV**

Agabus prophesied that, *indeed, Paul would be bound.* He went as far as to say that the Jews would bind the owner of the belt. Only that is different from how it played out. Paul was bound, he did have a conflict with the Jews, and he ended up in the Gentiles' hands.

First, when looking at this text, you can see that the Jews didn't deliver him into the hands of the Gentiles. Instead, the Romans, whom Agabus' prophecy was referring to, pretty much stepped in and saved Paul's life! For the Jews were beating him! Secondly, the Jews in the text didn't bind Paul; it was the Romans who placed two chains on him.

*Then **the commander** came near and took him, and **commanded him to be bound** with two chains; and he asked who he was and what he had done.*

—Acts 21:33

Does this mean Agabus missed it? Not at all. Here is why it is important in the New Testament to receive the heart of the prophecy. In the Old Testament, the prophet spoke directly on behalf of God. In the New Testament era, all God's people can hear Him. Agabus is part of the body of Christ and can participate in the Spirit-filled life. All believers can discern what the Lord is saying by weighing things out in what seems best by the Scripture and the Holy Spirit. Acts 15:28 says, "For it seemed good to the Holy Spirit, and to us."

The point is that there may be more than one vantage point when the Lord shows something to a prophetic voice. There is also a lot to consider when working in one of the four types of prophecy. Word of knowledge can be accessed more easily than a trance and open vision. It may be that word of knowledge because it is mixed with the person's mind, will, and emotions, can have the probability of mixture over someone experiencing a trance, vision, or prophetic visitation. The difference is when there is a prophetic moment involving a trance or intense vision, it comes upon a person. It is almost involuntary. Like John the Revelator on the Island of Patmos. Word of knowledge, as Agabus was working, using Paul's belt as a prophetic act, can have subjective fragments attached to it.

WAS AGABUS A FALSE PROPHET

Agabus was not a false prophet; he was working in all the light he had, and the Holy Spirit was present to make up the difference. Could it be that Agabus saw it accurately? The Jews were going to bind Paul only through the prayers of the saints, and a bad situation did not become worse due to some unforeseen escalation. The Holy Spirit saw to it that the commander of the Romans stepped in and rescued Paul.

The bottom line is vantage points, and the nature of prophetic accuracy is different today than in the days of the Old Testament.

DEPTH PERCEPTION

Depth perception in prophecy is an issue for new prophetic people and veterans alike. The Bible is clear about this by saying *we know in part* and *prophesy in part*. We see through *a glass dimly*, meaning that no one has it all figured out, nor does anyone have all mysteries and limitless prophetic insight nailed down to a science.

INTERPRETING SIGNS AND VANTAGE POINTS

One of the greatest areas of education has been in the arena of *interpretation*. Through a lot of pain and expense, it has been a life lesson the Lord used, *not caused*, to make it glaringly evident why proper interpretation is paramount when navigating prophetic encounters.

TWO HANDS PROPHECY

One day I received a phone call from two wonderful minister friends. They were very trusted and moved in the gifts of the Spirit. It was delightful to hear from them. They had been praying, and suddenly, one of the men on this call told me the Lord had spoken strongly to him about me! He shared a clear word, saying, "I saw two hands held out in front of you. One was of God, one was not, but you will know which one was of Him when the time is right." He went on to say it was important for me, and vital, that I heed this word. I thanked him and sensed the seriousness of this word.

Within a couple of days, someone I had known many years previous showed up during a very pivotal time in our lives. Heather had just received a kidney transplant and was experiencing a very difficult recovery that involved many challenges to her mental and physical health. We had just planted a new ministry work and were preaching around the nation, sometimes five times per week. So much was happening around this time, and some huge decisions were about to be made which would involve a good part of our future.

When this individual showed up, I had concerns and even paused due to certain flags in my heart about him being part of what we had going on. He came with great advice, great enthusiasm, and insightful counsel.

Through his insight and intervention, we saved a lot of money on a business situation we had no idea about, as we had never been businesspeople. Many things pointed to this person being great for our ministry and future. Besides that, many people knew this person, and he had a reputation for helping ministries and was on various boards at very reputable places.

I was still very hesitant about a few things that made me concerned. Being a young minister at the time and quite naïve, I kept a good attitude and thought, *God may be sending this person here to help me build and sustain a very large entity.* However, from the check in my heart, I was reluctant to step forward and commit to bringing him closer and giving him a voice and leadership status in our structure at the time.

He wanted to be trusted, and at every turn, it would seem he was going above and beyond to earn my trust and the trust of those around me. I thought that even though there were a few things others had warned me about with this person, and though I had an uneasiness in my heart, I was willing to walk this out with him until I received a green light.

THE SCRIPTURE SPOKE TO ME

One morning I woke up and heard in my heart prophetically so strong the words from Scripture. Second Thessalonians 3:2 (KJV) says, "And that we may be delivered from unreasonable and wicked men: for all men have not faith."

That word bore witness in me, and it became clear that we should stop in our journey with the ministry but remain friends. Shortly after, I requested a meeting with him to tell him I wasn't interested in going any further in our relationship or placing him in leadership.

STRANGE SIGN

We had no place to meet as we were away from the offices, so we stepped into an available RV. As we were talking and I was about to let him know we were going to go in another direction, suddenly the radio, which was shut off, crackled on. At a blaring volume, these scratchy, fuzzy words came through in a song, "Take my hand, it is yours to have," or something close to that. Then the radio shut off and completely cut out again. We all sat there and looked at each other briefly because of how unbelievably odd it was! There was no power on, and the vehicle was ultimately off! It made no sense at all and kind of flipped us all out for a moment.

Suddenly, the prophetic word I had received recently about the two hands came back to my mind. So, against all the mixed concerns I carried in my heart, I thought this was a sign from God, and I was going to obey it!

I jumped up and said, "That song is the fulfillment of a prophecy I received several days back, and God is making it clear what we are to do! I'm taking your hand and ready to work together." This was one of the worst decisions I ever made.

These people cost Heather and me an embarrassing amount of money, nearly cost us our ministry, and stirred up strife in a way I had never experienced. It took a very long season to get past what transpired but thank God, we came out of it all. I'm not so sure today if that wasn't a form of witchcraft or demonic interference. One thing is for sure, a sign like that will not be my determining factor ever again. Signs can accompany them, but they are not directional.

Looking back on that moment, it dawned on me that God had spoken to me through a still, small voice. I was looking for the spectacular and missed the supernatural! The prophetic word I received about two hands was accurate, and the Lord had another person we were to work with who came into the picture simultaneously. Thankfully we came through it and have since learned not to use a sign as a final decision.

Patterns determine capacity, which is required to understand anyone you want to work with long term or before making a relatively permanent decision regarding working relationships.

GOOD INFORMATION BRINGS PEACE

It is important to remember that even with negative supernatural and prophetic encounters, we are not to despise prophesying, as there is much good in it, especially when it involves good protocols, interpretation, and application. The Word of God is designed to bring peace to your heart and answer the fight inside. It will offer spiritual information that will correct what is out of alignment. We must trust the Bible over any prophetic word, as it is the highest form of good information and brings peace.

Dear reader, you can move in prophecy and grow in it. God wants you to hear His Voice even more than you want to. God also wants you to be a conduit of His Voice more than you want it. Remember, it is about the heart of a word and having ears to hear what the Spirit is saying.

CHAPTER TEN

SENSUS PLENIOR

DEEPER
FULLER MEANING

That which has been is what will be, that which is done is what will be done, and there is nothing new under the sun. Is there anything of which it may be said, "See, this is new"? It has already been in ancient times before us.

—Ecclesiastes 1:9-10

We are about to examine and walk into interesting territory, there is one thing we must always keep close in mind concerning Scripture—not one of us is above the Word of God. As we venture into topics open to *interpretation*, remember there is a crucial verse for those stepping into the revelatory spaces. First Corinthians 4:6 says, "Learn from us not to think beyond what is written." A point for every prophetic person to memorize and keep in disciplined practice—it will keep you from *error*.

*Now these things, brethren, I have figuratively transferred to myself and Apollos for your sakes, **that you may learn in us not to think beyond what is written,** that none of you may be puffed up on behalf of one against the other.*

—1 Corinthians 4:6

SENSUS PLENIOR

There is a phrase first used in the 1920s labeled *Sensus Plenior*. It is a *Latin phrase* that means a *fuller sense* or *a fuller meaning*. It is a way to define something as holding a deeper, fuller meaning. *Sensus plenior*, by its definition, has a significant space within prophecy. It also relates (at least in part) to much of the Jewish mind, which sees prophecy as a *pattern*.

PROPHECY AS PATTERN

There is much to consider regarding prophecy, which can induce more than one point of conversation. Prophecy exists throughout Scripture and has been declared at least once, in its context, for that time and event in which it was spoken and written. It may then apply again for *another time* and a *similar event* in the future—thus, a pattern.

We see this several times throughout the Psalms and the major and minor prophets as they *profoundly* describe or give subtle statements regarding the Messiah's life, death, and resurrection!

As believers, it is helpful whenever you can recognize a pattern and are able to "unpack" the ways in which it was fulfilled and how it can be applied to a future time. One such example is Jesus being seen as the completion or fulfillment of the biblical Passover. We will look at what I mean in a moment.

There are many *types* in the Bible that often provide the key to deeper understanding.

BEYOND THE PREDICTION FULFILLMENT MOTIF

To those impacted by a Western way of thinking, when we hear the words "prophecy" or "prophetic," our minds typically race toward some form of prediction/fulfillment motif. In contrast, the Eastern mind looks for *patterns*—then fulfillment.

EXAMPLE OF PROPHECY AS PATTERN USING THE PASSOVER

The following scripture passage is the example of Jesus being the completion or fulfillment of the biblical Passover. Again, as believers, it is vital to recognize and ascertain the *patterns* like the ones we are about to consider. Within Scripture, Jesus can be seen as the completion or the *fulfillment* of Messianic prophecies.

Prophetic Messianic implications involving Passover carry some of the most fundamental and foundational Messianic pattern/prophecy involving the Feasts. For example, notice the original instructions found in Exodus as it relates to Passover. See if you recognize any prophetic symbolism written for that time that still applies to you today.

> ...*On the tenth of this month **every man shall take for himself a lamb**, according to the house of his father, a lamb for a household.* [4] *And if the household is too small for the lamb, let him and his neighbor next to his house take it according to the number of the persons; according to each man's need you shall make your count for the lamb.* [5] ***Your lamb shall be without blemish**, a male of the first year. You may take it from the sheep or from the goats.*

*6 Now you shall keep it until the fourteenth day of the same month. Then the whole assembly of the congregation of Israel shall kill it at twilight. 7 **And they shall take some of the blood and put it on the two doorposts and on the lintel of the houses where they eat it.** 8 Then they shall eat the flesh on that night; roasted in fire, with unleavened bread and with bitter herbs they shall eat it. 9 Do not eat it raw, nor boiled at all with water, but roasted in fire—its head with its legs and its entrails. 10 You shall let none of it remain until morning, and what remains of it until morning you shall burn with fire. 11 And thus you shall eat it: with a belt on your waist, your sandals on your feet, and your staff in your hand. So you shall eat it in haste. It is the Lord's Passover. 12 For I will pass through the land of Egypt on that night, and will strike all the firstborn in the land of Egypt, both man and beast; and against all the gods of Egypt I will execute judgment: I am the Lord. 13 **Now the blood shall be a sign for you on the houses where you are. And when I see the blood, I will pass over you; and the plague shall not be on you to destroy you** when I strike the land of Egypt. 14 So this day shall be to you a memorial; and you shall keep it as a feast to the Lord throughout your generations. You shall keep it as a feast by an everlasting ordinance.*

—Exodus 12:3-14

The symbolism and ultimate reality are powerful, both for the children of Israel but clearly for you and me!

DEEPER FULLER MEANING

Messianic Scriptures are tremendously prophetic, and in this instance, are describing the blood of Jesus and the salvation He provided through His blood. It *holds a deeper, fuller meaning*. Indeed, the narrative above was a mighty experience. Every Israelite had the blood of a lamb covering their doors while death passed through the area. Yet it is the application of this command as it applies to Jesus Christ and our New Testament experience that is the greater fulfillment.

Death drifted through that region, taking the lives of those not under the blood! Today we have that same experience through Jesus' blood. In a dying world, and upon the end of this life, the blood of Jesus keeps us from the *second death*, which is eternal damnation. The more in-depth *meaning* here is that His blood saves all who apply it to the doorposts of their life!

BLOOD OF THE LAMB

Pattern is found in the initial action of the Israelites covering their doorposts with the *blood of a lamb*. Today, pattern finds another *deeper, fuller meaning* of fulfillment when Jesus shed His blood.

Finally, we are the recipients of the highest fulfillment of this prophetic pattern. What started in Exodus arrives in our present day as all who call on the name of the Lord are saved and covered *by the blood of Jesus!*

From blood on the doorposts, blood on a cross, and His blood covering us, a pattern is concealed in one distinct truth and symbolic action and is powerfully revealed in the fulfillment of that action.

Through the death and resurrection of Jesus Christ, which leads to those who enjoy the cleansing power of His blood, the prophetic pattern of Passover is fulfilled!

Sensus plenior is also used in biblical exegesis to describe the supposed deeper meaning, which was intended by God but not by the human author.

PRESENT TRUTH

*For this reason I will not be negligent to remind you always of these things, though you know and are established in the **present truth**.*

—2 Peter 1:12

Present truth simply means the Holy Spirit emphasizes something that has always been there. It is brought to light in the current time and season.

It is not new truth—*there is no such thing as new truth*. People who attempt to say that they have a new truth are working in deception as scripture is closed and there is no new truth, only what the Bible has presented us with. Deception left unchecked, even at a low level, can cause those who listen to it to wander or eventually can lead a person onto the road of *perdition* (the road to hell).

Present truth is simply when the Holy Spirit emphasizes something that has always been available. For example, the Azusa Street Revival reignited the Pentecostal experience and speaking in new tongues.

There was nothing new about the baptism in the Holy Spirit. It was already demonstrated to us in Acts 2. It was, however, new to the generation who began to experience it for themselves.

That is one example of present truth, something that needs to be correctly emphasized but then comes to light with the help of the Holy Spirit.

GENUINE INSPIRATION OF THE HOLY SPIRIT

> *Knowing this first, that no prophecy of Scripture is of any private interpretation,* [21] *for prophecy never came by the will of man, but holy men of God spoke as they were moved by the Holy Spirit.*
>
> —2 Peter 1:20-21

Let us embrace that no one and that means no one, has any private interpretation of Scripture or some hidden meaning that only they know how to interpret for their followers.

WILLFULLY LIMITED TO SCRIPTURE

The Holy Spirit speaks to every believer, and it is vital that we stay within what the Bible allows. We do this by choosing to be *willfully limited* to the confines of Scripture, never violating or breaking the barrier of what the Bible does *not* qualify.

REMEMBERING THE WORD FROM A PREVIOUS GENERATION

*This will be **written for the generation to come**, that a people yet to be created may praise the Lord.*

—**Psalm 102:18**

The understanding of present truth is an issue of remembering, like King Josiah, who found what the Word of God said to his generation or those who study revivals and ask, "Where is the earth-shaking move of God that those in past generations witnessed?" The real culprit isn't always that hearts grow cold or even backslide against a move of God. The simple answer, maybe it is due to the passing of time.

GENERATIONAL REPETITION: PHINEHAS AND MATTHIAS

Patterns repeat when the occasion calls for it, and every generation has an opportunity to drive out wickedness from the land.

The two stories mirror one another. One listed in Numbers 25 details Phinehas and his anger toward the blatant sin on display at the door to the Tabernacle. The second one is an extra-biblical but historical narrative about Judah Maccabees, aka "The Hammer," who encountered a similar situation when his father, Mattathias, stood up to a violation of Jewish tradition. Mattathias acted against Gentile ordinances being forced upon the Jewish people. He lunged at a Jew who was compromising and going to comply with the demands of the land to offer a sacrifice that violated God's law. Mattathias killed this man right on the altar! This act led to a conflict involving his son Judah who ultimately held off the Romans in a dramatic way. The following account references Phinehas and his zeal.

> *And indeed, one of the children of Israel came and presented to his brethren a Midianite woman in the sight of Moses and in the sight of all the congregation of the children of Israel, who were weeping at the door of the tabernacle of meeting. ⁷ Now when Phinehas the son of Eleazar, the son of Aaron the priest, saw it, he rose from among the congregation and took a javelin in his hand; ⁸ and he went after the man of Israel into the tent and thrust both of them through, the man of Israel, and the woman through her body. So the plague was stopped among the children of Israel. ⁹ And those who died in the plague were twenty-four thousand. ¹⁰ Then the Lord spoke to Moses, saying: ¹¹ "Phinehas the son of Eleazar, the son of Aaron the priest, has turned back My wrath from the children of Israel, because he was zealous with My zeal among them, so that I did not consume the children of Israel in My zeal. ¹² Therefore say, 'Behold, I give to him My covenant of peace; ¹³ and it shall be to him and his descendants after him a covenant of an everlasting priesthood, because he was zealous for his God, and made atonement for the children of Israel.'"*
>
> **—Numbers 25:6-13**

> *Many from Israel came to them; and Mattathias and his sons were assembled. ¹⁷ Then the king's officers spoke to Mattathias as follows: "You are a leader, honored and great in this town, and supported by sons and brothers. ¹⁸ Now be the first to come and do what the king commands, as all the Gentiles and the people of Judah and*

those that are left in Jerusalem have done. Then you and your sons will be among the friends of the king, and you and your sons will be honored with silver and gold and many gifts." [19] *But Mattathias answered and said in a loud voice: "Even if all the nations that live under the rule of the king obey him, and have chosen to do his commandments, every one of them abandoning the religion of their ancestors,* [20] *I and my sons and my brothers will live by the covenant of our ancestors.* [21] *Far be it from us to desert the law and the ordinances.* [22] *We will not obey the king's words by turning aside from our religion to the right hand or to the left."* [23] *When he had finished speaking these words, a Jew came forward in the sight of all to offer sacrifice upon the altar in Modein, according to the king's command.* [24] *When Mattathias* **saw it, he be burned with zeal and his heart was stirred.** *He gave vent to righteous anger; he ran and killed him upon the altar.* [25] *At the same time he killed the king's officer who was forcing them to sacrifice, and he tore down the altar.* [26] **Thus he burned with zeal for the law, as Phinehas did against Zimri the son of Salu.** [27] *Then Mattathias cried out in the town with a loud voice, saying: "Let every one who is zealous for the law and supports the covenant come out with me!"* [28] *And he and his sons fled to the hills and left all that they had in the town.* [29] *At that time many who were seeking righteousness and justice went down to the wilderness to live there.*

—1 Maccabees 2:16-29
New Revised Standard Version

THE PASSING OF TIME

As one generation's time ends and another begins, the memory of what God did in the previous generation begins to diminish until many no longer practice that truth and revelation of the former generation. Time's *gnawing abstractness* can turn a powerful *revealed truth* for one generation into a forgotten formality when a new generation supersedes the former.

I'm reminded of the riddle presented to Bilbo Baggins to solve in the classic book by J.R.R. Tolkien, *The Hobbit*. Gollum, a character in the story, challenges Bilbo to answer a riddle.

> This thing all things devours;
> Birds, beasts, trees, flowers;
> Gnaws iron, bites steel;
> Grinds hard stones to meal;
> Slays king, ruins town,
> And beats mountain down.

> —*The Hobbit*, J.R.R. Tolkien

In *The Hobbit, An Unexpected Journey*, Bilbo answers the riddle: "Time, the answer is time."

THE FORCE OF TIME

> *But, beloved, do not forget this one thing, that with the Lord one day is as a thousand years, and a thousand years as one day.*

> —**2 Peter 3:8**

For a thousand years in Your sight are like yesterday when
it is past, and like a watch in the night.

—Psalm 90:4

Next to God and His Word, not many things can stand up to the force of *time*. In the natural, time is an undefeated contender. This is why we must contend for the *present truth* that God may choose to emphasize in a new generation.

PRESENT TRUTH AND YOUR RESPONSIBILITY

It may shock you that your great God desires to reveal missing parts, seemingly absent from a generation, through you! It is His will that all people discover what He has provided. Discipleship and servanthood are not just healthy development for you. They are necessary for equipping those around you. Because, you see, we are all pressing against time itself. We only have so much left to reach those around us with whatever gifts you may be presented with.

An encouraging thought when considering time and the window we are given is that your life in the hand of God can produce present truth, which is a purpose accomplished by His Word working mightily through you.

It takes surrender and focus until the day arrives when we are taken from the clutches of natural time, in eternity future with Jesus, beyond the veil. Time is something we must consider when grasping the issue of the present truth and what God may be revealing at this current season.

Part of time management, as it relates to the present truth, is to simply remember. We remember by reading the entirety of Scripture and conforming to it. Then give away what we have at every available occasion.

SENSUS PLENIOR THROUGHOUT THE AGES

A *deeper, fuller meaning* has a connotation of history repeating itself. As a matter of fact, the antichrist has had to be prepared to appear in every generation! Why? Because historical cycles repeat themselves, and no one knows the actual day or hour in which the Son will return. Thus, the enemy must always be prepared from one generation to the next to fulfill his wicked schemes for the end of the world.

Consider all the wicked overlords such as Nero, Domitian, Hitler, or the evil dictators throughout the ages up to our modern history; it might be understandable that each of these was placed in their time to fill the role of antichrist. Now add our unbelievable technological advancements, and we can see we are closer than ever to the end of the age.

KAIROS MOMENTS THE FULLNESS OF APPOINTED TIMES

In Luke 18:8, Jesus said, "When the Son of Man comes, will He really find faith on the earth?" This verse suggests that things don't just happen without the cooperation of God's people. For prophetic events to manifest in their proper time and season requires cooperation by those alive in each generation.

In Matthew 23:37, Jesus said, when speaking to Jerusalem, "I wanted to gather your children together, as a hen gathers her chicks under her wings, but *you were not willing!*" In reference to prophetic moments, Jesus said to John the Baptist in Matthew 3:15 (NIV), "*Let it be so now*; it is proper for us to do this to fulfill all righteousness." A principle can be considered that suggests there are *kairos* moments when God is looking for willing vessels to cooperate with Him or, as

Jesus said to John, "Let it be so now," which is sometimes necessary for the fulfillment of His prophetic will.

Matthew 24:20 alluded to an interesting prophetic point made by Jesus when He said regarding things to come, "Pray that your flight may not be in winter or on the Sabbath." Suggesting that it is possible to alter, not stop, but alter the time trajectory of prophetic events. If this is the potential case, then agreement or disobedience to the call of God means believers should be in position—in the right place at the right time is highly important to the will of God being accomplished.

When His *kairos* moment arrives, we must be ready and in prayer; this is the admonition given in the Epistle of Peter, saying we can hasten the return of the Lord.

> *Therefore, since all these things will be dissolved, what manner of persons ought you to be in holy conduct and godliness,* ¹² *looking for and* **hastening the coming of the day of God,** *because of which the heavens will be dissolved, being on fire, and the elements will melt with fervent heat?*
>
> —2 Peter 3:11-12

By faith, lay hold of what God has for you and your family today! Agree with His perfect will for your life and watch the things intended to be fulfilled in a previous generation come to pass in your life according to His purpose for you. Yes, your family has a purpose, a destiny. In Jesus' name, I release a revelation of all you are called to seize and walk in now at this time!

CHAPTER ELEVEN

THE MYSTERY OF APPOINTED TIMES AND PEOPLE

Then He also said to the multitudes, "Whenever you see a cloud rising out of the west, immediately you say, 'A shower is coming'; and so it is. [55] And when you see the south wind blow, you say, 'There will be hot weather'; and there is. [56] **Hypocrites!** *You can discern the face of the sky and of the earth, but* **how is it you do not discern this time?**

—Luke 12:54-56

UNDERSTANDING TIME: CHRONOS, KAIROS, EPOCHS

Of the sons of Issachar who had understanding of the times, to know what Israel ought to do.

—1 Chronicles 12:32

There are *three basic understandings of time* relating to our natural experience. The following definitions may assist in grasping how God hides a truth and reveals it in certain seasons.

One example of this would be the Church! The Church was a concealed truth in the Old Testament but revealed in the New Testament! While the Church was a mystery in the Old Testament, it fully manifested after Jesus' death, which was an appointed time.

The following are the three basic understandings of time:

Chronos

1. Chronos: A Greek word meaning a sequential chronological time or a particular time and season.

An example of this word from Scripture is in Luke 4:5, where we see the devil taking Jesus up on a *high mountain* and showing Him a snapshot of all the world's kingdoms in a sequential *moment of time.*

> *Then the devil, taking Him up on a high mountain, showed Him all the kingdoms of the world in a **moment of time.***
>
> **—Luke 4:5**

One way *chronos* might be understood is to think of time as a river going along. It is a sequential series of events. It is time that plays out by one event leading to the next. It is the normal time we are all acquainted with.

Kairos

2. Kairos: A Greek word meaning the right, critical, or opportune moment in time.

An example of *kairos* is in Matthew 16:3, where Jesus speaks of discerning the times or a *kairos* moment they lived in.

He answered and said to them, "When it is evening you say, 'It will be fair weather, for the sky is red'; ³ and in the morning, 'It will be foul weather today, for the sky is red and threatening.' Hypocrites! You know how to discern the face of the sky, but you cannot discern the signs of the **times.**"

—Matthew 16:2-3

Kairos moments have more of a *prophetic edge* as destiny is attached to these moments of fulfillment, or assigned events, even prophecies that must be fulfilled. Jesus' return is a *kairos moment* in that no one knows the day or the hour, only the Father in heaven.

Yet it is a designated window that will appear in the sequential flow of *chronos*. Prophecy works this way, sometimes in a pattern, sometimes by prediction and fulfillment.

The following are some examples from Scripture of *kairos* moments related to prophecy via the prophets in Scripture. It would seem, in some instances, that prophecy may not automatically come to pass, at least to a certain degree. As you can see from the following verses, there is a sense of cooperation with what has been prophesied for it to fully manifest. Statements in the following verses such as, "that it might be fulfilled," or "that it might fulfilled which was spoken by the prophet," and "these things were done that the Scripture should be fulfilled."

Yet He warned them not to make Him known, ¹⁷ that it might be fulfilled which was spoken by Isaiah the prophet.
—Matthew 12:16-17

Saying to them, "Go into the village opposite you, and immediately you will find a donkey tied, and a colt with her. Loose them and bring them to Me. ³ And if anyone says anything to you, you shall say, 'The Lord has need of *them,' and immediately he will send them." ⁴ **All this was done that it might be fulfilled which was spoken by the prophet, saying:** ⁵ **"Tell the daughter of Zion, 'Behold, your King is coming to you, lowly, and sitting on a donkey, a colt, the foal of a donkey.'"***

—Matthew 21:2-5

For these things were done that the Scripture should be fulfilled, "Not one of His bones shall be broken." ³⁷ And again another Scripture says, "They shall look on Him whom they pierced."

—John 19:36-37

*When evening had come, they brought to Him many who were demon-possessed. And He cast out the spirits with a word, and healed all who were sick, ¹⁷ **that it might be fulfilled which was spoken by Isaiah the prophet, saying: "He Himself took our infirmities and bore our sicknesses."***

—Matthew 8:16-17

*So they gave Him a piece of a broiled fish and some honeycomb. ⁴³ And He took it and ate in their presence. ⁴⁴ Then He said to them, "These are the words which I spoke to you while I was still with you, that **all things must be fulfilled which were written in the Law of Moses and the Prophets and the Psalms concerning Me."***

—Luke 24:42-44

THE THIRD SEGMENT OF TIME

The first two are the most referenced; however, a third reference is worth mentioning. We could talk about the first two, and although it would be sufficient, this next one carries interesting subtleties and offers additional insights into time. It complements the other two but has a seasonal implication.

Epoch

3. *Epoch*: is a distinct period in history or a person's life marked by notable events or particular characteristics.

Epoch was first used in the 1610s as a point in time marking the start of a new period. For example, the founding of Rome or the birth of Jesus would be described as an *epoch* in time.

The Hebrew equivalent is the word *zeman*, meaning *appointed time or season marked with historical and significant value.*

Esther 9:27 describes the *appointed time* for the *feast of Purim.* Although this does have characteristics of *kairos* in it, being *an appointed time*, it goes beyond an appointed time and develops into a season or time in history.

> *The Jews established and imposed it upon themselves and their descendants and all who would join them, that without fail they should celebrate these two days every year, according to the written instructions and* **according to the prescribed time.**
>
> —Esther 9:27

There was a season of peace after the rescue of the Jewish people in the book of Esther. A celebration known as the Feast of Purim began and remains today, commemorating the great deliverance of the Jews through the actions of Esther and Mordecai while under the Persian Empire. Nehemiah 2:6 refers to an *appointed time* to return from a journey (indicates the time set by Nehemiah to inspect the broken walls of Jerusalem after receiving permission from the king).

This action was also the beginning of an *epoch* or a season of time when the wall was rebuilt, and the people of God could return. An *epoch* occurs in an often-quoted verse in Ecclesiastes 3:1, which says, *"To everything there is a season."* It says that everything has a *predestined time.*

> *I said in my heart, "God shall judge the righteous and the wicked, for there is a time there for every purpose and for every work."*
>
> **—Ecclesiastes 3:17**

> *He who keeps his command will experience nothing harmful; and a wise man's heart discerns both time and judgment, ⁶ because for every matter there is a time and judgment, though the misery of man increases greatly.*
>
> **—Ecclesiastes 8:5-6**

> *A man has joy by the answer of his mouth, and a word spoken in due season, how good it is!*
>
> **—Proverbs 15:23**

APPOINTED PROPHETIC MOMENTS IN TIME

Jesus predicted the destruction of Jerusalem which was fulfilled in AD 70. The prophetic word shared by Jesus made the destruction of Jerusalem an appointed time in history.

> *Then Jesus went out and departed from the temple, and His disciples came up to show Him the buildings of the temple. ² And Jesus said to them, "Do you not see all these things? Assuredly, I say to you, **not one stone shall be left here upon another, that shall not be thrown down.**"*
>
> —Matthew 24:1-2

> *"Therefore when you see the '**abomination of desolation**,' spoken of by Daniel the prophet, standing in the holy place" (whoever reads, let him understand), ¹⁶ "then let those who are in Judea flee to the mountains. ¹⁷ Let him who is on the housetop not go down to take anything out of his house. ¹⁸ And let him who is in the field not go back to get his clothes. ¹⁹ But woe to those who are pregnant and to those who are nursing babies in those days! ²⁰ And pray that your flight may not be in winter or on the Sabbath."*
>
> —Matthew 24:15-20

> ***But when you see Jerusalem surrounded by armies, then know that its desolation is near.*** *²¹ Then let those who are in Judea flee to the mountains, let those who are in the midst of her depart, and let not those who are in the country enter her. ²² For these are the days of vengeance, that all things which are written may be fulfilled. ²³ But woe to those who are pregnant and to those who are nursing*

babies in those days! For there will be great distress in the land and wrath upon this people. ²⁴ *And **they will fall by the edge of the sword, and be led away captive into all nations. And Jerusalem will be trampled by Gentiles until the times of the Gentiles are fulfilled.***

—Luke 21:20-24

Jesus gave the word before His death and resurrection. The fulfillment of His word came about in AD 70. A powerful prophecy and fulfillment. However, some believe this could indeed be *sensus plenior* as the prophecy has last days and end-time implications to it. Those predictive words of Jesus hold a *deeper, fuller meaning* and prophetically were not only for Jerusalem's fateful day in AD 70. They are words laced with end-time predictions!

HIS-STORY REPEATS ITSELF

*That which has been is what will be, that which is done is what will be done, and **there is nothing new under the sun.*** ¹⁰ *Is there anything of which it may be said, "See, this is new"? It has already been in ancient times before us.* ¹¹ ***There is no remembrance of former things, nor will there be any remembrance of things that are to come by those who will come after.***

—Ecclesiastes 1:9-11

It is a striking realization when you begin to understand that history repeats itself. As one intelligent person once said, "It is, after all, His-Story," meaning it is God's story from the beginning, and He will bring closure to things at the end.

You might say that along the lines of *chronos* are cycles or opportunities throughout history for the purpose and will of God to manifest in each generation fully. Again, Ecclesiastes states there is *nothing new under the sun*, and it could be that history will repeat itself until the fullness of time has come, or there has been the proper fulfillment of prophecy.

THE GREAT PROPHETIC CO-MISSION

God speaks through His Word, prophesying the future and what will come. Every generation can hear and line up with His will or wait for the next generation to rise. This may be why it has taken 2,000 years for Jesus to return!

Unfulfilled words in the Scriptures must be accomplished. It has always been true of the great commission that it is a cooperation between God and His people to reach the world with the gospel of His kingdom. God with us puts the "CO" in commission.

Kairos moments in time appear, and if preparation is not readied for the opportunity, it may be that the Spirit of the Lord says the exact words Jesus spoke—"Jerusalem, I longed to hold you in My arms, but you would not have it."

> *O Jerusalem, Jerusalem, the one who kills the prophets and stones those who are sent to her!* **How often I wanted** *to gather your children together, as a hen gathers her chicks under her wings,* **but you were not willing!**
> —**Matthew 23:37**

> *O Jerusalem, Jerusalem, the one who kills the prophets and stones those who are sent to her! How often I wanted*

to gather your children together, as a hen gathers her brood under her wings, but you were not willing!

—Luke 13:34

How about the future consideration Jesus stated: when the Son of Man returns, will He find faith on the earth?

When the Son of Man comes, will He really find faith on the earth?

—Luke 18:8

SOBERING STATEMENTS FOR A KAIROS MOMENT YET TO COME!

These statements above should make us think. Are we the last generation? Most people view their generation as the last one. We have seen more prophetic fulfillment than any generation leading up to this one. Yet it still begs the question, "Have the prophetic utterances in Scripture been fulfilled to a satisfactory level to the Lord? Are we the ones whom He has chosen to see His return?"

I cannot judge that, as God knows when He will send Jesus back. However, it is a very interesting thought that none of us should take lightly.

*Now there is in store for me the crown of righteousness, which the Lord, the righteous Judge, will award to me on that day—and not only to me, but also to **all who have longed for his appearing.***

—2 Timothy 4:8 NIV

Consider the time and season we are living in. Ask yourself the question—Are you eagerly longing for Jesus' appearance?

THE MILLENNIAL REIGN EPOCH

Often some people don't fulfill their *kairos* mandate to usher in an *epoch*. Take Adam, for example. One day I found myself asking the Lord, why does there have to be a millennial reign of Jesus on earth, correcting everything only to destroy the earth and heaven and re-create them both?

> And so it is written, "**The first man Adam became a living being.**" *The last Adam became a life-giving spirit.*
> —**1 Corinthians 15:45**

After prayer and study, the Holy Spirit answered me by saying Jesus is the last Adam. Not the second Adam, but rather the *last Adam*. Why is this significant? Because Jesus came to fulfill what Adam was assigned to accomplish but instead gave up his authority to the devil.

JESUS SHIFTED THE AXIS OF POWER

For thousands of years, Adam's loss was the devil's gain. Throughout the Old Testament, the devil traversed the earth doing as he pleased and was left unrivaled. That is, until Jesus arrived on the scene and shifted the axis of power back to the *Ekklesia*, the Church. After Jesus won, conquered sin, and paid the ultimate price, He was seated at the right hand of God.

The question I asked about this was, why did He stop there? Why not eradicate darkness forever? Why not just take over the world, melt it all down, and start again? The answer is that Adam still has a commandment to subdue the earth. Jesus is the last Adam and carries the anointing of the Holy One to accomplish and fulfill the assignment of the first Adam. One thousand years of Jesus ruling over planet Earth might very well be, among other things, Jesus fulfilling God's desire from the beginning.

> Blessed and holy is he who has part in the first resurrection. Over such the second death has no power, but they shall be priests of God and of Christ, and **shall reign with Him a thousand years.**
>
> —Revelation 20:6

Another way of looking at it is that Jesus had to fulfill what God spoke over the earth. It is a fulfillment of prophecy. You see, God gave Adam dominion over the earth. I suspect Adam had a specific window of time to accomplish tending to the garden and taking dominion over the earth. He forfeited it. Jesus is finishing what Adam was to start and complete.

A THOUSAND YEARS TO FINISH ADAM'S ASSIGNMENT

Therefore, the *thousand-year reign* must likely take place to liberate creation and have it arrive at its destiny and purpose. A timeline set by God can be seen in part when considering the following three verses listed. Particularly in the word *expired*. As if to say there is a seasonal time or epoch that has been appointed, but it will run its course. God always fulfills what He says from the beginning. "Expired" is likely the end of Adam's lease on the earth. A lease that was legally hijacked by the devil with Adam's permission. Jesus had to come and legally take back what the devil had acquired. Imprisonment is a legal action initiated by God when the legal requirements are met to cast him chained for the remainder of the lease.

- Revelation 20:3, *Till the **thousand years were finished.***
- Revelation 20:5, *The rest of the dead did not live again **until the thousand years were finished.***
- Revelation 20:7, *When the **thousand years have expired.***

When the lease is up, the devil gets out, possibly due to him being a free agent again, no longer under the nullified authority of Adam. Upon the end of the millennium, the deceiver will have his liberty with no hindrance to influence anyone who will hear him—one last time.

LUCIFER'S FINAL COUP D'ÉTAT ENDS ABRUPTLY

Judgment of fire straight from heaven results from his final coup d'état! So long, Lu!

> *Now when the thousand years have **expired**, Satan will be released from his prison* [8] *and will go out to deceive the nations which are in the four corners of the earth, Gog and Magog, to gather them together to battle, whose number is as the sand of the sea.* [9] *They went up on the breadth of the earth and surrounded the camp of the saints and the beloved city. And **fire came down from God out of heaven and devoured them.*** [10] *The devil, who deceived them, was cast into the lake of fire and brimstone where*

the beast and the false prophet are. And they will be tormented day and night forever and ever.

—Revelation 20:7-10

In the end, heaven and earth will all be done away with, but not until the purpose of God's design for the earth is fulfilled.

Then I saw a great white throne and Him who sat on it, **from whose face the earth and the heaven fled away.** *And there was found no place for them.*

—Revelation 20:11

Again, prophecy occurs in *kairos* moments and an *epoch*—in this case, a thousand-year reign of rightsizing God's creation. There is a great lesson to be learned through understanding the various times and seasons by which God operates.

INTERPRETING THE TIMES YOU LIVE IN

Then He also said to the multitudes, "Whenever you see a cloud rising out of the west, immediately you say, 'A shower is coming'; and so it is. 55 And when you see the south wind blow, you say, 'There will be hot weather'; and there is. 56 Hypocrites! You can discern the face of the sky and of the earth, but **how is it you do not discern this time?"**

—Luke 12:54-56

Discerning the times is crucial for each of us in our generation. How do we do this? Get to know God through His Word and copious amounts of time in prayer. So much of what is happening in the world must be spiritually discerned. Look at the patterns of biblical prophecy, but with the discernment cultivated by knowing the Author of all creation and what His Word says about everything.

Remember, it was the sons of Issachar who not only knew the times and seasons, but they also *knew what to do* about it!

> *Of the sons of Issachar who had understanding of the times, to know what Israel ought to do, their chiefs were two hundred; and all their brethren were at their command.*
>
> **—1 Chronicles 12:32**

Three things the sons of Issachar did:

1. Understood the times
2. Knew what Israel should do
3. Had the proper alignment and structure to act

More goes into interpreting the times than simply recognizing what is happening in the world. Proper alignment and a plan of action are also required. A point I often make when speaking is to say God doesn't call you to live wherever you choose. You must make sure you are where God has called you. If you do not know for sure, it is vital to seek Him over His will for your life now. So He can supernaturally align you to who, what, where, when, and how you are to walk out the times and seasons in which you are living.

Start seeking Him today, re-sensitize your heart to His Word and what the Holy Spirit is leading you to do.

It's only forever!

SECTION THREE

DARK POWERS AND
STRANGE ENCOUNTERS

CHAPTER TWELVE

GATEKEEPERS TO THE SPIRIT REALM

*So I sought for a man among them who would make a wall, and **stand in the gap before Me on behalf of the land**, that I should not destroy it; but I found no one.*

—Ezekiel 22:30

When moving in the prophetic, it is crucial to understand that it is a gift that interprets what God, who is a Spirit, wants to say to His people in the natural. Spiritual encounters and experiences, including prophecy, are not authorized to operate without human cooperation and permission.

By permission, the light and dark sides of things operate this way. God designed human beings as infinite beings, not finite creations. A better way of saying this would be to say mankind was created from the realm of the spirit, not the other way around. The natural did not give birth to the spirit when God spoke creation into existence!

Then God said, "Let there be light"; and there was light.

—Genesis 1:3

MAN ONCE HAD SIMULTANEOUS ACCESS TO BOTH REALMS

We were made to live and fellowship with our great God forever! With the fall of man in the garden, our capacity to enjoy a full life with *simultaneous access* to the natural and spiritual realm was altered. The realm of the unseen became all but entirely removed from mankind's perception. Five basic senses are where humanity arrived after stepping down from the plane of a supernatural connection with the living God. Once broken, it was very difficult to access the realm of the unseen without assistance from God and His angels.

ADAM WILLINGLY CHOSE REBELLION AGAINST GOD

God was also, in a sense, cut off from the realm He had given to Adam to take dominion over, to subdue it, and to tend to it. Adam wasn't deceived when the devil deceived Eve—he knew what he was doing and chose to rebel against God when Eve offered him the fruit. In 1 Timothy 2:14 (NIV), Paul subtly points out the distinction between Adam's sin and Eve's sin: "And Adam was not the one deceived; it was the woman who was deceived and became a sinner." Eve fell into sin because of deception; however, Adam was *not* deceived, so he chose to sin. When Adam took the fruit from his wife, he fully knew what he was doing. He was not misinformed or misled; he simply decided to rebel against God's command.

> *Then to Adam He said, "Because you have heeded the voice of your wife, and have eaten from the tree of which I commanded you, saying, 'You shall not eat of it': "Cursed*

is the ground for your sake; in toil you shall eat of it all the days of your life."

—**Genesis 3:17**

Now the human experience is mainly limited to the confines of the natural—only when an individual becomes born again in Christ Jesus, they are reconnected to God the Father on a spiritual level. This spiritual level is the realm where everything we need is provided for us. Additionally, scripture tells us that we consist of three parts—*spirit, soul, and body* and it is vital that we say it in that order as that is how it is listed in the scripture. Knowing we are first and foremost a spirit being and in the Spirit we have everything we need. However we also have a soul and live in a physical body. What is required is to get what is done in the spirit to manifest in the natural realm. Or the arena our body is in. This requires a supernatural reaction! I will show you what I mean in a moment.

> *Now may the God of peace Himself sanctify you com-pletely; and may your whole* **spirit**, **soul**, *and* **body** *be preserved blameless at the coming of our Lord Jesus Christ.*

—**1 Thessalonians 5:23**

As three-part beings, as the Word of God teaches us, we must understand that there is far more to us than just our five senses. Although humanity fell and we were all born into original sin, it is as if humanity sank into a *cage of flesh.* The human experience was cut off from the supernatural without understanding or knowing anything about the other remaining places of their existence.

GETTING A SUPERNATURAL REACTION

However, the spiritual is not first, but the natural, and afterward the spiritual.

—1 Corinthians 15:46

The gap is the space between the realm of the natural and the spirit. Cooperation is required for the realm of the spirit to access the realm of this natural world. First Corinthians 15:46 references the spirit not being first, but the natural then comes the spirit. This is in reference to Adam being a natural being, and then Jesus came as the life-giving Spirit as God in the flesh. What is interesting is the idea of the natural being first and not the spirit. There is a principle that can be considered here.

In the natural, we don't automatically *walk in the spirit* or experience spiritual things. Instead, we must take a natural action of faith to induce a supernatural reaction. Examples of this follow:

- **Receiving Salvation:** Romans 10:9 says, "That if you confess with your mouth the Lord Jesus and believe in your heart that God has raised Him from the dead, you will be saved." *Confessing with your mouth* is a natural action with a supernatural response.

- **Laying hands on the sick:** Mark 16:18 says, "They will lay hands on the sick, and they will recover." *Laying hands on the sick* is a natural faith action that induces a supernatural response.

- **Sowing and reaping:** Hebrews 7:8 says, "Here mortal men receive tithes, but there he receives them, of whom it is witnessed that he lives." This scripture reveals the here-and-there principle. Here, the natural *tithe is given*—there, in the realm of the spirit, He receives them!

There is a supernatural reaction waiting on your faith-action in the natural.

PERMISSION AND VETO POWER

Permission is granted based on authority. As gatekeepers to the natural world, we carry an authority that allows or vetoes supernatural activity in the natural. Even the mighty God, the Creator of the universe, could not simply come down and save humankind as He willed. Instead, Jesus had to come. As referenced earlier regarding Mount Sinai, He didn't arrive on the scene as God with thunderbolts and lighting. No, Jesus came in the flesh. Why is this so vital? Because He had to come in a way that He would destroy the works of the devil and condemn sin in the flesh. All of this required a physical body!

> Jesus answered, "Most assuredly, I say to you, unless one is **born of water** and the Spirit, he cannot enter the kingdom of God."
>
> —John 3:5

Here Jesus tells us that one must be born of water, then of spirit. You must be born of a woman or born into the natural world where water breaks in the birthing process. Consequently, many implications come to light when considering this point made by Jesus. Unless a person is born of a woman by natural means and pure DNA, they cannot be born of the spirit or even saved! The issue of transhumanism and cloning comes up if you follow this thought far enough.

Jesus tells us that a physical body is needed to operate in the world because that is what Adam had. That is why Jesus had to be born via Mary, and therefore He was also called the Son of man—a reference to His humanity and point of authority on earth. Demons were never cast out of humans until the God-Man combo of Jesus, God in the flesh, showed up! For the first time, God could operate legally in man's arena. The results were devastating whenever God Himself tried to show up in the Old Testament in His pure, holy, and spiritual form! Again, think of *Sinai with all the drama and terror.* Now we see Jesus, the exact representation of God in the flesh, doing good and destroying the works of the devil.

> *Jesus said to him, "Have I been with you so long, and yet you have not known Me, Philip?* **He who has seen Me has seen the Father;** *so how can you say, 'Show us the Father'?"*
>
> —John 14:9

PHYSICAL BODIES ARE POSITIONS OF AUTHORITY

What does this mean for you and me? As born-again believers, we have the ultimate authority to tread on snakes and scorpions and overcome all the power of the enemy. The enemy is also limited to the realm of the spirit, having no physical body.

Thus, *the war is over who influences humanity.* If those who possess physical bodies are overtaken with evil and witchcraft, they will allow evil spirits access to this natural realm. However, when a born-again believer fully submits to Jesus, walks as a disciplined follower of the Word of God, and uses their authority—look out, darkness! Because the Kingdom of God is being granted permission to operate!

Knowing that physical bodies provide a position of authority and are the gateway of operation in the natural is sobering. If we were only in the spirit and did not possess bodies, we would be completely at the mercy of the spirit realm. Only we are not in that realm—we live in the natural realm where choices, actions, and what we believe determine the level of activity that any spiritual force (good or evil) may have in the natural. The spirit realm needs your permission to do any spiritual activity here!

> The spirit of a man is the lamp of the Lord, searching all the inner depths of his heart.
>
> **—Proverbs 20:27**

A fascinating discovery is to recognize that the spirit of every man and woman is still a lamp. It is ever searching for its origin, searching for the source by which it was created—your spirit knows it is not destined to an end. All spirits will live forever, somewhere.

God uses our very spirit, or the God-breathed part of our existence, as a *light* to search out the inward parts and determine what is good or bad within that vessel.

> But the natural man does not receive the things of the Spirit of God, for they are foolishness to him; nor can he know them, **because they are spiritually discerned.** [15] But he who is spiritual judges all things, yet he himself is rightly judged by no one.
>
> **—1 Corinthians 2:14-15**

The human spirit is the God-breathed part, the essence of life and existence, whether born again or lost. The breath of God is the life force, and it keeps us alive. Hebrews 1:3 says, "Upholding all things by the word of His power." The Word of God formed all creation, including the spirit of every human. Experiencing the life force given to every living person by God does not mean everyone is saved!

CREATION OR CHILDREN

There is a significant difference between God's creation and children. Children of God receive Jesus as their Lord, giving their lives to Him and staying committed to living for Him. His creations are those wandering around in life, and although they have His spirit force keeping them alive—*they are destined for eternity in hell and the lake of fire.* His creations are those on the broad path, with many who find it. Jesus is the narrow path, the narrow way, and He came so that those who died spiritually can be reconnected to God the Father!

> *And when He had said this, He breathed on them, and said to them, "Receive the Holy Spirit."*
> —John 20:22

Jesus reconnected His disciples to God the Father in John 20:22 when He breathed on them. The phrase "breathed on them" to receive the Holy Spirit, is the Greek word *pneuma* and is the dynamic equivalent to God breathing life into the dust and placing His breath, or Spirit, within Adam! In this instance, Jesus was not filling them with a baptism in the Holy Spirit. *He was filling them with God Himself!* He was reconnecting their spirits to the Father of all spirits—He was saving them!

After the resurrection, Jesus had the *power and the right* to save His own who believed in Him! Salvation means their spirits are *perfected* and reconnected to God the Father. The disciples went from being God's creations to His children, as their disconnected spirits were made perfect upon being reconnected to the Father.

> *To the general assembly and church of the firstborn who are registered in heaven, to God the Judge of all, **to the spirits of just men made perfect.***
> —Hebrews 12:23

EVERY LIVING PERSON WILL LIVE FOREVER, SOMEWHERE

This is also why the doctrine of annihilation, or the destruction of a created individual, is impossible. As every living person has the life of God in them, they will exist forever. That does not mean they are saved. It simply means that just like all of creation is held together by the word of His power, so are those who live without God. His Spirit is all life, and that is why every person is destined to live forever, somewhere.

DEATH DOESN'T COMPUTE WITH ANYONE

We were not created to die. We were created for eternity. Therefore, death is an emotional issue, and funerals are difficult for many. Because no human was designed to deal with coming to an end, it doesn't compute. However, some believe when an individual dies, they cease to exist. "That's it," they say, "No more. It's the end of the line."

If they are honest, those same people cannot even imagine *nothing*. Try right now and imagine nothing yourself. If you're like me, you might have imagined dark emptiness. Maybe you imagined a mystical void of nothingness, likened to the lights going out, as if you were to pull the plug on a computer. That's it; the power is off.

However, you are not a computer, you were made in the image of God, and no matter what you attempt to imagine about nothing, it is impossible! Because whatever image you see in your mind is still something, it suggests that we cannot imagine what nothing is because it is not part of our makeup. It is not part of our divine programming.

Your Great Creator programmed you for eternal thinking. Saying all of that to make the point: Although we live in a natural corporeal body, there is more to us than simply that!

Enter the realm of the spirit. The realm of the unseen is not a science. It is not simply measurable. It is different from what we think we know.

SPIRITUAL THINGS CAN BE OFFENSIVE TO THE CARNAL

Carnal-minded religious voices often say, "I don't believe in healing, I don't believe in tongues, I don't believe in prophecy, I don't believe in miracles, I don't believe, I don't believe, I don't believe!" Well, like a tremendous ministry friend of mine named Dave Duell used to say, "Don't worry about it, brother! It won't happen to you!"

Imagine if the apostle John explained his revelation to the church of Ephesus, and they responded by saying, "Wow, you're off your rocker!" How about Peter having a trance while hungry and praying on a rooftop?

> *The next day, as they went on their journey and drew near the city, Peter went up on the housetop to pray, about the sixth hour.* [10] *Then he became very hungry and wanted to eat; but while they made ready, he fell into a trance* [11] *and saw heaven opened and an object like a great sheet bound at the four corners, descending to him and let down to the earth.* [12] *In it were all kinds of four-footed animals of the earth, wild beasts, creeping things, and birds of the air.* [13] *And a voice came to him, "Rise, Peter; kill and eat."*
>
> —Acts 10:9-13

Peter went up to the rooftop; he was very hungry while he was praying. I'm sure Peter could hear the quiet rustling of preparation downstairs, and while praying in the Spirit, he suddenly was exposed to the power of God via a trance. We know the story, and something very significant happened at that moment, which changed the entire trajectory of the Christian Church! Gentiles were welcomed to the gospel!

What if someone told Peter, "You're all hopped up on something. You need to go back to sleep and dream up something less nuts."

PHILIP'S UNIQUE ENCOUNTER

Take Philip, the evangelist, and the time he was caught away and taken to another territory. Can you imagine him breaking that story down for unbelieving people?

> Now when they came up out of the water, **the Spirit of the Lord caught Philip away,** so that the eunuch saw him no more; and he went on his way rejoicing. [40] But **Philip was found at Azotus.** And passing through, he **preached in all the cities till he came to Caesarea.**
>
> —Acts 8:39-40

It is interesting to realize that Philip, led by the Holy Spirit, ministered to an Ethiopian. That step of obedience led him to the territory he would finally settle in. Philip had a prophetic unction, he obeyed it, and it was that act of obedience that led him to his destination. Doing whatever God tells you to do will align you to the place He has in store for you.

In Philip's case, it was the territory of Azotus, then on to Caesarea, as you see in Acts 8:40. The point is this: When free moral agents surrender to the realm of the spirit God's way, not only can the Voice of

God be released via the prophetic but miracles, displays of power, and all things of the Holy Spirit will manifest! A supernatural act is when a person surrenders to God and makes way for the super to get on their natural—permission is granted for the supernatural to engage, and anything is possible!

CHAPTER THIRTEEN

MYSTERIES AND STRANGE HAPPENINGS

*Let a man so consider us, as servants of Christ and **stewards of the mysteries** of God. ² Moreover it is required in stewards that one be found faithful.*

—1 Corinthians 4:1-2

But God has revealed them to us through His Spirit. For the Spirit searches all things, yes, the deep things of God.

—1 Corinthians 2:10

"LABEL CAGING" THE SUPERNATURAL

Metaphors reign where mysteries reside.

—Unknown

T his quote makes a great statement regarding the way many explain supernatural encounters. When some do not understand a thing, they devise a saying for it or label it via *catchphrases* and *metaphors*—one of religion's favorite mechanisms.

Understanding encounters and experiences deserves a far more valuable approach than using the Christian nomenclature of familiar labeling. Placing a spoken label on an experience induces a containment moniker acting as an effective mechanism of religion when relating to most things not understood—a corral of inherited words used to prod anything not agreed with into a nice, safe little box. An action I call "label caging" or, as already explained, simply labeling something to control it, dismiss it, or direct it.

WHAT DOES THE BIBLE SAY?

Identifying and finding what the Word of God conveys about such things is of greater value. Grasping encounters and supernatural happenings that are *difficult to understand* is essential, or those who have encounters are in danger of being word-caged and unable to discover the biblical reality of what they are experiencing.

There is no perfect way to cover the entire scope of experiences and encounters, yet we will touch on a variety of them here. I desire to offer clarity and a sense of peace to those who have encounters but haven't known *how to quantify it*. Please remember, no matter how unique or fantastic an experience might be, we *must **always stand firmly on the written Word of God**—the ultimate standard of safety and truth.

> ...*that you may learn in us **not to think beyond what is written**, that none of you may be puffed up on behalf of one against the other.*
>
> **—1 Corinthians 4:6**

ENCOUNTERS ARE HIGHLY SUBJECTIVE

Prophecy and supernatural encounters are often highly *subjective*, and although we have our measuring line, the final and ultimate authority is the written Word of God; this is our standard. As already stated, unique things can and do happen in the supernatural and it is the unwavering discipline to the Word, mixed with faith, that will produce an outcome of healthy supernatural encounters.

Even if you have an unexplainable scenario take place in your life, you are still in the driver's seat of how to respond. I have had some very unusual encounters, things that are not easily found in the Scripture. My response is, if it doesn't line up with Scripture, or if there is something that violates Scripture, *cast it away*. As far away as possible!

UNIQUE PHENOMENA

Further, we are going to define and look at various phenomena. Two things can transpire as onlookers observe the realm of encounters as it relates to those observing and hearing about such things.

1. They either *fully embrace what they hear with a reckless open-mindedness poised with zero questions*—which is a mistake.

2. They *completely throw every encounter out*, calling it not of God or, even worse, of the devil.

There are certainly many examples of how God speaks and various kinds of supernatural encounters that take place in the Bible. Once the door to the spirit realm is accessed, supernatural experiences may happen more frequently.

*It is doubtless not profitable for me to boast. I will come to **visions and revelations of the Lord:** ² I know a man in Christ who fourteen years ago—whether in the body I do not know, or whether out of the body I do not know, God knows—such a one was **caught up to the third heaven.** ³ And I know such a man—whether in the body or out of the body I do not know, God knows—⁴ how **he was caught up into Paradise and heard inexpressible words, which it is not lawful for a man to utter.***

—**2 Corinthians 12:1-4**

I have often asked the Holy Spirit, "Why do we see in visions, dreams, symbols, and the like? How is it that You don't just tell me plainly, much like a friend would tell someone about an event they have seen or that is upcoming?" One day He answered me on this issue.

WHY VISIONS, DREAMS, SYMBOLS, AND THE LIKE?

What dropped into my heart surprised me. I knew it was God's Voice when He answered. It was a simple yet straightforward answer—"I want to be pursued." The word came to me that plain—God wants to be pursued. It was that simple! Such a basic but profound revelation it was to me that He loves it when people seek Him. To seek Him is to seek His will, and He is a *relational* God.

It is the glory of God to conceal a matter, but the glory of kings is to search out a matter.

—**Proverbs 25:2**

THE SCOPE OF ENCOUNTERS

The supernatural is an interesting space that is more real than this natural world; in understanding that, we will look at a few strange happenings, mysterious encounters, entities, and revelatory experiences and understand that they are all part of the spectrum in prophetic reality. However, we must determine case by case where each moment falls in the scope of encounters. We are going to take a look at many of the issues you may have heard of or even experienced and talk about them in a relatable way.

Although we will by no means cover the entire scope of encounters and experiences, we will offer thought and insight into some. I desire that you have a purposeful consideration as you see encounters through a biblical lens as a takeaway regarding what to do as encounters and situations present themselves, which are not mentioned in this book. Remember this—*the answer is always the same*. Surrender to Jesus, which means surrender to His Word.

And the spirits of the prophets are subject to the prophets.
—1 Corinthians 14:32

As we explore some unique encounters and prophetic experiences, remember the scripture from 1 Corinthians 14:32, "The spirits of the prophets are subject to the prophets." Prophets should be subject to the voice of other prophets and able to control their vessel.

Controlling oneself and the gift of prophecy (including wild physical manifestations) is always in your ability. Are there exceptions? Yes. The Holy Spirit may invade a surrendered vessel's space, similar to how John the Revelator experienced the apocalypse. His experience resulted in writing down some of the most dramatic revelations the world has ever been exposed to. However, God is not the author of confusion, nor is He giving people complicated gifts that do not draw people closer to the Word of God and Christ Jesus the Son.

CRUCIAL

What we are about to talk about is crucial to anyone venturing into the realm of prophecy or any spiritual encounter. You are responsible for managing yourself and holding command of the gift God has entrusted you with—you are also to biblically wield prophecy or any power gift God has entrusted you. Remember, if you find yourself resonating with encounters as we look at them or have an unction to step out in prophecy, stay with the Bible, be honorable, have class, don't over-dramatize, and when in doubt, use people skills!

Encounters are *subjective* in that they are difficult to quantify for those hearing and trying to understand as an outsider looking in. This is also why deception is so rampant in the prophecy space. Because anyone can simply say, I have had a vision. I just went to heaven, or an angel just spoke to me, etc.

The Lord has given us His Word as the absolute standard and a powerful source for accuracy and propelling legitimate prophetic ministry to a heightened position.

GOD'S WRITTEN WORD IS A PLACE OF REST

Remember that God's written Word is a *place of rest* for your heart! When you receive the Word of God by faith, it creates a sense of ease, and you will be able to cease your striving and start *flowing*. As a result, this is what you will convey to others—a flow, a sense of ease and peace rather than tension. Safety is found in His Words of life, and He will never violate what He has said.

Here and now, before we venture into some of the strange and mysterious aspects of prophecy and the supernatural, *remember your foundation must be on God's written Word.* As it will keep your heart safe in that place of rest—stay safe, dear reader.

YOU ARE SOPHISTICATED

You are a powerful agent, and as a free moral agent, a person is highly capable of inducing experiences.

The human mind alone is a sophisticated and extremely complex mechanism that can be altered or step out of its normal designated function. If you meditate on sensational things enough, a delusion can set in. Your mind and will can create things that are not real.

UNIQUE SUPERNATURAL ENCOUNTERS

I'm about to go into an arena that is sensitive to talk about but happens to believers and unbelievers alike.

I have experienced many unique encounters over the years but have learned to stand on the Word of God and refuse to go beyond what is written. If the Scripture doesn't support a thing, then teaching it should be avoided altogether. The following is a sampling of what sensitive people can and sometimes experience.

Remember, it doesn't matter what the experience might be—*the Word of God is your final authority.* It must be, or subjective conjecture about what is legitimate becomes based on how someone "feels" about the event.

It is imperative that you know you can *control* your experiences. This is a highly important truth to be understood regardless of what you might think or what others have taught you. *Controlling yourself* is required to become mature in the prophetic.

Following is a number of experiential occasions that happen more to those who are prophetically inclined. This is, of course, a *partial scope* of encounters or experiences. Yet we must acknowledge the unique encounters so many seem to have. We will look at a list of encounters or simple explanations. Let's begin.

SYMBOLISM, SIGNS, AND STRANGE ENCOUNTERS

I have chosen to list many things I have encountered and have had others come to me about over the years. The terminology for some of these experiences and events is words I utilize to label and explain some of these experiences.

Traffic

*To another the working of miracles, to another prophecy, to another **discerning of spirits**, to another different kinds of tongues, to another the interpretation of tongues.*
—1 Corinthians 12:10

Traffic is a term we have used for many years. It is a word we use to describe recurring experiences and encounters with the unseen. It is typically in reference to supernatural, emotionally impacting data that happens when in the proximity of people, events, or even when there are conversations pertinent to you or something you are picking up on about a person, place, or thing.

I have come to believe traffic is a heightened level of *discerning of spirits* as listed in 1 Corinthians 12:10. The Greek word for "discern" is *diákrisis* which means *to distinguish, decide,* or *judge.*

DEFINING TRAFFIC

Traffic is emotional and informational data. In my experience, it is a "ripple effect" of either information within a person or a precursor to a prophetic encounter due to an event about to take place or an event that has already happened. It is the gift of discernment arbitrarily picking up on unseen movement in the form of words, actions, and intentions.

At times traffic in the negative sense works this way. Imagine if someone was yelling in your face, saying the meanest and harshest things, and telling you heart-wrenching information. You likely can imagine the feeling to a degree of what I'm describing. Now remove the data, the words, and any logical connection to what was said. All that remains is the sensation on the inside. You now understand what I call traffic.

One of the best ways to navigate traffic you don't understand or where it is coming from is to pray out loud, speak the Word of God out loud in faith, and press in by speaking in tongues. Spending time in the Spirit by speaking in tongues will help you discern and lessen the negative effects of traffic.

Traffic is not something you look for but something you walk into—like the wind. Traffic is being exposed to random data. It can be emotions or feelings—not always read right or interpreted accurately, by the way. Something emotional or informational that comes from seemingly nowhere.

Having been in situations when emotion overcame me leads me to believe that Jesus may have been so moved for the people involved with Lazarus and for Lazarus himself, it drove Him not to cry, but to weep. It is very possible that Jesus could feel their pain. Potentially, the most extreme form of *traffic* Jesus encountered was manifested in the sweating of blood (*see* Luke 22:44).

This term, *traffic*, which is in the scope of discerning spirits, encounters the semi-unknown. It can predicate an encounter, either good or bad. It is an elusive experience, yet very real. A person who is sensitive to the things of the spirit and not full of the Word of God might feel like a bystander—it's not something you are looking for, but rather a sensory encounter induced by people or events.

Déjà vu

Déjà vu is a French term meaning *already seen*. Déjà vu is that sensation of familiarity or the sense that you have been in a particular situation before. It varies in intensity and the depth of familiarity it provides. For one person it may relate to what they are currently experiencing. Another individual might see or sense much more, to the point of names and moments they can call right before they happen.

When I attended university, studying psychology, déjà vu was one of the things we learned. It caused me to take somewhat of a deeper interest in it, primarily due to the fact that I have experienced intense moments of déjà vu. My takeaway from studying and experiencing it led me to believe there are two aspects to it. One purely natural, the other and a far less common experience touches the prophetic realm.

Let's look at the natural explanation through the lens of what certain psychoanalysts say.[9] Some attribute déjà vu to wishful thinking; some psychiatrists cite mismatching in the brain, causing us to *mistake* the present for the past.

Some researchers offer speculation that déjà vu is an occurrence of a *mismatch in the brain* during its continual attempt to gather data and create a perception of what is around it, having only a limited amount of input.

Researchers also refer to your memory and how it only requires small bits of *sensory information* (such as a familiar smell) to bring forth a detailed mental recollection of an event or moment in your life. Some believe déjà vu is a "mix-up" between sensory input and memory-recalling output.

Another related theory states that déjà vu is a fleeting malfunctioning between the long and short-term circuits in the brain. Researchers postulate that the information we take in from our surroundings may "leak out" and incorrectly shortcut its way from short to long-term memory, bypassing typical storage transfer mechanisms. When a new moment is experienced—which is currently in our short-term memory—it *feels* as though we're drawing upon some memory from our distant past.

A similar hypothesis suggests that déjà vu is an error in timing. At the same time we perceive a moment, there is a parallel release of sensory information that may simultaneously be re-routing its way to our brain's long-term storage. This causes a delay and, perhaps, the unsettling feeling we've experienced the moment before.

One characteristic is common to all déjà vu experiences: we are completely conscious that they are occurring, implying that participation of the entire brain is unnecessary to produce the phenomenon.

Over the years, researchers have pinpointed disturbances of the medial temporal lobe as the culprit behind déjà vu.[10] Studies of epileptic patients investigated via intracerebral electrodes demonstrate that stimulation of the rhinal cortex (such as the entorhinal and perirhinal cortices—structures involved in episodic memory and sensory processing) can actually induce a déjà vu episode.

A study published in an issue of *Clinical Neurophysiology* analyzed the patterns of electroencephalography (EEG) signals from the rhinal cortices, hippocampus (involved in memory formation), and amygdala (involved in emotion) in epileptic patients for whom déjà vu could be induced by electrical stimulation.

The researchers found that synchronized *neural* firing between the rhinal cortices and the hippocampus or amygdala was increased in stimulations that induced déjà vu. This suggests that some sort of coincident occurrence in medial temporal lobe structures may "trigger" activation of the recollection system.

There may be additional theories that researchers and professionals postulate over. What can be taken away is that there is a natural phenomenon involving your brain's perception and memory which gives many this sensation known as déjà vu.

THE PROPHETIC SIDE OF *DÉJÀ VU*

The other side of déjà vu may have much more to do with the prophetic spectrum. This would be in the sensory prediction category. It could be that, at times, you walk into a setting, and suddenly you are reminded of a dream or vision. Sometimes it can be much more involved, such as a familiar event begins to play out in front of you. Only you know what will happen next, like a film you have seen before plays out before you. It's as if you know the lines, the setting, and who will arrive, as well as knowledge of what will happen following each moment. This can last a few brief seconds or a minute. It is my opinion that this is within the realm of prophetic visions, dreams, and word of knowledge.

Sensory Issues

*And Jesus said, "**Who touched Me?**" When all denied it, Peter and those with him said, "Master, the multitudes throng and press You, and You say, 'Who touched Me?'" [46] But Jesus said, "Somebody touched Me, for I **perceived power going out from Me.**"*

—Luke 8:45-46

Sensory issues are interesting. Mainly because they are subjective, I will try and explain this for the sake of helping someone. One of the only reasons I bring this issue out is because, on more than one occasion, when talking to prophetic people, this is part of the way their prophetic gift works.

Here is what I mean. Sometimes, there are moments when a person touches me, and that information will come to me about them—their life, past emotional issues, good, bad, and the ugly. An example of this is when I had a minor outpatient surgical procedure that required a little scalpel cut followed by a few stitches. I couldn't move, and thankfully, Heather was with me.

When the doctor placed her hand on me around the halfway point of the procedure, I had a flash vision of this person's life. I calmly said, "Oh, I see you play piano during the holidays." She said, "Well, yes, I do," and I proceeded to see and say things in detail about her life. Because of the proximity and close quarters of the doctor, it was like seeing into this person's life.

I only shared a few things when this doctor began coughing violently and manifesting a demon! This is before I was to be stitched up! Meaning there was blood starting to roll as she coughed. Heather spoke up, saying, "Um, um, are you okay?" to the doctor, and the situation got worse until we prayed for peace in the scenario. Immediately the doctor was able to rush back over to me and finish.

Another time, I was having a routine blood draw, and with the needle in my arm, I saw something about the nurse who was holding my arm, and she burst into tears, which caused me a fair amount of pain! While Heather was hugging her, the nurse received a breakthrough in getting to know Jesus because of the prophetic moment.

Heather said to me, "Next time, wait until after the medical procedure before saying what you see!" Today, I take Heather's advice!

My point in sharing these two stories is that there is a point of contact that draws on a certain spectrum of prophetic people.

RIGHT HAND LEFT HAND

Sometimes information comes in a different manner based on what hand is laid on people when praying for them. If my right hand goes onto a person, it is like an impartation or giving. If my left hand is laid on a person when ministering to them, information can come to me in a clearer way. It reminds me of Kenneth E. Hagin, who would talk about sensing fire in one hand and healing would manifest at a powerful level. Other notable ministers have commented about similar experiences.

At times my left hand will open an emotional response in me when I lay it on people. An embarrassing thing, depending on the scenario, is that much of what a person has been dealing with will rush to me in an emotional way. I've learned to be stronger and emotionally prepared when laying hands on a person with my left.

Hands with different receptivity is something I don't completely understand but is something I have experienced for many years, and I know others who are the same.

Signs, Prophetic Symbolism, Numbers, etc.

*Truly the signs of an apostle were accomplished among you with all perseverance, in **signs** and **wonders** and mighty deeds.*

—2 Corinthians 12:12

There is a level of subjective interpretation in the area of *signs* and *wonders*. Spiritual encounters can have a unique perception based on the recipient's position. This applies to nearly all signs, wonders, prophetic symbolism, and *numbers* you see repeatedly or even wake up to in the middle of the night.

Therefore the people who stood by and heard it said that it had thundered. Others said, "An angel has spoken to Him."

—John 12:29

A great example is in John 12:29, where we recognize that *some thought it thundered, and others said, an angel has spoken.* This was the perception of those near the audible Voice of God. Jesus replied in the following verse by saying, "This voice did not come because of Me, but for your sake" (John 12:30). Interesting that the words were to affirm Jesus; however, the real purpose was for the sake of those around Him!

Yet even with the sign directly from God, the perception was not all the same.

So what is a sign? One way to describe a sign would be to call it a *marked event*, token, or miracle with a spiritual end and purpose. Signs are miracles that lead to something out of and beyond themselves, like the fingermarks of God. Signs are not valuable for what they are or the scene they might make—but their purpose is for what they indicate.

SIGNS GET ATTENTION

Signs are events, sights, moments, or strange out-of-the-ordinary occurrences that your inner person perks up to. It can also be a prophetic sign where something happens that you just know was for you. It either confirms or jars you to pay attention that something is taking place. Maybe it is a transition or a new event about to happen in your life, and God wants you to pay attention to it.

Signs manifest in a variety of ways and are part of prophetic symbolism. Some people see a billboard or a license plate with an unexpected message for them. Others may catch a glimpse of a particular animal at a unique moment, and it speaks to them. Many years ago, there was a meeting being held, and the purpose was to vote on allowing perversion to be recognized as leadership in the clergy of a denomination. Right as the vote was happening, and it was obvious who would win it, a tornado destroyed the church's steeple! They joked it off, but it must be said that was a sign!

> *Truly **You are God, who hide Yourself**, O God of Israel, the Savior!*
>
> **—Isaiah 45:15**

Even as I'm writing this, there was a crack from a bolt of lightning near Cheyenne Mountain in Colorado Springs that I can see from our location. In a humorous way, yet with sincerity, I take that as a sign that I'm writing about something good right now!

RECURRING NUMBERS

Again, signs arrive in a variety of ways. One of the more common ways it can take place is through recurring numbers that you wake up to in the middle of the night or see throughout the day. This all falls under the category of signs and wonders. A repeated number can simply mean God is with you. Sadly, many believers chase dream interpretation to an extreme and certainly beyond what Scripture offers on the topic. Remember, numbers and unique prophetic signs are often a simple reminder that God is with you. When you don't know what else to do with recurring numbers, pray.

SIGN OF THE BROKEN MUG

Recently I was with a friend. He had a special cup he drank out of every day. I sensed something about the cup and would even comment about it as I felt it had significant meaning. One day as he walked with it, the cup fell out of his hand and broke!

The Lord spoke to my friend, saying, *A breaking into the new.* It was a significant moment, and I happened to be present right after it happened. We both knew it meant a breaking into the new! This might sound kind of arbitrary, but I assure you, when these kinds of things happen, the Holy Spirit bears witness that something shifted in the realm of the spirit and should be noted.

DO NOT MAKE DOCTRINE OUT OF SIGNS

Signs are not to make doctrine out of, nor should we look to make all these things into something more than what they are meant to be. A sign is a sign. It means something is happening, or we need to pay attention. They are meant for you but can also be for a nation, a culture, a church, and many things. A wonder is something that happens that makes you wonder. It is a unique and peculiar event or sign that blows your mind or causes a sense of wonder.

DREAMS

Understanding dreams has also been an overly complicated issue for many. It technically shouldn't even be on the list of strange occurrences, but it is worth looking at based on how many people have asked me to interpret their dreams over the years. Dreams are a way that God speaks to us, but it must be said that dreams are very *subjective* experiences. A whole lot of capitalization has been made from books and materials on dream interpretation, and I'm certainly not saying that there is not some value in those things, but there is a point when we must stick with the Bible. However, please do develop your dream language, only firmly stand on the understanding that dreams are subjective.

More on Dreams

Most often, the best person to interpret a dream is the dreamer! It might be that there is something puzzling about it, and they know it has more meaning yet are unable to grasp it. There is nothing wrong with a prophetic person helping interpret someone's dream in a word of knowledge or with a word of wisdom; but most of the time, the one who had the dream has a better sense of what was being conveyed in their dream.

We know from Scripture that one of the gifts and abilities Daniel the prophet worked in was to solve enigmas and interpret dreams. Today, however, we have the infilling of the Holy Spirit, and He guides us into all truth.

START A DREAM JOURNAL

For years, I've instructed people to consider making a *dream journal*. Write down (or record) your dream as soon as you remember and date it. The reason is if the thing you dreamed about begins to happen or comes to pass, it is important that you identify what you saw and how you saw it. What were the symbols and scenarios? What were the places and things of interest? These can be recurring language symbols that help discover what the Lord is saying for a future situation the next time you see that symbol. I have had this happen many times.

Another word on dream interpretation. Many people give what I call a prophetic calculus equation for how dreams should be interpreted, just like those who say numbers mean something at every turn. These things can have merit, and I do not desire to discredit anyone who has helped people in the areas of dreams and numbers. Still, when things become deeper and deeper, with an overly complicated grid to work through, it has evolved beyond what is written, and it may simply be time to get back to your Bible.

Staying grounded in the Word has always been my discipline with signs in the form of dreams. Simply take the heart of the matter from any dream experience. When we get caught up in a system not clearly laid out in Scripture, we are headed for confusion and can misinterpret God.

In my experience, I have had dreams that were so clear and pointed at something so directly, only to see it happen in the natural a day or week of the time it was dreamt. Those predictive dreams are self-explanatory and need little explanation when they manifest. If you dream something demonstrative occasionally and nothing continues to happen with each passing dream, it might be time to consider that you have a vivid imagination—there is nothing wrong with that!

BE HONEST WITH YOUR OWN HEART

It is always good to be very honest with your own heart. If you violate your own heart, you will start down a path of not trusting others or yourself. It will also damage your faith. Be honest with yourself about encounters. Don't sensationalize it or try to make more out of something than what it was. Yes, encounters and legitimate things happen, but be sure not to add to something or go beyond what is actually happening. Now there are legitimate encounters that need a little explanation.

STRANGE ENTITIES

This is a unique topic and worthy of some discussion. I have had personal experiences with dark entities that would try and speak or visit. They have stood in my room; they have been in the form of an intense presence that would wake me at night. When I was a small child, there were many terrifying encounters that really scared me. As a result, it took me years to overcome my fear of the dark.

Regarding seeing strange entities, we must be aware that there are always extremes with people. They can mistake a shadow or something going around in the night as a presence when it could simply have a natural explanation. As a practice, one of the things I will immediately check first is my natural disposition. It is possible that I experienced something that has a perfectly natural explanation.

STRANGE ENTITY OUT OF JOB

Let's talk about strange entities for a moment. Job 4 is a great biblical example of this. Eliphaz recounts the story of an entity that arrived on the scene.

Job 4 gives insight into the devil's contempt for God and his hatred toward mankind. Eliphaz, one of Job's friends, is within earshot of a rhetorical conversation the devil is having with himself. This leads to Eliphaz involuntarily eavesdropping on the moment.

> *Now a word was secretly brought to me, and my ear received a whisper of it. [13] In disquieting thoughts from the visions of the night, when deep sleep falls on men, [14] fear came upon me, and trembling, which made all my bones shake. [15] Then a spirit passed before my face; the hair on my body stood up. [16] It stood still, but I could not discern its appearance. A form was before my eyes; there was silence; then I heard a voice saying: [17] "Can a mortal be more righteous than God? Can a man be more pure than his Maker? [18] If He puts no trust in His servants, if He charges His angels with error, [19] how much more those who dwell in houses of clay, whose foundation is in the dust, who are crushed before a moth? [20] They are broken*

*in pieces from morning till evening; they perish forever,
with no one regarding.* [21] *Does not their own excellence go
away? They die, even without wisdom."*

—Job 4:12-21

Eliphaz sensed a presence, the encounter was a terrifying scenario that induced trembling, bones shaking, and the hair on his body stood up. At this same moment, he could identify a formless entity before his eyes until, finally, a voice spoke. This was a strange entity, the main antagonist, a fallen angel—the devil.

This one should be the biggest and worst encounter of all the entities that would manifest to someone. Because this is in the Old Testament, we must remember that Jesus was not on the scene yet. Mankind was basically on its own with this mutinous angel.

THEATRICS OF DARKNESS

If Eliphaz could have seen past all the theatrics—meaning the fear, darkness, and sense of dread—what is left is a voice that begins to complain to itself, basically throwing a tantrum. This scenario is a strange moment experienced by Eliphaz as he was eavesdropping on the devil, who was whining and telling himself that he is so much better than humans.

From different encounters I have personally experienced with entities stepping into the room, a realization has come to me over the years. In this narrative, we see the devil, the A-List fallen angel, who was basically ruling earth at this time under the authority he lied away from Adam. What would his mode of operation be in the background? What was the nefarious thing he was doing within earshot of Eliphaz? When considering the text, it may surprise many to learn his MO was

MYSTERIES AND STRANGE HAPPENINGS

to walk around and complain to himself! As stated, he was throwing a tantrum. Most likely, the same behavior was displayed as Michael, the Archangel, kicked him out of heaven.

Demonic entities are divas and love attention. They feed on it. One night in particular, my wife, Heather, was very ill from being on dialysis for two years. She desperately needed a kidney transplant (which she miraculously received after the time of the story I'm telling you). She was asleep in our bed, and I was lying by her and comforting her. After falling asleep for what seemed like a moment, as it was late into the middle of the night, something entered the room.

It was not something in my mind or a sense I was having. Instead, I could see it with my eyes. Standing about 8 feet tall, a large, skinny-bodied, human-like creature stood at the foot of our bed. Its face was stretched forward with squinty eyes and long, stringy gray hair.

DISESTEEMING THE DEVIL

In our bedroom, this entity stood at the end of our bed, leaning forward with intensely squinted eyes, and I knew it was there for my wife. It wanted to raise its hand toward her. Next, the most curious response happened, faith rose in my heart while looking at that thing, and I began to chuckle dismissively. If my memory serves me correctly, I chuckled and said, "Whatever." Rolled over and completely ignored the looming entity! Years before that moment, the response would have been warring emergency tongues and instant out-of-bed marching and praying loud! Commanding every demon to flee would have been a full-on Pentecostal moment!

Rather than all that, my spirit was chuckling, and I rolled over with a sarcastic "Whatever!"

Guess what? Instantly peace came in, all was well, and we were at rest. Sometimes disesteeming the darkness by not giving it the time of day is a powerful force of action. The power of disesteeming darkness had quite the desired effect that evening.

A good point of understanding about signs—which do happen, as with the things we looked at in the chapter—is to remember to keep things simple. You will know if the Holy Spirit is engaging you in a heightened manner. If that is not the case, relax and continue functioning in the grace He has given you.

Anything that gets too far down the fortune-cookie path can end up sensational, with your heart and mind becoming overly developed to look at numbers and signs nonstop.

We should be meditating on the Word of God, and from that position, God can speak. Numbers and looking at numbers, their meaning, and more is not wrong; there might be moments that are helpful for some through this means.

But never replace the Word of God; if any system of hearing God is utilized over the written Word, an error is right around the corner.

> *Knowing this first, that no prophecy of Scripture is of any private interpretation.*
>
> **—2 Peter 1:20**

THE "SPECIAL ONES"

Anyone who tells you that only the special ones, or the prophets alone, can interpret Scripture is lying. There is a principle in the Word of God that no prophecy of Scripture is of private interpretation. That same principle is true of prophetic encounters. Although the Holy

Spirit will undoubtedly speak a personal word to you, there is no such thing as secret knowledge that only you know about, as far as revelatory things go.

> *Surely the Lord God does nothing, unless He reveals His secret to His servants the prophets.*
>
> —**Amos 3:7**

God will absolutely reveal secrets with you, and He does that with His prophets, as in Amos 3:7.

A major point is that we do not need special revelation to know what God is saying. Like many generations before us, we are again seeing a rise of strange doctrines and encounters taught by prophetic voices. Getting special insight and fortune-cookie type of theological ideas, mixed with supernatural experiences, is not the purpose of prophetic ministry.

Prophets are to relate to the body of Christ as servant leaders who edify and equip the saints. They are not gurus, nor are they the *enlightened ones* who alone carry special insights unavailable to everyone else. An unhealthy practice is put into place when this type of teaching or culture is elevated. Those caught up by it will likely find themselves wandering through life, not truly coming to the high call of God in their life. Often these types of issues are the result of a cult of personality rather than the reliance on the Word of God. They become ever learning but have yet to come to a solid conclusion. It creates the desire for the next mystical word, number, dream, or experience.

Dreams, numbers, visions, and more in the path of a mature believer are wonderful, but must be in their proper position and locale for the believer.

The answer is to be filled with joy, get to know Jesus, walk in the power of the Holy Spirit, and continue to be a daily reader of the Bible. Let unique experiences come to you as God wills and as you grow in the realm of the Spirit. In the long game, that is how real winning is done, and it will bear fruit the way God intended!

CHAPTER FOURTEEN

ANGELS OF LIGHT AND DOCTRINES OF DEMONS

Let no one cheat you of your reward, taking delight in false humility and worship of angels, intruding into those things which he has not seen, vainly puffed up by his fleshly mind.

—Colossians 2:18

A worthy conversation is a topic that has gained more momentum in recent years. It is the growing *infatuation* with all things supernatural and the wide acceptance of *extra-biblical encounters.*

When it comes to a greater fascination with the supernatural, a lesser emphasis on the written Word of God is always a path to error, at the very least, or it could lead all the way into occultic behavior and witchcraft.

In my book *Servants of Fire*, a deep study of angels is presented, and many of the points in this chapter will reflect facts and information from that book.

OUT-OF-BIBLE EXPERIENCES

Regarding the prophetic spectrum, *infatuation can turn into deception.* On the very basic level, wandering will occur in the lives of *naïve*, simple individuals who listen to every wind of doctrine, especially sensational stories. It is concerning that there is an intense rise of *out-of-Bible experiences*, a play on words from the supernatural phenomenon known as out-of-body experiences. I say this because many tell fantastic tales of what they have seen and where they have gone, which leave question marks.

We must first acknowledge supernatural encounters do happen! Yet they must find a foundation in the written Bible. Without that foundation, a growing trend of out-of-Bible experiences will lead to deception and masses of good-hearted believers being impacted.

Through bad teaching and the influence of sensational mechanisms, improper belief systems can be put into practice. Opening believers to influences or realms of darkness is a legitimate danger, as it induces a floating sense of acceptance from the voices of misguided influencers. Deception is an issue on several levels, one of the most common being those caught in it tend to wander. We will deal with this issue more as we go into the topic of false prophets.

IF THERE IS A COUNTERFEIT, THERE IS A REAL

Now please understand there is nothing wrong with desiring the supernatural as it relates to God and the Holy Spirit. First Corinthians 14 even encourages us to "desire spiritual gifts," which are supernatural. Many of our encounters with Jesus are filled with supernatural moments. However, the infatuation with the supernatural minus a deep love of the truth allows deception to position itself right around the corner and spring open the door for counterfeit experiences.

You see, experiences are wonderful when they involve the supernatural movement of the Holy Spirit. My life has been forever impacted by dramatic supernatural encounters, which I thank God for.

What is of great concern is how many people place experiences (or the deep desire for them) in such a high regard that it leads to irresponsibility. An encounter alone should not be the verification for any scenario when it comes to supernatural events—especially in the arena of the prophetic as it relates to angels, heaven, and various outlandish scenarios.

Please listen to me carefully, as it is vital for the days we are living in. More than ever, there is a mania related to these things. The concern comes down to more than false experiences and specific individuals who may sensationalize an encounter for attention.

Although this is very unhealthy and can and does happen, it is the listener who believes the sensationalized story that was never true to begin with. Damage ensues, leading the listener to have false expectations based on smoke, mirrors, and storytelling. Jesus takes the misleading of His sheep very seriously.

There will be a day of accountability for those who would not surrender or repent of knowingly deceiving susceptible people in the body of Christ. Giving them a false image based on fairy tales that produce little to nothing and ultimately derail them from their God-given destiny.

For all encounters, it is of utmost importance that we do not sensationalize, as it can lead to deception.

SELF-DECEPTION

One of the most tragic forms of deception is *self-deception*. Someone might ask, "Why is that so tragic?" Well, self-deception takes shape in a person's life when they are not honest with themselves about experiences or their encounters. If a person embellishes the truth and knows they are doing so, it will eventually lead to self-deception and ruin their own heart's confidence in themselves.

Sometimes when speaking with people about their encounters, I am led to conclude that they have intellectually rationalized what they have experienced or testified to. In all reality, their encounter or experience is an imagination they have chosen to embrace as a revelatory experience. When these things are as easy to experience as having a thought, then these people are walking on dangerous ground.

WHY INNER INTEGRITY MATTERS

We must tell the truth of a matter for the sake of *our hearts*, so we have inner integrity. Self-deception lays a foundation that is very unhealthy to build on. Beyond this is the issue of outside deception. Supernatural forces are always looking for avenues to enter through. The first step is bending the truth, then doing it repeatedly until, ultimately, a violation of the gospel can take place.

THE GOSPEL TRUMPS ENCOUNTERS

We notice that Paul refers to two points when referencing the authority of the gospel he was preaching. In Galatians 1:8, he states, "But even if *we*, or an *angel* from heaven." His statement in this scripture aligns with 2 Corinthians 11:13, where Paul again warns his listeners about false teachers and ministers operating by cloaking themselves as legitimate ministers.

> *For such are false apostles, deceitful workers, transforming themselves into apostles of Christ.* [14] *And no wonder! For Satan himself transforms himself into an angel of light.*
>
> **—2 Corinthians 11:13-14**

It is fascinating that Paul speaks of false fivefold ministers and angels in the *same context*. Often, this scripture has given me pause when dealing with the realm of the supernatural.

LEGITIMATE ENCOUNTERS BEAR FRUIT UNTO JESUS

Now for those who are mature, having their senses exercised to discern both good and evil, this is not a problem. Even true angels would always direct all glory to the Lord Jesus Christ. For example, the angel in Revelation 19:10, who saw that John was falling to worship him, said to John, "See that you do not do that!" and "Worship God!" going on to say, "The testimony of Jesus is the spirit of prophecy."

This is how *legitimate* supernatural encounters go, according to Scripture, with an outcome that always points to God the Father and Jesus the Son. A growing area of concern, especially in prophetic circles, is many runaway notions regarding supernatural interactions.

Very seldom do these encounters have a scriptural basis, especially when few even care to question the validity of these moments. Many of these could very well be legitimate encounters. Still, regardless, we must hold fast to the Word of God when considering the narratives of those who have frequent encounters with the unseen realms and have fantastic tales to substantiate them.

DECEIVING GOD'S PEOPLE

For false christs and false prophets will rise and show great signs and wonders to deceive, if possible, even the elect.
—Matthew 24:24

The Bible says that in the last days some will be deceived. We read that there will be false christs and false prophets equipped and ready to deceive the masses. Not only will these arise, but the enemy will also use people to share things that didn't happen. To stretch the truth, so to say.

Those not in tune with the Holy Spirit and the Word of God could be deceived. *It is so crucial for every believer to test the spirits!* (See 1 John 4:1.)

It can be highly offensive to someone having an experience or an encounter to then be questioned about its authenticity. Some will *believe anything they experience, fabricate an encounter,* or *even worse*—intentionally *create narratives* for deception. Sadly, some will intentionally deceive others by fabricating an encounter and using people's gullibility for their agenda.

The angel of light is deception at its finest. If you are gullible to encounters that are off, willing to bend the Word of God to fit a sensational narrative, but only *mildly,* then falsehood can creep in until full-blown deception takes hold.

An angel of light might have little trouble deceiving such individuals pre-filled with this type of self-deception. These are the sort who, upon any encounter, are wildly blown away, having little foundation to bring balance. These easily surrender to deceptive persuasions.

FALSE EXPERIENCES WANTING DARK ACCESS

Angels of light appear for permission. For the non-discerning, they would be just another angelic messenger, beautiful and arrayed in glorious splendor. After all, *humanity is not used to seeing into the spirit realm,* so even the lowest level manifestation could rock the non-discerning into compliance and willingness to cooperate.

I bring this issue to light because many people not rooted in the Word of God play along with strange encounters. Some entities and experiences may come across as not evil at all. They may be presented in an engaging, intriguing, or even kind way. I found that the answer to any experience is to not go beyond what is written (1 Corinthians 4:6), and you will never go astray.

GENERATIONAL GIFTS TARGETED BY LIGHT AND DARKNESS

As we touched on earlier, it is sad to realize that spiritual gifts can be similar, much like a person who has a gift to sing—who can either use it for the world or in a church. Let me explain.

Encounters with spiritual forces can lead to the wrong conclusion without having a relationship with Jesus. Those who don't understand how gifting works (and who is the real author of such gifts) may begin to dabble in dark things such as psychic activity, believing their gift is for clairvoyance and various forms of witchcraft.

Nothing could be further from the truth, as God is the Author of every good and perfect gift. It is an agenda of darkness to pervert these wonderful gifts given by God.

A true conversion with Jesus Christ is the real answer for navigating the gifts in anyone's life. Once a person gives their life to Jesus, what must take place is a dedication to the written Word of God. God's Word is the plumb line that rightsizes experiences.

Like so many gifted young people, what these voices were competing over was me. These two voices—the Holy Spirit and the other a demonic force—were calling me. One was to enter the prophetic calling God had ordained for me; the other was a psychic spirit wanting me to give it access to a variety of evil.

YOU'RE NOT TALKING TO GRANDMA!

This scenario is a gateway to talking to what many believe are spirits of the departed, but the entities they are in contact with are not grandma! They are familiar spirits who are well acquainted with your family from generations past. These use familiarity and many other evil tricks to gain access into your life and your family by permission.

DARKNESS NEEDS COOPERATION

Darkness needs cooperation from people, especially those more sensitive to the spiritual realm. When individuals engage in any supernatural experiences that are not of God and His Word, they are giving access via permission to enter their lives!

PERMISSION TO MANIFEST

Could it be that supernatural dark entities have the ability to appear because so many have given permission to them? This may indeed be part of such phenomena as UFOs—what some would consider alien entities—and the encounters many have talked about. What if many of the paranormal issues that seem to be rising are simply "angels of light" or the opening of rogue spiritual gateways from permission, people's belief in them, and even the desire to interact with them? Could they be exercising their ability to manifest into the natural world in various shapes and bodily forms, all due to the permission they are being granted from occultists and naïve believers who love wild supernatural encounters far more than being lovers of the truth? It is eye-opening to consider that much of the nefarious supernatural activity going on in the world may, in part, be to the tolerance of an anything-goes point of view regarding supernatural experiences—ultimately leading to permission.

THE GODLY AND THE WICKED— BOTH ARE GATEWAYS

How are spiritual forces, both light and dark, empowered to manifest? The answer is similar to the angels of God. God's angels, *the servants of fire*, manifest by the Voice of God and in a place where the Kingdom of God is being enforced through human beings.

The same is true on the opposite side of humanity, wherever there is a compromise, evil, fear, false beliefs, or anything else that goes contrary to the Word of God and His Kingdom system. Proverbs 29:2 says, "When a wicked man rules, the people groan." However, Proverbs 14:34 says, "Righteousness exalts a nation, but sin is a reproach to any people."

Additionally, Matthew 18:18 says, "Assuredly, I say to you, whatever you bind on earth will be bound in heaven, and whatever you loose on earth will be loosed in heaven." Think about how horrible it must have been in cultures where *human sacrifice* was customary. Evil was celebrated and, in a way, even legislated! This type of culture would certainly empower nefarious supernatural activity through human permission, allowing access to the natural world.

Through their insidious deceptions, demonic entities are granted much more latitude to do what they desire when a culture allows it corporately. Therefore, we must be alert and watch for our enemy, the devil, who prowls around like a roaring lion seeking whom he may devour (*see* 1 Peter 5:8). He seeks whom he may devour by putting his voice out in front of unwitting individuals.

Those who take on his persuasion begin acting out on his suggestions through thoughts, emotions, and the human experience. If this persists, permission is granted by cooperation with those thoughts or fiery darts of the enemy. Cooperation means permission and access are granted. A host of evil actions can manifest greatly by this type of access, which includes demonic, fallen angel manifestations.

Society is falling deeper and deeper into deception, being fixated on darkness and evil and embracing a variety of wickedness. This results in more reports of strange things in the sky, unusual paranormal encounters, and even a heightened volume of angel experiences. One of many reasons we resist the devil through the Word of God is to avoid encounters with powers of darkness and angels of light!

PERMISSION BY REQUEST

It needs to be repeated that access comes through the forces of permission. A request must be made to gain permission, and the number-one way a request is made by darkness is through *persuasion* and *deception*.

Anyone should be very cautious when venturing into things they have not seen. Why? Because stories and testimonies are subjective, they can be fabricated, even purposefully crafted to deceive. But even more critical is the high potential of encountering something or deceiving your heart to the point that deep deception takes root. This is the desire of evil entities, demons, or fallen angels. Let's look at the following scripture from 2 Peter.

CLOUDS WITHOUT WATER, ETC.

These are wells without water, clouds carried by a tempest, for whom is reserved the blackness of darkness forever. [18] *For when **they speak great swelling words of emptiness, they allure through the lusts of the flesh, through lewdness, the ones who have actually escaped from those who live in error.** [19] While **they promise them liberty**, they themselves are slaves of corruption; for by whom a person is overcome, by him also he is brought into bondage.*

—**2 Peter 2:17-19**

This is a fascinating scripture as it gives insight into the heart of deception and the deceivers. These are wells without water. They are clouds carried by a tempest. They speak great swelling words of emptiness. They allure through the lusts of the flesh.

ALLURE

Notice whom they draw away or allure. "Allure" is the Greek word *deleázō*, meaning *to bait, entrap*.

Notice how deception regarding spiritual encounters begins as "wells without water, clouds carried by a tempest" and goes into the speech of "great swelling words of emptiness." This leads to the allure or bait and entrapment.

NO QUENCHING OF THIRST

The progression goes as follows: *wells with no water* or the image of places that are supposed to quench thirst but are empty. *Clouds carried by a tempest* are storms with no rain yet lots of show. Next comes *great swelling words* or amazing stories and testimonies that are mind-blowing! Finally, this progression of deception even takes away the purity of those who have escaped from those who live in error. How do they lose their purity? Through the *temptation of lewdness*.

Deceivers who tell tall tales of supernatural encounters or bait believers through the lust of the flesh, Scripture points out, are those who have once already escaped these types of people only to be captured again by their tall tales and the lust of the flesh.

They become captivated through lewdness or lasciviousness, and a person can be entangled in every indulgence. It's as if these individuals telling their stories (that they have not truly ventured into) are so self-deceived that they develop a deep-rooted false narrative that becomes a stumbling block and temptation for previously delivered believers.

SUSCEPTIBLE TO HIGHER FORMS OF EVIL

Deception starts with just a little storytelling. *Tall tales grow more and more outlandish until the hearers compromise their discernment.* After refusing to check what is being stated, individuals eventually allow their hearts to become hardened. A symptom of a hardened heart is the susceptibility to higher forms of evil, which ultimately leads to gross perversion. By the way, this is where nearly every cult ends up— gross perversion. It all begins with not loving the truth; or a better way of saying it would be, they quit loving the Word of God and all it says.

We must check our supernatural experiences and certainly consider the discernment God gave us when we hear others' stories.

> But solid food belongs to those who are of full age, that is, those who by reason of use have their senses exercised to discern both good and evil.
>
> **—Hebrews 5:14**

When Hebrews references "those who have their senses exercised to discern both good and evil," it speaks of your *five senses.* We are to take our five senses and train them by the written Word of God! That's correct—you read that right. What you can see, smell, taste, touch, and feel must be subject to the Word of God. Safety will be the result for any believer who surrenders their natural impulses to the Word of God. This is very beneficial for spiritual encounters and discerning the encounters of others. A shield is also in place against the perversion often accompanying spiritual deception.

LOVERS OF THE TRUTH

When humankind ventures into realms that God does not permit them to go into, it is rebellion; additionally, it is a place of great deception. If any person or believer accesses the realm of the spirit outside of what God has authorized, they are open to spiritual deception. If a person believes something from the realm of the spirit that God does not authorize, they have empowered deception.

> *For such are false apostles, deceitful workers, transforming themselves into apostles of Christ.* [14] *And no wonder! For Satan himself transforms himself into an angel of light.* [15] *Therefore it is no great thing if his ministers also transform themselves into ministers of righteousness, whose end will be according to their works.*
>
> **—2 Corinthians 11:13-15**

THE GREAT MIMIC

When looking at the passage in 2 Corinthians 11, we see the word *transform*. The Greek word for "transform" is *metaschēmatízō*. It means *to give a certain form to something, to change in fashion or appearance*. It carries the idea of a disguise.

In context, this means that the devil and his workers will attempt to *mimic* or *disguise* themselves as workers of God. Second Corinthians 11:13-15 shows us that angels of light and false apostles have one thing in common. They transform or *disguise themselves* for deception. Again, we ask the question, "Why the deception?" The answer is that deception opens up a gateway through what a person will allow based on what they believe. Angels of light or any other form of demonic influence come with overt tactics or the basic fiery darts of the enemy. All of these things are to gain access by permission from a human being. A better way of saying it would be, whatever you believe or engage from the spirit realm is also like giving it permission for activity in your life. Both God and the devil are territorial, and whoever gets permission is the one who gains the territory.

An example from early extra-biblical Jewish tradition tells how the devil *disguised* himself to influence Job's wife as an angel or in other ways. Some texts suggest he turned himself into a beautiful woman; others say as a beggar. The point is that throughout history, the devil has been seen as capable of disguise.

DEALING WITH DECEPTION IS SIMPLE

Today, his only weapon against the believer is deception and influence until an embracing of what is being introduced takes place. Discernment comes from time in the Word of God, prayer, and exercising our five senses for the service of God's Word. Dealing with deception is simple.

Knowing the truth keeps you free of the devil's devices. God's truth and loving the truth will keep you free.

> *Lest Satan should take advantage of us; for we are not ignorant of his devices.*
>
> **—2 Corinthians 2:11**

I am so grateful to my friend Rick Renner for his insights on the word "devices," which can be interpreted from Greek as *mental devices and can carry the idea of mind games*. The devil wants to get you involved in mind games, confusion, and his influence. Keep your mind clear, walk soberly, and stay in the faith that ultimately comes from His Word!

REBELLION AS WITCHCRAFT

A certain element that goes along with deception is the issue of rebellion. Rebellion is encouraged and taught as a good thing in much of today's culture. The statement, *"rebellion is as the sin of witchcraft,"* gets quoted often but it may not be fully understood. Let's briefly look at the following scripture reference and what this means in greater depth.

> So Samuel said: "Has the Lord as great delight in burnt offerings and sacrifices, as in obeying the voice of the Lord? Behold, to obey is better than sacrifice, and to heed than the fat of rams. ²³ For **rebellion is as the sin of witchcraft,** and stubbornness is as iniquity and idolatry. Because you have rejected the word of the Lord, He also has rejected you from being king."
> —**1 Samuel 15:22-23**

When taking this scripture into context, we can ascertain a definition for the phrase, "Rebellion is as the sin of witchcraft." First, we need to recognize that rebellion is a violation of authority.

VIOLATION OF AUTHORITY

In the case of Saul and Samuel, it was a violation of God's authority. But how is this tied together with witchcraft? The answer is man's will over God's will. When a man decides he will place his desires or actions above what God has instructed him to do, this is an act of rebellion. Regarding spiritual things, acts of rebellion are defined by a person who wants to access the realm of the spirit by their means.

Behavior such as this is tragic. Saul attempted to play it off; however, God was not pleased. Later, we see Saul stepping into witchcraft by engaging with the witch of EnDor to pull Samuel up from the grave. Saul's action fulfilled what he started when he disobeyed Samuel's words, "To obey is better than sacrifice." The following is the account of Saul's encounter with the witch of EnDor.

THE WITCH OF ENDOR

*Now **Samuel had died**, and all Israel had lamented for him and buried him in Ramah, in his own city. And Saul had put the mediums and the spiritists out of the land. [4] Then the Philistines gathered together, and came and encamped at Shunem. So Saul gathered all Israel together, and they encamped at Gilboa. [5] **When Saul saw the army of the Philistines, he was afraid, and his heart trembled greatly. [6] And when Saul inquired of the Lord, the Lord did not answer him, either by dreams or by Urim or by the prophets.** [7] Then Saul said to his servants, "Find me a woman who is a medium, that I may go to her and inquire of her." And his servants said to him, "In fact, there is a woman who is a medium at En Dor." [8] So Saul disguised himself and put on other clothes, and he went, and two men with him; and they came to the woman by night. And he said, "**Please conduct a séance for me, and bring up for me the one I shall name to you.**" [9] Then the woman said to him,*

"Look, you know what Saul has done, how he has cut off the mediums and the spiritists from the land. Why then do you lay a snare for my life, to cause me to die?" [10] And Saul swore to her by the Lord, saying, "As the Lord lives, no punishment shall come upon you for this thing." [11] Then the woman said, "Whom shall I bring up for you?" And he said, "Bring up Samuel for me." [12] **When the woman saw Samuel, she cried out with a loud voice. And the woman spoke to Saul, saying, "Why have you deceived me? For you are Saul!"** [13] And the king said to her, "Do not be afraid. What did you see?" And the woman said to Saul, "I saw a spirit ascending out of the earth." [14] So he said to her, "What is his form?" And she said, "An old man is coming up, and he is covered with a mantle." And Saul perceived that it was Samuel, and he stooped with his face to the ground and bowed down. [15] **Now Samuel said to Saul, "Why have you disturbed me by bringing me up?"** And Saul answered, "I am deeply distressed; for the Philistines make war against me, and God has departed from me and does not answer me anymore, neither by prophets nor by dreams. Therefore I have called you, that you may reveal to me what I should do." [16] Then Samuel said: "So why do you ask me, seeing the Lord has departed from you and has become your enemy? [17] And the Lord has done for Himself as He spoke by me. For the Lord has torn the kingdom out of your hand and given it to your neighbor, David. [18] Because you did not obey the voice of the Lord nor execute His fierce wrath upon Ama- lek, therefore the Lord has done this thing to you this day. [19] Moreover the Lord will also deliver Israel with you into the hand of the Philistines. And tomorrow you and your sons will be with me. The

Lord will also deliver the army of Israel into the hand of the Philistines." [20] Immediately Saul fell full length on the ground, and was dreadfully afraid because of the words of Samuel. And there was no strength in him, for he had eaten no food all day or all night. [21] And the woman came to Saul and saw that he was severely troubled, and said to him, "Look, your maidservant has obeyed your voice, and I have put my life in my hands and heeded the words which you spoke to me."

—1 Samuel 28:3-21

Saul had gone from disobeying Samuel to fully exercising witchcraft! An interesting thought is just as the servant had a quick answer about where to find a witch, there are many who are ready to assist someone in unintentionally disobeying God! Watch who you surround yourself with!

WITCHCRAFT IS AN UNAUTHORIZED USE OF SUPERNATURAL POWER

We can see a glaring example of rebellion and witchcraft going hand in hand through the story of the Tower of Babel.

Nimrod was a ruler and built a city in the Valley of Shinar. One of the most infamous structures in history was fashioned in this location—the Tower of Babel, a tower to reach the heavens.

And they said, "Come, let us build ourselves a city, and a tower whose top is in the heavens; let us make a name for ourselves, lest we be scattered abroad over the face of the whole earth." [5] But the Lord came down to see the city and the tower which the sons of men had built. [6] And the Lord said, "Indeed the people are one and they all have one language, and this is what they begin to do; now nothing that they propose to do will be withheld from them."

—**Genesis 11:4-6**

Not only was this a *wonder* of the world at the time, but some accounts suggest it was a high tower well into the sky, while others suggest it may have been more of a ceremonial structure. As a ceremonial structure, it might have been a *ziggurat*, much like the Mayans and Aztecs utilized for their worship of deities.

REACHING INTO A DIFFERENT DIMENSION

What this story is talking about is a tower that was built to reach another dimension. Nimrod and his followers were looking to access the realm of the spirit without the permission of God. Therefore, God had to come down and strike the language. The Lord wasn't concerned about mankind building a tower up into the sky and the heavens; instead, this was a tower to access the realms of the spirit or supernatural without God's permission.

NIMROD—WE REBEL!

An interesting point is found in the name of Nimrod. His name means "we rebel," and that is what these people came together to do—rebel.

In this case, they wanted to encounter all things supernatural, only without God.

This Tower of Babel was likely part of their evil agenda. The watchers or angels with a wicked agenda also needed permission from mankind to access the natural realm fully. This could be the reason behind the tower being built.

As speculative as it sounds, something was taking place that was serious enough for God to intervene. It was all brought on by a rebellion that wanted to access the unseen realm without God.

UNAUTHORIZED ACCESS TO THE REALM OF THE SPIRIT

Witchcraft is unauthorized access to the realm of the spirit. Those who do not obey authority in the natural and those who disobey on a spiritual level are the same. Both are unauthorized violations of authority.

> But even if we, or **an angel from heaven**, preach any other gospel to you than what we have preached to you, let him be accursed.
>
> —**Galatians 1:8**

Many things could be taking place regarding those who claim things they likely have not truly seen or experienced. Here are three I have considered over the years that you may find helpful.

1. **Fake encounters:** Simply experiences contrived by misguided people's imagination desiring the experience more than the truth.

2. **Self-deception:** As unique as it may sound, through my experiences with the prophetic, I have seen such a need for people to be validated that they will imagine encounters

and call them real. It's almost as if they give themselves to their imagination and call it visions, dreams, etc.

3. **Demonic encounters**: Demonic persuasion or experiences involving agents from the kingdom of darkness having access to the mystical through ignorance.

KEEPING PROPHECY CLEAN

Prophecy can be highly controversial because experiences are subjective to the one having them. It is imperative to the heart of the person delivering an experience to be very honest. If they are not, it begins a journey of self-deception, and it could even become the first step into becoming a false witness, false voice, and, God forbid—a false prophet.

How they communicate their revelation to others and what they are experiencing, even to themselves, is of the utmost importance. When laying hold of a revelatory moment, there is a process to how it should be conveyed to others, or even what you tell your heart about what is happening.

For those not reading the Bible and praying and not having an established foundation in the Word of God, there can be a fine line between prophetic encounters and a psychic/soulish mixture.

THE WORD OF GOD WILL CHECK YOU

You have an inner conviction of what is right and wrong. You have internal integrity for the truth. The Word of God, in your heart, will check you subtly, and it will check you directly. God's Word will encourage you when you are walking in love and will make you wince at night or in the morning for having wrong thoughts or if you are disingenuous about something.

The Word of God will check your honesty with yourself and keep you on the rails. All issues that happen to prophetic people usually stem from not honoring the Word of God first. If you allow the Word of God to speak to you, it will keep you solid. When a person does have the Word in their mind and heart but chooses to violate what they know is true, that same person will develop a calloused heart.

UNCALLOUSED MATURITY

Years ago, I taught a series titled "Uncalloused Maturity." The crux of the message stated is that you can know a lot, but unless it affects you at a heart level and manifests in how you treat people, you will remain immature.

If you violate self-honesty, others may not know you are confabulating an experience, but your heart knows it. You may fool others, but if you choose to continue pressing past honesty for the sake of sensationalism, your own heart knows it.

All believers, especially prophetic people, must learn faith with honesty. Why? Can you imagine if the Bible was written the way some people share their confabulated testimonies? We wouldn't know what to believe. There would be no standard. I believe you are a person of integrity and will walk in the supernatural full of faith while keeping an intense love of the truth! It is God's highest and best for you!

SECTION FOUR

RIGHTSIZING THE PROPHETIC

CHAPTER FIFTEEN

HARNESSING THE EXPERIENCE

*But solid food belongs to those who are of full age, that is, those who by reason of use **have their senses exercised** to discern both good and evil.*

—**Hebrews 5:14**

Character is both emotional and behavioral development. It is the staying force keeping a prophetic person on the rails. Without character, every gifted person will eventually falter horribly. Character is the opposite of being led off by wild experiences. Character is empowered by the Word of God—your solid foundation.

Without character, a person is unable to harness whatever experience they might have. They will be the servant of the experience rather than the master and one who is submitted to Jesus Christ by His Word.

SUPERSTITION

When considering a better way to deal with experiences, it might be shocking to realize that without the Word of God and proper character development, the issue of superstition can become the basis for some individual's prophetic operation.

Something many might not be quick to agree with is that any supernatural operation, without a Bible foundation, will develop a false construct of why, what, or how something is happening, thus *superstition*.

The word "superstition" is defined in Dictionary.com as: a belief or practice resulting from ignorance, fear of the unknown, trust in magic or chance, or a false conception of causation or an irrational abject attitude of mind toward the supernatural, nature, or God resulting from superstition.

Simply put, superstition is a way of grappling with the unknown apart from the Word of God.

> ...so that you may learn from us the meaning of the saying, "Do not go beyond what is written." Then you will not be puffed up in being a follower of one of us over against the other.
>
> **—1 Corinthians 4:6 NIV**

TRAINING IS IN ORDER

Gifts in the prophetic need training and practice. Often the untrained prophetic individuals cause the most harm and are the most dramatic.

A desire or a motivation to prophesy grows in a person who has observed another more tenured prophetic voice in operation. This leads the untrained novice to emulate or attempt to do what they witnessed another doing. This is a good thing as long as there is a grounding in the Word of God and good teaching on the subject as well as a safe environment for prophecy to be exercised in biblical order.

Training is in order, and good healthy Bible teaching is a must! Anyone who is not dedicated to the Word of God yet carries a gift of prophecy is destined for error.

AWAKENED SENSE OF DISCERNMENT

Along with this awakening and desire to prophesy often comes a heightened sense of discernment that can lead to hearing, seeing, and sensing a variety of things, sometimes helpful, other times it can be troubling. When trained, a person with good discernment is a very helpful individual as they can sense what is happening in another person's life and appropriately minister to them.

EMOTIONAL INTELLIGENCE

According to Wikipedia.org "emotional intelligence" is *the ability to perceive, use, understand, manage, and handle emotions.* People with high emotional intelligence can recognize their own emotions and those of others, use emotional information to guide thinking and behavior, discern between different feelings and label them appropriately, and adjust emotions to adapt to environments.

Lacking *emotional intelligence* is a form of lacking true humility; by not learning awareness or emotional intelligence, prophetic ministers keep themselves in an elevated position and limit their effectiveness. Through learning emotional intelligence, they are humbling themselves and can better read the needs of the person they are ministering to.

INTENSE TRAFFIC

Let's take a deeper look at the notion of being untrained. By untrained, as it relates to sensing and feeling things prophetically, it takes a higher level of emotional maturity to manage some of the experiences which can have a strong impact on a prophetic person's emotions. The experiences I am referring to are intense emotional sensations which are hard to navigate without understanding as to what is happening. Again referring to the word I use to label these experiences—traffic—it is a reference to some of the spiritual and soulish feelings which rise within prophetic individuals. Feelings can be so intense, and if not prepared for them, can cause a very challenging encounter for the prophetic person experiencing them.

Years ago, at the beginning of my prophetic ministry, I recall being driven to an event where I would speak. While going to that meeting, a challenging feeling was suddenly inside my stomach. The intense sensation was followed by sensory information. An awareness had engaged in my life that was very in tune with the words and emotions of others, even if I was not present where they were being spoken. So much so that it would be overwhelming at times. In this instance, I could make out words being spoken with strong emotions attached to them.

They were speaking critical things and stating how much they did not like what was about to happen at the meeting I was driving to. They began to talk about a person and say negative things about a person.

Suddenly it dawned on me! The person being discussed and the one they were dialoguing about was me! It was quite intense for me, and the information kept getting stronger on the inside until, at a zenith of emotional overload, it almost caused me to nearly cry.

Something about their unkind words was grating to my soul and painful, but the added issue was that there was no escape from it.

Nothing would make it cease or relax. The sense and the experience grew stronger and stronger until it became so intense that I wanted to cry, and I had to fight back, bursting into tears. I didn't really know what to do. So I told a friend who was driving, "There are people gathered, three or four of them, and they are speaking about me and what we are about to do in the meeting we're heading to. These individuals don't want me here, and they are being very vocal about it. They are standing in the facility's entryway we are about to enter, and they are in a group."

Upon entering the facility, sure enough, there was a group of people in the exact spot I saw them; and upon walking into the facility, it was clear they didn't expect us to arrive this early. At one point, I walked over to the group of people, thinking it would help the situation by casually saying the words I heard them speaking before I arrived. That is what I did. It flipped them out, and they didn't know what to do, so they left—all walked away and left me alone.

Following this, they pulled my friend aside and began to tell him to reconsider doing this meeting. These people were concerned that so many people were coming to our meetings that it would diminish the meetings they wanted to do. Everything went well, though, and we ended up having the meeting—it went wonderfully. Jesus was glorified, and much fruit for the gospel came out of it.

Now the reason it was necessary to share this story is that it was something that deeply hurt me. As I went to the Lord with it and as this prophetic gift in my life grew, this scenario of sensing things happened repeatedly. Sometimes it was in a positive way. Other times, it was in a negative way.

UNBEARABLE EMOTIONS

On one occasion, because of additional similar experiences, I even cried out to my wife, saying, "If this is what God has for me, I don't want it!" It was difficult for me. Not only do you hear data, but the amplified emotion of it comes as well, especially in those early days when people would be saying unkind things. It hurt internally, making me want to disappear and not have to speak to any people and never have to feel them again.

It was something no one had prepared me for and has been the hardest part of dealing with the prophetic in my life.

One day the Lord showed me something that changed my perspective on the experience. As I was wrestling with that same sensation again, the Voice of the Spirit suddenly said, "This is a little of how I feel when My people attack one another." Wow, did that hit me hard. Then I was directed to the book of Ecclesiastes.

> For there is not a just man on earth who does good and does not sin. [21] Also do not take to heart everything people say, lest you hear your servant cursing you. [22] For many times, also, your own heart has known that even you have cursed others.
>
> —Ecclesiastes 7:20-22

It was an eye-opening moment for me. Prophetically, I was experiencing God's heart and hurt over this topic. It helped me adjust—rather than saying to myself, "These horrible people, how dare they," I saw what the scripture said. "Also, do not take to heart everything people say, lest you hear your servant cursing you. For many times, your heart has also *known that even you have cursed others.*"

TRAIN PAST THE PAIN

Ecclesiastes 7:20-22 got my attention. In other words, gifting that is in your life doesn't make you special. God graced you with it to develop and utilize it for the good of the body of Christ. We must learn to *train past the pain* and what we now label traffic. By *training past the pain*, I mean you must get your emotions subject to you. There is no place for a highly sensitive prophetic person to allow what they feel to run them around. Prayer, speaking in tongues, praise and worship, and extended amounts of time in the Word of God have been a tremendous source of life regarding that intense traffic.

Among several reasons it is necessary to train past the pain is that traffic and sensations are a dangerous inroad that carries with them the potential to make a prophetic person mentally unstable.

Years ago, there were times I would visit people in the mental hospital or dementia units. Seeing those who had lost their minds due to a variety of reasons often shared a common trait, they believed God was speaking to them constantly. Some individuals I met suffered from chemical imbalances, whereas others I found were prophetically inclined people damaged by religion. These operated in a guilty conscience or continued to walk down a brakeless pathway of emotionalism with their encounters until it broke them. A road that led to institutionalizing them, medicating them, and keeping them in a hospital setting. Not checking those intense and sensitive encounters can become an inroad for demonic activity to take a foothold.

The natural mind is not made to process supernatural experiences; only a mind renewed to the Word of God can have the stamina and fortitude to process the supernatural in a healthy and lasting way.

CAN HE TRUST YOU WITH HIS SECRETS?

*Surely the Lord God does nothing, unless He **reveals His secret** to His servants the prophets.*

—Amos 3:7

It is refreshing to see someone who, although they can see and sense things in the spirit, act as normal as possible without sensationalizing what they experience. That is someone the Lord will trust with His secrets.

Anyone who gets their tongue under control is a person who oversees their own life, especially the prophetic!

ANY GIFTING WITH THE ABILITY TO MOVE A HEART YET REMAINS UNTRAINED CAN BE DANGEROUS. —JOSEPH Z

Thus says the Lord: "Heaven is My throne, and earth is My footstool. Where is the house that you will build Me? And where is the place of My rest? ² For all those things My hand has made, and all those things exist," says the Lord. "But on this one will I look: on him who is poor and of a contrite spirit, and who trembles at My word."

—Isaiah 66:1-2

When it comes to walking out the life of a believer, these scriptures apply—but so much more for the prophetic. These two scriptures are saying heaven and earth belong to Him. He has everything, so what kind of a house could a man possibly build the Lord? He answers that question in Isaiah 66:2, "But on this one I will look: on him who is poor and of a contrite spirit, and who trembles at My word."

THE POWER OF HUMILITY

Contriteness and trembling at His Word, simply put, is talking about someone who is deeply humble and places God's written Word above all else. The further a person develops into this space, the more God will look upon them. This is a very encouraging thought, but even more so should be the goal of every prophetic person. It causes God's attention to come upon you, and I believe this is a safety feature to keep the prophetic person's mind stable.

HUMILITY AND THE WORD STABILIZE HEARTS AND MINDS

But He gives more grace. Therefore He says: "God resists the proud, but gives grace to the humble."

—James 4:6

What a statement! This means even if you are not the sharpest tool in the shed, but practice humility and fear His Word, you will have a special grace from God!

MUST DIE TO SELF

Without a serious understanding of death to self and surrender to the Word of God—offense can steal years from your life or even hijack your destiny altogether. Some of the most *profoundly gifted people* can often be those with a gift under assault.

The issue might be that they are correct in people talking about them or some other clear thing they are encountering. Two things usually are part of this experience:

1. They desperately want to be validated.

2. They want to create a mystical sense about themselves to others by showing they experience these kinds of things.

STOP BEING SO SENSITIVE

At one point in my journey, I arrived at a place of frustration due to all the sensory impact these encounters had on me. It caused a heightened sense of protectiveness and even suspicion. The Holy Spirit spoke to me, saying, "*Stop being so sensitive!* Do what I tell you to do and ensure you are grounded in the Word of God." The Word of God is *always* the answer for prophetic discourse and when it comes to rightsizing any issue around the topic.

We become overly sensitive when not grounded in the Word and training our hearts by it. These days we must be Word people more than ever, especially the prophets.

All Scripture is given by inspiration of God, and is profitable for doctrine, for reproof, for correction, for instruction

in righteousness, [17] *that the man of God may be complete,*
thoroughly equipped for every good work.

—2 Timothy 3:16-17

PROPHETIC PEOPLE CAN
CONTROL THEIR GIFT

Part of harnessing the experience is realizing that a gift can sometimes work just because it is a gift. Sometimes a prophetic person will be out in a public setting, or in a restaurant, and they begin to get information from people randomly.

I liken this to identifying color. Did God cause you to see color? In a roundabout way, yes, by giving us eyes that process color to our brains. Yet when you see color, it is not because God turned on your ability to see it and suddenly you can perceive whatever color you are being exposed to. Instead, you can see color because the ability is always with you.

Identifying color is very similar to prophetic people with a legit-imate gift of prophecy. They will identify and see it because the gift operates without trying.

Gifts can work a lot like seeing color. They function not always at will, but for some, they rarely shut off. This is where, again, mastering the experience is all about managing or controlling the gift. Is that possible? Someone might ask. The answer is yes, as we see in 1 Corinthians 14:32:

And the spirits of the prophets are subject to the prophets.

—1 Corinthians 14:32

The spirits of prophets are subject to the control of prophets.

—1 Corinthians 14:32 NIV

RELAYING A REVELATION

A revelation is pure Holy Spirit knowledge transferred from the realm of the spirit to your soul. Often it can become lost or fuzzy in translation. This is not because prophecy isn't legitimate or that revelatory experiences are not real. It is the vessel, the recipient of a revelation, who can fail in properly relaying information upon communicating what they received.

Prophecies sometimes fail because the person delivering the word doesn't communicate what they are seeing well, or those receiving prophetic information have little understanding to extract the heart of what the Spirit is saying through the vessel. Again, this is why we need a better hermeneutic in prophecy.

PICKING UP ON THOUGHTS AND INTENTIONS

*And at once some of the scribes said within themselves, "This Man blasphemes!" [4] But **Jesus, knowing their thoughts**, said, "Why do you think evil in your hearts?*
—Matthew 9:3-4

*But **He knew their thoughts**, and said to the man who had the withered hand, "Arise and stand here." And he arose and stood.*
—Luke 6:8

It may come as a surprise for many to learn that there are times when those on the prophetic spectrum may suddenly know the thoughts and intentions of those around them. I have personally had this happen and have been in meetings when this took place. It was life-giving and even had a positive course correction in telling a person's thoughts in real time. Jesus did this, and it was to call out these religious leaders.

THE SPIRIT KNOWS ALL THINGS

These are the things God has revealed to us by his Spirit. The Spirit searches all things, even the deep things of God. [11] For who knows a person's thoughts except their own spirit within them? In the same way no one knows the thoughts of God except the Spirit of God.

—1 Corinthians 2:10-11 NIV

How is it possible that Jesus, or a gift in His body, can read thoughts or internal issues inside another person? We recognize that "the Spirit searches all things, even the deep things of God" (1 Corinthians 2:10). The next verse tells us something revealing, "Who knows a person's thoughts except their spirit within them?" It additionally says, "In the same way no one knows the thoughts of God except the Spirit of God." If we have His Spirit within us, we can know God's thoughts and anything else His Spirit chooses to show us—even the thoughts of another person.

SARAH LAUGHED WITHIN HERSELF

Then one of them said, "I will surely return to you about this time next year, and Sarah your wife will have a son." Now Sarah was listening at the entrance to the tent, which was behind him. [11] Abraham and Sarah were already very old, and Sarah was past the age of childbearing. [12] So Sarah laughed to herself as she thought, "After I am worn out and my lord is old, will I now have this pleasure?" [13] Then the Lord said to Abraham, "Why did Sarah laugh and say, 'Will I really have a child, now that I am old?' [14] Is anything too hard for the Lord? I will return to you at the appointed time next year, and Sarah will have a son." [15] Sarah was afraid, so she lied and said, "I did not laugh." But he said, "Yes, you did laugh."

—Genesis 18:10-15 NIV

The Spirit of the Lord knows all things. After all, the Lord said to Sarah, "But you did laugh." Meaning the Lord heard her without "hearing her." It is a humorous story in that Sarah must have been embarrassed being called out for laughing. She technically didn't laugh where anyone could hear it. She laughed to herself. This could have meant no audible sound—her laughter was more internal than external. It was a laugh meant for her to be heard only to herself.

It wouldn't be a far leap to say it was in her private thoughts. This is why she lied about it when Sarah was called out for laughing! She was likely responding to the statement by emotionally denying it because it was her point of view that no one heard her. But the Spirit of the Lord knows all things and hears all things. Reading the thoughts and intents of the heart is common for the Spirit!

PETER SAID

When Simon saw that the Spirit was given at the laying on of the apostles' hands, he offered them money [19] and said, "Give me also this ability so that everyone on whom I lay my hands may receive the Holy Spirit." [20] *Peter answered: "May your money perish with you, because you thought you could buy the gift of God with money!* [21] *You have no part or share in this ministry, because your heart is not right before God.* [22] *Repent of this wickedness and pray to the Lord in the hope that he may forgive you for having such a thought in your heart.* [23] ***For I see that you are full of bitterness and captive to sin."*** [24] *Then Simon answered, "Pray to the Lord for me so that nothing you have said may happen to me."*

—Acts 8:18-24 NIV

Peter used the phrase, "*I see*." Think about that for a moment; he said, "*I see*." This is a prophetic insight into the heart of Simon the sorcerer. Word of knowledge came through, with *chazah*, as Peter gazed right into the heart of this sorcerer and stated, "*I see*."

This is the same kind of prophetic operation that takes place in 1 Corinthians 14:

But if all prophesy, and an unbeliever or an uninformed person comes in, he is convinced by all, he is convicted by all. [25] *And thus the secrets of his heart are revealed; and so, falling down on his face, he will worship God and report that God is truly among you.*

—1 Corinthians 14:24-25

Notice how 1 Corinthians 14:24-25 states if all prophesy, two things can happen. The unbeliever and uninformed person have an encounter that causes them to fall on their face worshiping God. This is because they had the secrets of their heart revealed. According to this passage, a gift of operation is available to every believer. If all prophesy, this can indeed be the result.

IF ALL PROPHESY

Therefore tongues are for a sign, not to those who believe but to unbelievers; but prophesying is not for unbelievers but for those who believe. [23] *Therefore if the whole church comes together in one place, and all speak with tongues, and there come in those who are uninformed or unbelievers, will they not say that you are out of your mind?* [24] *But if all prophesy, and an unbeliever or an uninformed person comes in, he is convinced by all, he is convicted by all.* [25] *And thus the secrets of his heart are revealed; and so, falling down on his face, he will worship God and report that God is truly among you.*

—**1 Corinthians 14:22-25**

According to 1 Corinthians 14, prophecy is not only edification, exhortation, and comfort, as pointed out at the beginning of Chapter Fourteen, but also a *word of knowledge.*

The level of word of knowledge mentioned is strong enough and accurate enough to cause people to cry out to God, as verse 25 says. This point alone is a wonderful scenario, but let's consider what this reveals.

Among those in the body of Christ who believe in prophecy, many would say prophets are only to encourage, comfort, and bring edification, according to 1 Corinthians 14.

Although this is correct, it needs to be completed. The greater vantage point is understood later in that chapter when it speaks of *all.* If *all* prophesy, all means *all* in each congregation.

Someone might say, "Wait, brother, this type of ministry is only for prophets!" Well, prophets do prophesy. But according to the Word of

God, it may be surprising to recognize that anyone can prophesy at a high level.

Let me say it in an even clearer way. There is a difference between those who prophesy and those in the office of the prophet. One is simply a gift of prophecy, and the office is a responsibility to a segment of the body of Christ.

MANY THINK PROPHECY IS WEIRD UNTIL

Many think prophecy is weird until it happens to them. The uninformed or unbelieving may put their face on the ground, worship God, and confess that "God is among you." What is the cause of this level of convincing and conviction? First Corinthians 14:25 clearly states that it is due to the secrets of his heart that have been revealed.

Imagine worship services where this becomes the norm! The Bible gives instructions to the body of Christ in this chapter. It shows us how the Holy Spirit would like to deal with unbelievers and uninformed people who might be visiting your church.

This sounds wild, but this is what Paul was saying, rather than everyone speaking in tongues when these two types of people come in—prophesy to their heart!

God is more interested in reaching people on the heart level than displaying any other gifts. Ultimately, this is why Paul wrote *to desire gifts, but especially prophecy!*

OFFICE AND GIFT ARE NOT THE SAME

The ultimate responsibility of any office gift (apostle, prophet, evangelist, pastor, teacher, listed in Ephesians 4:11) is to empower disciples and equip them with the Gospel.

This includes taking the topic of strange encounters head-on. For many years at the end of meetings, people come forward to let me know they felt crazy and didn't realize they could have a way to quantify and put their experiences in order. Sometimes I've had to tell people they were unstable and possibly having a mental issue and should get healed or seek professional help.

However, many more individuals have had real encounters and do not know what to do with them or what they mean. Some of this type is very easy to work through with people once they are given clear biblical information.

There are also the high-responsibility prophets, who, in particular, carry the mantle to mentor those who want to train the gifts of prophecy. Training the gifts of prophecy is essential to sharpen the potential of discovering a growing gift of the office of the prophet.

Let's be clear, word of knowledge, seeing into the future, dreams, or any other prophetic function does not make someone a Prophet. The office of the prophet is defined by responsibility, or a calling to disciple through edifying and equipping a segment of the body of Christ. Uniquely enough, many who function in the prophetic powerfully are often not prophets! Someone may say, "How is this possible?"

It is possible because the Holy Spirit moves in all His people. But like Paul says in Romans 12:3, "For I say, through the grace given to me..." this was referencing his apostolic office. The grace given to a person is in reference to their office also. The office of the prophet is a grace office where an individual is endowed with responsibility for a segment of the body of Christ.

GAIN SAYING

Let me give an example from my own life. One day I had a powerful encounter; it was just after a broadcast where I finished the final session of a two-week series regarding angels.

At the end, after employing biblical prayers that engage angels, I had an encounter with one. I heard a powerful voice that began saying things about a message from the throne to me.

Heather was in the room with me as the power of God became so evident, and we were both caught up in the moment. It was intense. Much of what was said to me came to pass regarding people, scenarios, and the assignment of our ministry.

The temptation after this encounter was to add to what had happened, to falsify the details of the actual story. Or overly dramatizing the encounter. There were moments when it seemed as if it would be so simple just to spice it up a bit, and therefore, I would have the listeners' attention.

Yet I refused to do that. Over the years, others have stepped in front of Heather and me because they had a word from the Lord, and they would release it with demonstrative flair and a lot of color, but often not a lot of substance. We promised God we would only say what we see; even if we see it, we only say it if we are supposed to.

"Gain saying" is the adding to a prophetic word by spicing up a prophetic encounter with additional narrative that was not part of the actual event. Self-deception can take root if gain saying becomes a practice in anyone's life.

The Holy Spirit wants to move through honest and clear vessels. Let's be that for Him!

SUPERNATURAL HYSTERIA

The Voice of God has taken the blame for many issues. Including but certainly not limited to church splits, rivalries, discord, or the classic "The Lord has led us to leave this church." A fortune would be accumulated, but the currency it represented would be subjective and far more self-serving than being an actual word from God.

Supernatural experiences are so subjective that the slightest offense or conflict for believers will often cause them to desire a reprieve. Obsessing over an issue they are walking through can lead to an escape hatch. "*I feel led*" is the type of phrasing heard when people reach for the escape hatch.

THE BEST FORM OF DELIVERANCE

Any believer can and will go the distance and outlast hardship if they keep themselves full of faith and the Word of God.

Ongoing healthy teaching is the highest form of deliverance. It will destroy strongholds and force your mind into a Christlike position until you hear the Lord more clearly than you've ever heard Him before. Complete surrender to sound Bible teaching is paramount to a successful experience with the Voice of God. Positioning yourself under a great pastor-teacher of the Word is vital. Not only will areas of your life experience deliverance, but you will remain delivered through that continual washing as with water of the Word of God (*see* Ephesians 5).

TORTURING THE DATA WILL GET A CONFESSION YOU DON'T WANT

One of my favorite Bible teachers used to say, "If people torture the data long enough, they can make it confess to anything!" It was a saying used in technology. How appropriate for hearing the Voice of God.

Sometimes believers want something so badly to happen or desire something to take place that they will tell themselves honest lies or even full-out falsehoods to get what they want out of something. Much of this has risen out of the Spirit-filled camps within the Church. When taught with accuracy and clarity, the Spirit-filled churches are tremendous and full of the life of God!

Spirit-filled cultures that emphasize moving in the Holy Ghost over being grounded in the Word of God via healthy ongoing teaching are headed for issues on a small scale or disaster on a large scale. A torturing of the data can take place when those not trained in the Word of God begin emphasizing spiritual encounters over the foundation of the written Word.

Text without context is used to explain away strange, even weird, behaviors in the name of the Holy Spirit. When excuses are made, or a loose scriptural foundation is laid down as a basis for supernatural weirdness, it creates a culture of dysfunction. Usually, it leads to perversion in teaching and, ultimately, even morals.

CORRECTING SUPERNATURAL HYSTERIA

The church of Corinth is a clear example of supernatural hysteria. A good way to explain what was happening would be that these believers were sensationalizing the spectacular—and missing the Spirit. Believers in the church community in Corinth were very spiritual in the sense they desired to see the gifts of the Spirit at work. First Corinthians 12 even lists the nine manifestation gifts in which these worked. Paul had to lay out clear guidelines on manifestation gifts and encounters due to the wild and ultimately immoral behavior surrounding the gifts of the Spirit.

This church loved to prophesy, and they enjoyed speaking in tongues. Yet in the middle of all the supernatural things they chased after, the immorality of the highest order was taking place within that church community. Let's look at Paul's words to the Corinthian believers regarding this topic.

IMMORALITY AND GIFTS

A mature place of harnessing the experience begins with walking with strong moral integrity. This comes from practicing strong character and ethics. Especially in the prophetic, as it is a very sensory-driven space. The church of Corinth had this issue. Corinth was a culture that loved spiritual gifts and was known for being radically immoral due to the environment and the paganism that the city was inundated with. As the church grew, there was a bleed over from the immorality of the Corinthian culture. Corinthian believers who came from a background of idolatry and moral depravity also had a desire for spiritual things, and the two were intermingling. Paul had to bring correction. Gifts and spiritual experiences without a good foundation in the Word of God and strong character development can allow mixture from the surrounding culture.

It was so out of control that Paul was forced to take action in more instances than one!

It is actually reported that there is sexual immorality among you, and such sexual immorality as is not even named among the Gentiles—that a man has his father's wife! ² *And you are puffed up, and have not rather mourned, that he who has done this deed might be taken away from among you.* ³ *For I indeed, as absent in body but present in spirit, have already judged (as though I were present) him who has so done this deed.* ⁴ *In the name of our Lord Jesus Christ, when you are gathered together, along with my spirit, with the power of our Lord Jesus Christ,* ⁵ *deliver such a one to Satan for the destruction of the flesh, that his spirit may be saved in the day of the Lord Jesus.* ⁶ *Your glorying is not good. Do you not know that a little leaven leavens the whole lump?* ⁷ *Therefore purge out the old leaven, that you may be a new lump, since you truly are unleavened. For indeed Christ, our Passover, was sacrificed for us.* ⁸ *Therefore let us keep the feast, not with old leaven, nor with the leaven of malice and wickedness, but with the unleavened bread of sincerity and truth.* ⁹ *I wrote to you in my epistle not to keep company with sexually immoral people.* ¹⁰ *Yet I certainly did not mean with the sexually immoral people of this world, or with the covetous, or extortioners, or idolaters, since then you would need to go out of the world.* ¹¹ *But now I have written to you not to keep company with anyone named a brother, who is sexually immoral, or covetous, or an idolater, or a reviler, or a drunkard, or an extortioner—not even to eat with such a person.* ¹² *For what have I to do with judging those also who are outside? Do you not judge those who are inside?* ¹³ *But those who are outside God judges. Therefore "put away from yourselves the evil person.*

—1 Corinthians 5:1-13

FLEE SEXUAL IMMORALITY

All things are lawful for me, but all things are not helpful. All things are lawful for me, but I will not be brought under the power of any. [13] *Foods for the stomach and the stomach for foods, but God will destroy both it and them. Now the body is not for sexual immorality but for the Lord, and the Lord for the body.* [14] *And God both raised up the Lord and will also raise us up by His power.* [15] *Do you not know that your bodies are members of Christ? Shall I then take the members of Christ and make them members of a harlot? Certainly not!* [16] *Or do you not know that he who is joined to a harlot is one body with her? For "the two," He says, "shall become one flesh."* [17] *But he who is joined to the Lord is one spirit with Him.* [18] *Flee sexual immorality. Every sin that a man does is outside the body, but he who commits sexual immorality sins against his own body.* [19] *Or do you not know that your body is the temple of the Holy Spirit who is in you, whom you have from God, and you are not your own?* [20] *For you were bought at a price; therefore glorify God in your body and in your spirit, which are God's.*

—1 Corinthians 6:12-20

One of the number-one ways immoral behavior can transpire is by consistently emphasizing the supernatural more than the Word of God. Some cultures are far more inclined to run after the sensational and delve into the gifts of the Spirit yet won't crack open their Bible—this can be a costly mistake.

Your word I have hidden in my heart, that I might not sin against You.

—Psalm 119:11

Here is why it can be a costly mistake; spiritual gifts, prophecies, healings, visions, dreams, and seeing angels have no power to curb carnal impulses. Only the Word hidden in a heart can rightsize or curb carnal sense, making them obedient to the will of God.

Compromise is right at the door when a person is exhausted and not thinking clearly. The Word of God will speak to your conscience.

Now these things, brethren, I have figuratively applied to myself and Apollos for your sakes, that in us you might learn not to exceed what is written, in order that no one of you might become arrogant in behalf of one against the other.

—1 Corinthians 4:6

HYSTERIA IS COUNTERED BY A LOVE OF THE TRUTH

Often in the same areas that allow wild sensationalism without emphasis on the Word of God and a foundation upon which revelation is judged, immorality and misguided culture can occur.

God gave us emotions, yet it must be understood that emotions themselves can be deceptive. The same can be said for experiences. I, for one, greatly enjoy experiences and encounters with the Holy Spirit! Your life is changed or altered through such events, yet if this is what people are searching for, a hysteria can occur to attempt to outdo the last experience. Sadly they will eventually be let down when the last high isn't surpassed by the next one.

What is needed is a foundation of unshakable trust in the Word of God. After all, the Word of God makes faith, not experiences. "So then faith comes by hearing, and hearing by the word of God" (Romans 10:17). If all prophetic experiences were grounded this way, there would be so much less disillusionment and hurt from the area of prophecy. Instead, in proper order, the prophetic could become one of the most potent gifts to bring clarity to the body of Christ while additionally convincing unbelievers and those who are uninformed regarding the power of the Holy Spirit working among us!

CHAPTER SIXTEEN

THE COUNTERFEIT ANOINTING

But the anointing which you have received from Him abides in you, and you do not need that anyone teach you; but as the same anointing teaches you concerning all things, and is true, and is not a lie, and just as it has taught you, you will abide in Him.

—1 John 2:27

The Greek word for "lie" is *pseudos* and can be interpreted as *false or falsehood*. This means there is a true anointing and a false anointing.

A false anointing looks like the real thing, but it is not—it's *pseudo or false*. It is a "form of godliness" or a way of operation that would lead those hearing to believe what they are experiencing is from God.

Mystical Christians fall prey to false anointing all the time. A false anointing appeals to the five senses; James 3:15 references a false anointing by saying, "This wisdom does not descend from above, but is earthly, sensual, demonic." Stepping into the realm of experience and being open to just about anything can be dangerous as it introduces encounters which are not grounded in truth.

CHRISTIAN MYSTICISM

The Oxford Dictionary of the Christian Church explains the topic of mysticism by referencing mystical theology. This is interesting, as it sheds light on what some believers in Jesus Christ could venture into without being grounded. These believers value strange encounters or fables from voices that will say just about anything to gain a following. Of growing concern is what I call "Christian Mysticism." Mysticism, by definition, generally refers to claims of immediate knowledge of Ultimate Reality (whether this is called "God") by direct personal experience; "mystical theology" is used to mean the study of mystical phenomena or the science of the mystical life.[11]

Paranormal phenomena, such as trances, visions, and locutions, are often regarded as "mystical," though their value and significance are assessed differently by different thinkers; they are usually not regarded as essential. For what we are looking at, mystical Christians are those caught up with a fairy-tale version of the Holy Spirit and encounters with the unseen realm.

Christian mystics will most likely fall for every wind of doctrine or new theory. The troubling issue regarding new theories and experiences is that many will be swept away into progressive deception without the Word of God.

JACOB MIMICKED
HIS OLDER BROTHER

As for you, the anointing you received from him remains in you, and you do not need anyone to teach you. But as his anointing teaches you about all things and as that *anointing is **real, not counterfeit**—just as it has taught you, remain in him.*

—1 John 2:27 NIV

It might look like that anointing seems like the anointing, but often it is simply a theatrical reproduction—a counterfeit of the genuine article. Jacob understood the value of the blessing, and in that narrative, he was able to pull off deceiving his father. Concerning how the blessing was transferred to Jacob is partly due to Jacob's deception, but the scripture says something quite scathing about Esau.

> *Lest there be any fornicator or profane person like Esau, who for one morsel of food sold his birthright.*

—Hebrews 12:16

> *That there be no immoral or godless person like Esau, who sold his own birthright for a single meal.*

—Hebrews 12:16 NASB1977

The NASB1977 version calls Esau a *godless person!* Why godless? He treated what was holy as if it was normal or ordinary. In this way, he despised his birthright. Jacob fooled him into giving up what was given to him by birth in exchange for a bowl of stew. An imposter will always be around to step in and mimic God's legitimate purpose in an attempt to hijack it!

A TALE OF TWO PROPHETS

In 1 Kings 13, there is a story about a young prophet sent on an assignment by the Lord with specific instructions. He was to keep those instructions until his task was finished. Everything was altered upon the arrival of an older prophet.

> *For a command came to me by the word of the Lord, "You shall eat no bread, nor drink water there; do not return by going the way which you came."* [18] *He said to him, "I also am a prophet like you, and an angel spoke to me by the word of the Lord, saying, 'Bring him back with you to your house, that he may eat bread and drink water.'" But he lied to him.* [19] *So he went back with him, and ate bread in his house and drank water.*
>
> [23] *It came about after he had eaten bread and after he had drunk, that he saddled the donkey for him, for the prophet whom he had brought back.* [24] *Now when he had gone, a lion met him on the way and killed him, and his body was thrown on the road, with the donkey standing beside it; the lion also was standing beside the body.*
>
> —1 Kings 13:17-19, 23-24
> NASB1995

When observing this chapter, the Bible isn't clear why this older prophet lied to the younger. Conjecture can be made as to why this took place, but we know that the older prophet deceived the younger.

So often, while walking out the call of God, it takes faith to hear and obey, and sometimes some voices seem as if they would assist, as it can be human nature to believe what someone else heard over what you know God said to you. As was the case with this younger prophet. The older prophet, among other things, represents a false anointing. It comes to hijack assignments, callings, and destiny. Our young prophet in this story yielded to the lie when he heard "an angel spoke to me, and you no longer need to obey the Voice of God for yourself. I am a prophet, so follow me." It was a decision that cost the young prophet his life.

Such has been the case for many, which may cost them a season, a calling, an opportunity. False anointings will disguise themselves as anointed, qualified, and caring.

STRANGE FIRE

One of the cloaks of a false anointing is strange fire, or false signs, wonders and even miraculous encounters. A false anointing may even be driven by strange fire. Let me explain below. The scriptures in Leviticus tell us that priests are to keep a fire burning, but not just any fire, the fire *lit by God.*

> *And the fire on the altar shall be kept burning on it; it shall not be put out. And the priest shall burn wood on it every morning and lay the burnt offering in order on it; and he shall burn on it the fat of the peace offerings.* [13] *A fire shall always be burning on the altar; it shall never go out.*
>
> **—Leviticus 6:12-13**

Fire lit by God shows up in the acceptance of an offering. Whenever fire from God shows up, it makes a powerful demonstration.

> *And Moses and Aaron went into the tabernacle of meeting and came out and blessed the people. Then the glory of the Lord appeared to all the people,* [24] *and fire came out from before the Lord and consumed the burnt offering and the fat on the altar. When all the people saw it, they shouted and fell on their faces.*
>
> **—Leviticus 9:23-24**

An interesting consideration point is how offerings were accepted or rejected in the Old Covenant. Solomon dedicated the temple, and much like the scripture in Leviticus 9:23-24, God consumed the offering with fire. Elijah built an altar as he opposed the prophets of Baal, resulting in God consuming the altar with fire.

It is a fair assumption that when Cain and Abel made offerings to the Lord, there was an instantaneous knowing if it was accepted, based on if God consumed the offering with fire or not.

MAN-MADE FIRE THAT MIMICS GOD'S FIRE

Fire that God started is holy fire. Strange fire is a form of false anointing that it is created by man and kept going by man under the premise that the fire is holy.

> *Then Nadab and Abihu, the sons of Aaron, each took his censer and put fire in it, put incense on it, and offered profane fire before the Lord, which He had not commanded them.*
>
> **—Leviticus 10:1**

COUNTERFEITS RISE ON THE COATTAILS OF THE REAL

A false anointing can be the result of encountering the real. When something legitimate is observed, and the corresponding result is produced, those who do not know the Spirit and have not paid the

THE COUNTERFEIT ANOINTING

price for the anointing may attempt to manufacture what they have observed.

SIMON THE SORCERER

A good example is in Acts 8 when Peter came into contact with Simon, the sorcerer. Simon had witnessed the power of the Spirit being transferred by the laying on of hands. Not knowing what to do, Simon asked if he could purchase the power!

> *And when Simon saw that through the laying on of the apostles' hands the Holy Spirit was given, he offered them money,* [19] *saying, "Give me this power also, that anyone on whom I lay hands may receive the Holy Spirit."* [20] *But Peter said to him, "Your money perish with you, because you thought that the gift of God could be purchased with money!* [21] *You have neither part nor portion in this for your heart is not right in the sight of God.* [22] *Repent therefore of this your wickedness, and pray God if perhaps the thought of your heart may be forgiven you."*
>
> **—Acts 8:18-22**

Simon is the perfect example of someone *not understanding the anointing* and trying to attain it in his own carnal way. It is interesting to consider that the devil doesn't have an anointing, so he uses natural devices to accomplish his plans.

This whole idea of a false anointing is dangerous territory and of great concern, as it can create a *snowball effect*. Once a mode or method is advanced that is not of God yet is called a work of God, it has the potential of turning into a practice that is not rooted in God. People who marry that method fortify falsehood and allow a stronghold to be instituted.

FALSE ANOINTING AND SPIRITUAL ENCOUNTERS

There is an issue whenever an emphasis on experiences supersedes the gospel.

Please hear me—there is a place for desiring spiritual gifts and the things of the Spirit, but *never* should it replace the gospel. A culture more interested in these things than good and healthy doctrine is of great concern.

By and large, believers have been exposed to less and less Bible, resulting in no bearing and no understanding of right and wrong. Ultimately, the biblically malnourished arrive at a place of little to no discernment—the result is deception.

RIGHTSIZING A FALSE ANOINTING

The kingdom of darkness does not mind if these believers are caught up in desiring the supernatural. Believers baptized in the washing of the water of His Word are what darkness fears, as the Word of God alone brings a rightsizing to spiritual encounters.

Some might say, "Why is this such a concern and such a big deal?" The Word of God shows us that it is human nature *to exchange the truth of God for a lie,* which means that if we take anything as truth over the Word of God and then navigate life by that understanding, the lie will take hold—especially in the areas of spiritual things (*see*

Romans 1:25). To rightsize there must be a return to the love of the truth—the Word of God.

GOOD NEWS

The good news is you can rise to your God-given potential in faith and discernment! Be encouraged, read your Bible, pray in the Spirit, and things will become clear. Do not be led along by every new wind of doctrine or every new experiential thing that comes along. Test the spirits by the Word of God, listen to ongoing healthy teaching, and you will successfully navigate the new mystical things that seem to arrive on the playing field with every generation.

A FALSE ANOINTING DOES ALL THE RIGHT THINGS FOR THE WRONG REASONS

When a false anointing is in operation, it significantly affects those who don't know much. The naïve are quick to end up in a false anointing. The way out of this is a correction—even a rebuke.

CORRECTION IS GOOD FOR YOUR SOUL

Whoever loves instruction loves knowledge, but he who hates correction is stupid.

—Proverbs 12:1

I hope to simply cause a love for the Word of God. As there are many things taking place around the world with a variety of unique manifestations, we should be looking at them only from the perspective of the Word of God and keeping our focus on the lordship of Jesus Christ.

BEWARE OF CONSPIRACIES

> *You are not to say, "It is a conspiracy!" In regard to all that this people call a conspiracy, and you are not to fear what they fear or be in dread of it.*

> **—Isaiah 8:12**
> **NASB1995**

This is a great scripture to consider when dealing with conspiracies and unique issues. Notice it says, "Do not say 'a conspiracy' concerning all that this people call a conspiracy." In other words, do not run along with everything labeled a conspiracy—keep your head on straight!

CONSPIRACIES HIJACK WHAT YOUR FAITH IS DESIGNED TO DO

Conspiracies highjack what your faith is designed to do. We must return to the firm foundation of the Word of God, no matter what comes our way. Yes, some conspiracies are shown to be true. However, the real reason we don't run down the conspiracy trail—even if the conspiracy is proven true—is it can take our focus away from the Word of God and lead to an obsession over conspiracies.

This generation will be exposed to more strange and weird phenomena than any generation before it. Christians who are prone to conspiracies and the sensational, not having the reins of the Word of God governing their hearts, will fall prey to much of what is coming.

THE ANSWER FOR EVERY BELIEVER IS TO POLISH THE GLASS

Think about looking through a dirty window into an old house—something I did at a very young age with abandoned houses in the country where we lived. To look inside those dirt-worn windows required cupping my hands above my eyes and leaning tightly against the glass while standing on my toes.

Doing this allowed me to see through those dirty windows partially. Straining to see what was inside made me realize that I wouldn't be able to see much. The glass had a visually obstructing combination of dim lighting and dirty glass. This lack of light and murky glass nearly restricted my visibility altogether. The answer was to shine a light and *polish the glass!*

It was remarkable to see into this structure when there was light and the advantage of a newly cleaned window. This parallels many people's lives; they have no sensitivity to the Holy Spirit or the Word of God.

> *The lamp of the body is the eye; if therefore your eye is clear, your whole body will be full of light.* [23] *"But if your eye is bad, your whole body will be full of darkness. If therefore the light that is in you is darkness, how great is the darkness!*
>
> **—Matthew 6:22-23**
> **NASB1977**

Seeing through that dim glass is, among other things, a reference to your soul. Made up of the mind, will, and emotions. Clarity comes through the soulish arena as it is brought into order by the Word of God and prayer. If the soul is cluttered, so is everything else. David played the harp for Saul, and it caused a tormenting spirit to leave him, and peace would come to his soul (*see* 1 Samuel 16:23).

Today we have Jesus, and as a result, believers have a much higher level of access to the peace God provides. We find clarity and achieve greater insights into the spirit realm through peace.

THE MIRROR

This understanding of a dim mirror is very insightful. Now we see *in a mirror* is a reference to how we see our identity from the Word of God. The Word of God is the mirror!

James 1:23 describes the Word of God as a type of mirror, saying, "For if anyone is a hearer of the word and not a doer, he is like a man observing his natural face in a mirror." The understanding here is that when anyone hears the Word of God, they are given an image of who they are.

Their identity is being laid out before them. However, after leaving the presence of the revelatory reflection presented, they go away and forget what they looked like. The Word reflects who you are in Jesus. You forget the image you were meant to walk in when you do not renew your mind to what you heard.

Second Corinthians 3:18 drives this understanding home for us even more! "But we all, with unveiled face, beholding as in a mirror the glory of the Lord, are being transformed into the same image from glory to glory, just as by the Spirit of the Lord."

QUALITIES OF THE REFLECTION

We can unpack much from this verse but consider the reflection qualities listed here. This verse explains what happens when someone continues to behold the glory of the Lord as in a mirror! Here we see it again, the mirror of the Word of God.

BEHOLDING

Only now there is a beholding of the reflection or a beholding of what the Word of God says about you, and you become transformed into that same glory! You become the reflection!

> One thing I have desired of the Lord, that will I seek: That I may dwell in the house of the Lord all the days of my life, to **behold** the beauty of the Lord, and to inquire in His temple.
>
> —**Psalm 27:4**

Why is this so vital? Well, if we are going to become better hearers of the Spirit of God, then we must become better students and disciples in the practice of *beholding*.

Beholding the glory is to gaze in faith into the Word of God, to spend extended amounts of time in His presence through worship and prayer, and to be intimately acquainted with His promises.

To polish the glass is to develop a lifestyle of beholding every aspect of God!

Now take this understanding of polishing the dim glass of your soul until it gains clarity. What you have now is better sight into your identity and the things of God as it relates to the spirit realm.

THE FIVE SENSES

Let me again present to you that your soul is the dim glass. Your soul needs polishing! How is this accomplished? Let's look at Hebrews 5:14 for the answer: "But solid food belongs to those who are of full age, that is, those who by reason of use have their senses exercised to discern both good and evil."

The word "senses" here means *to perceive with the external senses or five senses.* What you can touch, smell, hear, taste, or see. We as human beings have developed these senses for our entire life. Suddenly we come into a relationship with the living God, which challenges our five senses.

God is not logical! He is the *faith* God. This natural world wants us to remain dependent on our five senses. Only we see in Hebrews 5:14 that we must exercise or train our five senses! For what purpose? So we may discern both good and evil. We could also distinguish what is of God and what is not, which is the beginning of discernment.

MIND RENEWAL

And do not be conformed to this world, but be transformed by the renewing of your mind, that you may prove what the will of God is, that which is good and acceptable and perfect.

—Romans 12:2
NASB1977

In the life of a believer, there is a process of mind renewal that is discipleship. Through growth in discipleship comes a level of spiritual activation by the infilling of the Holy Spirit. We are all called to walk in the gifts of the Holy Ghost, and according to 1 Corinthians 14:1, we are to *desire spiritual gifts especially that we prophesy.*

This issue at hand today is a culture in the body of Christ that is highly distracted! Focus, or the eye gate of our attention, desperately needs polishing.

> *Blessed are the pure in heart, for they shall see God.*
> **—Matthew 5:8**

MIRROR OR MIRAGE

The antidote is to *polish the glass!*

However, a false anointing offers a mirage of the real thing before they can get a hold of the true, which leads to a false image made up of human ideologies without the love of the truth attached.

The mirage is powerful. It is like *gravity for the carnal.* Suppose a believer runs for the mirage rather than the mirror. In that case, the result will lead to clouds without water, or on the other side, believers displaying no recognizable difference between themselves and the world.

The saddening end of chasing the mirage will ultimately make your heart cold. Therefore, so many believers are depressed or struggle with their faith.

When difficulties inevitably arise, what they have planted in their heart immediately stands up in defiance to faith and the life of God. Fear, sorrow, anger, hopelessness, and unbelief will manifest in the place of faith. In this stage, when a crisis hits, the carnal will sometimes frantically pray or bring God into focus. Usually mixing their prayers with accusations toward God or from a misinformed and wounded heart, asking, "Why?" Or, "What have You done or allowed, God?" When truthfully, their lens has been habitually darkened to respond from the flesh and not in faith.

THE MIRROR EXPOSES THE MIRAGE

The mirror is vastly different from the mirage. The mirror is the reflection of who the believer is in Christ! It is the Word of God mixed with faith! I have often stated the gospel you hear preached is correct! But it is only complete once it is working through you!

EFFECTS OF THE COMPLETE GOSPEL

The mirror shows who a person is and how to act. The mirror sensitizes you to the love and leading of the Holy Spirit. It offers you life and overcoming power that dumbfounds the carnal. It fosters peace that surpasses natural logic! Things can go super bad, but because of focusing on the mirror—victory is experienced even in difficulty.

The mirror is for believers. When someone turns to Jesus as their means of salvation, they receive an unveiled face, and they are then able to behold the glory of the Lord as reflected and radiant in the gospel.

REAL TRANSFORMATION

The more you behold, the more you are changed into what you're beholding! The mirror takes the weak and says, "You are so strong! In Christ, you are perfectly righteous! In Christ, you're as holy as you're going to get!" On a bad day, the mirror says, "In Christ, you are the best there is!" The mirror declares you a winner! When you soak and meditate on the reflection it presents, you will see the change that has already been done inside you and manifests to the outside!

The real answer is to *be preemptive* by mixing the Word of God with your faith today, right now! Become prepared for what's around the corner by transforming into the image you see in the mirror. It's effortless. All that's required is to behold!

Habitually cut out the distractions! Spend time with the *mirror*, and your life will change from the inside to the outside!

No false anointing or any strange fire can touch you!

CHAPTER SEVENTEEN

FALSE PROPHETS

And many false prophets will appear and will deceive many people.

—Matthew 24:11 NIV

*But there were also **false prophets** among the people, even as there will be **false teachers** among you, who will secretly bring in destructive heresies, even denying the Lord who bought them, and bring on themselves swift destruction. [2] And many will follow their destructive ways, because of whom the way of truth will be blasphemed. [3] **By covetousness they will exploit you with deceptive words;** for a long time, their judgment has not been idle, and their destruction does not slumber.*

—2 Peter 2:1-3

A clear-minded love of the truth is required when dealing with a topic such as false prophets. It is never right to subjectively navigate such matters while making conjectures and statements that sound good but are not rooted in the Scripture.

Lovers of the truth are qualified to venture into such a topic and come to the other side, full of the Word of God and walking in love. It was Jesus Himself who issued the prophetic warning regarding false prophets. They are here and have influence—some outside the Church's orbit and some within it.

One of the best quotes regarding how to deal with false doctrines, teachers, and prophets comes from D.L. Moody: "The best way to show that a stick is crooked is not to argue about it or to spend time denouncing it but to lay a straight stick alongside it."

LOVERS OF THE TRUTH

Remember, the purpose of identifying or having to deal directly with a false prophet is not because you hate the person. It is because you love the truth! Lovers of the truth, as stated, are those who value the Word of God, which is the one defense that shields all who embrace it from deception or delusion.

> *The coming of the lawless one is according to the working of Satan, with all power, signs, and lying wonders,* [10] *and with all unrighteous deception among those who perish, because* **they did not receive the love of the truth,** *that they might be saved.* [11] *And for this reason God will send them strong delusion, that they should believe the lie,* [12] *that they all may be condemned who did not believe the truth but had pleasure in unrighteousness.*
>
> —2 Thessalonians 2:9-12

A sobering observation can be made through the scripture in 2 Thessalonians 2. In context, it describes the coming of the antichrist—with all power, signs, lying wonders, all unrighteous deception. It explains that those who perish are susceptible to such things for a specific reason—That they did not receive the love of the truth, that they might be saved. Again, there is that phrase, the love of the truth.

We are admonished it is the truth that we know will set us free.

> *Then Jesus said to those Jews who believed Him, "If you abide in My word, you are My disciples indeed.* [32] *And you shall know the truth, and the truth shall make you free."*

> **—John 8:31-32**

We have clarity knowing the truth begins by abiding in His Word. This is what makes a legitimate disciple. From this abiding in His Word, the truth is known—which makes us free!

CLARITY DEVELOPS AUTHORITY

Armed with the truth and in a position of clarity, as the scripture prescribes, will induce a sense of authority, and not just any authority, but the Christ-in-you authority. You will be allergic to the false, and you will be intolerant of deceptive spirits.

There are two sides to false prophets, the individual who has ventured off the appropriate path for a prophet to walk on and the other side is those who allow it. Those who allow it are often biblically ignorant, average believers who take on the spectacular and routinely miss the Spirit of God. These desire miraculous sensationalism over clarity and soundness.

False prophets may be rotten from the beginning. These are the ones who have never had a relationship with Jesus and have their senses seared with a hot iron.

> *Now the Spirit expressly says that in latter times some will depart from the faith, giving heed to deceiving spirits and*

doctrines of demons, [2] *speaking lies in hypocrisy, having their own conscience seared with a hot iron.*

—1 Timothy 4:1-2

Those who have departed the faith have their senses seared with a hot iron, which applies to those who were never in the faith to begin with.

Jesus told the story in Scripture of those who would come before Him at the judgment to declare their worthiness based on all the things they did for Him in this life, such as casting out demons, healing the sick, and prophesying.

> *Not everyone who says to Me, "Lord, Lord," shall enter the kingdom of heaven, but he who does the will of My Father in heaven.* [22] *Many will say to Me in that day, "Lord, Lord, have we not **prophesied** in Your name, cast out demons in Your name, and done many wonders in Your name?"* [23] *And then I will declare to them, "I never knew you; depart from Me, you who practice lawlessness!"*

—Matthew 7:21-23

Among the list of virtues put forward by those who say, *Lord, Lord*—is the gift of prophecy. These prophesied in the name of Jesus. Often I have thought of 1 John 4:2, which says at face value that anyone who confesses Jesus came in the flesh is not a false prophet.

However, when looking into the context of that scripture and considering what Jesus said in Matthew 7:22-23, we must recognize the fullness of this picture.

> *Beloved, do not believe every spirit, but test the spirits, whether they are of God; because many false prophets have gone out into the world.* [2] *By this you know the Spirit*

of God: ***Every spirit that confesses that Jesus Christ has come in the flesh is of God,*** [3] *and every spirit that does not confess that Jesus Christ has come in the flesh is not of God. And this is the spirit of the Antichrist, which you have heard was coming, and is now already in the world.*

—1 John 4:1-3

Reading this scripture at face value would lead many to believe all they need to say is the magic statement, "Jesus came in the flesh." And it's all good!

GNOSTICISM

Yet without a historical background of what this meant, the wrong conclusion might be reached. When this scripture was written, false teachings and strange doctrines were attempting to infiltrate the Church, one of which was known as Gnosticism.

Without entering all the details of Gnosticism, it was a belief that aspired to transform the Christian creed, elevate its faith into philosophy, or reduce it to special knowledge and make this special knowledge supersede faith.

Gnosticism taught that matter was the power of evil, whose home is in the region of darkness. Minds that started from this fundamental view could only accept the incarnation provisionally and with reserve and must at once proceed to explain it away!

"The Word was made flesh," but the Word of God, the true light, could not be personally united to an actual material system called a human body that was plunged into this world of matter, darkened, and contaminated by its immersion.

Gnosticism taught that the human flesh in which Jesus appeared was fictitious. They insisted that the phantom of a Redeemer (Jesus) was nailed to the phantom of a cross, relegating Jesus as nothing more than a shadow made to appear real.

The evil deception of Gnosticism is the denial that Jesus truly came in the flesh. Thus, the statement in 1 John 4:2, "Every spirit that confesses that Jesus Christ has come in the flesh is of God," directly opposed the Gnostic heresy!

Interestingly, Gnostics called their teaching "the depths of God." There is a sarcastic slam by Jesus at their teaching in the book of Revelation when He calls their doctrine "the depths of Satan."

> *Now to you I say, and to the rest in Thyatira, as many as do not have this doctrine, who have not known the depths of Satan, as they say, I will put on you no other burden.*
>
> **—Revelation 2:24**

FALSE PROPHETS SAY THE RIGHT THINGS FOR THE WRONG REASON

There is a principle in this passage: not only should we agree with healthy doctrine that Jesus came in the flesh, but we should also recognize that false prophets are those who mangle the truth about Jesus in a way that appeals to the five senses as an attempt to supersede our faith!

Gnosticism said that *Jesus didn't come in the flesh! He was all spirit and could have never been an actual man.* That is a lie and denies the completeness of His work, such as how He condemned sin in the flesh and died in a natural body!

Today the argument is in the other direction. We no longer hear much about Jesus being all Spirit and only appearing as flesh; rather, we hear the opposite! Jesus was only a man and not the Son of God. He was all natural and not spiritual. This brings about all the same heretical problems as the Gnostic heresy, only flipped around the other way.

SOUND DOCTRINE IS THE ACTUAL TEST

My point is this. Simply saying Jesus came in the flesh doesn't get a false prophet off the hook! Rather soundness of doctrine must be applied to all areas of who Jesus is and what He accomplished. Sound doctrine is the first thing to consider when dealing with false prophets. They love to spin doctrine with a "special revelation."

Notice Matthew 7:22 says, "We prophesied in Your name."

Two things can be happening in the life and "ministry" of a false prophet. They can prophesy with accuracy and amazing revelation and declare the name of Jesus. As even Jesus said, they would do so in His name!

A SOBERING REALITY

Sobering is the only description when grappling with the truth of this issue as it relates to a false prophet. So what does a believer do when someone they are hearing and experiencing says all the right words? They talk about Jesus and how He is the Way. They prophesy accurately, but there is still something off about them. The Holy Spirit is giving a big caution sign regarding them.

First, speculation or suspicion is not the way forward. When interacting with a prophetic person who seems off, there must be measurable results. No one has the right to accuse or slander an individual because they don't like how they dress, walk, talk, or the demonstrative way they might minister.

It isn't even if the words they give always come to pass or not. We dealt with that earlier regarding Agabus and his prophetic word not being 100 percent accurate; it was only mostly accurate.

Measurable results come from the Bible and the fivefold ministry. You also have the Holy Spirit in you and are called to discern such matters for you and your family. If you are not in a place or position to speak to such things, then don't.

However, you can remove yourself from the orbit of anything that grates your spirit. You are also free to constructively speak about your sense to those with whom you have a relationship.

PROPHETS ARE EITHER *REAL, NOVICE,* OR *FALSE*

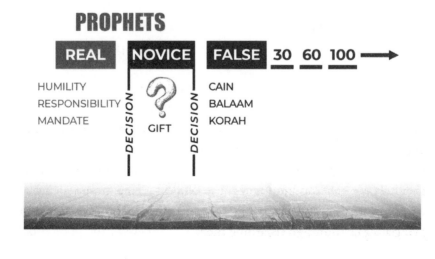

In this simple graph, there is a scale of placement for locating the development of prophets. When I teach this subject in meetings or on my daily broadcast, we go way into this with a whiteboard. I will try to convey it the best I can here in writing.

Of the utmost importance is to realize motive is the defining issue that tells what makes a prophet *real, novice,* or *false.* Once a prophetic person becomes aware of the requirements (via the Word of God) that must be met to qualify as a New Testament prophet, it leaves little room for any prophetic person to say they didn't know.

Motive is defined when the truth is realized and understood. A moment that leads to a decision! Will they humble themselves and walk according to the Word of God, submitting to leadership, taking responsibility, and walking out the mandate the Lord has shown them? Or will they decide their way is best and edge into the error of Cain, Balaam, and Korah? These are all those who were self-willed, rebellious voices. False prophets may come off smooth on the exterior, but their fruit will reveal them eventually.

Real Prophets

Therefore by their fruits you will know them.
—Matthew 7:20

You will know them by their fruits! Real prophets are constantly developing in humility. These are teachable individuals and lovers of the written Word of God and of the truth. Real prophets desire sound doctrine that doesn't make everyone scratch their heads or say, "Wow, that was so revelatory, but I'm not sure what it means." Legitimate prophets are generous and faithful to biblical giving and receiving. A generous prophet is showing they do not have a love of money problem, like Balaam, who was moved by monetary gain even though he could not curse the children of Israel. He still found a way around the issue and told the evil king how he might conquer them. All of Balaam's actions were driven by money (*see* Numbers 22). A true prophet will run from such things!

There are many excellent traits real prophets display; among them is the foundational gift of prophecy which is highly developed in the major spectrum in which they operate.

Novice

Not a novice, lest being puffed up with pride he fall into the same condemnation as the devil.

—1 Timothy 3:6

It has been my experience that many who are accused of being false prophets are novices—who don't know any better. They have a legitimate gift on the prophetic spectrum but have had everyone tell them how amazing they are, and they like it. These are standing in the valley of decision and will be confronted with growth that has the potential of taking them into the real.

Growth usually arrives in the form of a challenge or dying to self. Growth rarely comes in the form of an opportunity. The question for the novice is whether they will rise and grow in character or will they fall to offense, selfishness, and the like, which is a pathway to becoming false. An offense that remains is the sure way to drift toward the false.

A generic humility that is learned to gain favor is a major temptation for novices; they are tempted to do and say all the right things for all the wrong reasons. A father, like Paul was to Timothy, can bring correction and growth to this; being submitted to leadership, such as their pastor and other mature prophetic voices, can also temper this.

A novice will be tested by not getting promoted, not getting what they want, and still serving and keeping a clean heart inside—where only God sees and knows.

A tragedy in the body of Christ is the dereliction of duty some leaders display by putting novices into the public eye, giving them a platform and a microphone. It is a mistake.

If, however, the novice continues to rise through whatever hits them and they are generous, doctrinally sound, submitted, prophetically accurate, have a love for the truth, and will not be shaken, they have the potential to become a real prophet that God can use.

False Prophets

False prophets start by placing gifting above character and keep it that way. There may even be moments of good works, good operations, and even a mixed desire to do right. However, as you see on the upper right of the previous graph, the numbers 30, 60, and 100-fold are the biblical progression for growth. In this case, it represents negative acceleration, and there are stages to becoming reprobate.

From experience and working with many individuals in the prophetic space, there is a progression where those who did not start off as false but have drifted can be turned back by a rebuke, which leads to repentance. At 30- and 60-fold, they still can be corrected by confrontation or rebuking them. This requires telling them they are missing it and how it could be harmful to others. If they hear it, they just may have a spark of humility within them and choose to repent and turn their life over to Jesus once again.

However, when the 100-fold is reached, this is dangerous territory as it takes effort to walk into a place of deception until, finally, that deception turns to self-deception. A reprobate person has completely given themselves over to the powers of darkness and has rejected Jesus as Lord and Savior.

GOD KNOWS, GOD SEES

In my life, there were times when prophecy in my meetings was very powerful and got people's attention. I can recall individuals who thought I could read their minds and knew everything they were thinking. There are moments of intense prophetic operation, but it is not a nonstop inflow of people's thoughts, etc. A point came when I said to more than one person, "I'm not reading your thoughts; I know in part, and I prophesy in part."

This may seem like a small issue, but let me assure you that moments such as those have with them the temptation for individuals to manipulate by acting a little more mystical, a little more prophetic, and spookier. People go for that stuff. For me, it is repulsive on every level. So rather than act out a part or role to make the prophetic as strange as possible for the benefit of myself, I chose to be transparent.

Many who are in the prophetic understand the influence they can have by a simple innuendo. The people may not know it, but God does. Much like David in the cave when he poured out water which his men brought him (*see* 2 Samuel 23), there comes a time when the Lord is watching to see if we will pour out what we really desire.

False prophets may be able to fool many that they are God's special chosen vessel. They might be able to pull the wool over the eyes of believers, even other prophets and fivefold leaders. What they cannot do is hide the thoughts and intents of the heart from God, who sits in the heavens.

Again, we will know them by their fruits. The Word of God and sound leaders, along with the counsel of other tenured voices, can bring about clarity. If you stay deep in the Bible and prayer, listening to good strong teaching, you will not be led astray.

MOTIVE

Again as mentioned earlier, what is the real determining factor of a false prophet? Motive—a heart with a hidden agenda that does not line up with God or His Word. Motive, which is based on the will of man and filled with self-centered desires, is the foundation to build a persona and create a culture around such a persona until the false prophet has what he or she desires. Power, money, control, and oftentimes perversion comes with it. False prophets despise correction. Please hear me—no one is giddy about correction. Wise people hear correction and become wiser still (*see* Proverbs 9:9). However, false prophets despise correction and authority, and depending on the sphere or level of influence they are operating in, they will give several reasons why they don't have to listen.

Nearly every prophet I know has a gift that works very well externally. Meaning they have the ability to see for *others* from their spectral vantage point, yet they struggle to see for themselves. This is why even prophets need accountability and those who speak into their lives. Such as the other fivefold ministry offices. Especially the office of the apostle. Genuine apostolic authority carries a governing correction, direction, and a powerful foundation for all the fivefold, especially the prophet. Prophets and apostles have a unique relationship even by the way these two offices are placed together throughout the New Testament as a foundation-building team.

Motive is truly a positive or negative currency with God. He watches all and knows all.

> *And there is no creature hidden from His sight, but all things are naked and open to the eyes of Him to whom we must give account.*
>
> **—Hebrews 4:13**

STRANGE FIRE OF MAN

Here is the interesting thing about prophets. Sometimes those who have the biggest following or most clout line up closer to the woe that Jesus spoke of.

> *Woe to you when all men speak well of you, for so did their fathers to the false prophets.*
>
> **—Luke 6:26**

True prophetic voices will at times have to say the unpopular and hard truth of a matter.

Those who lean back when the Spirit requires them to speak may do so out of a form of self-preservation. A behavior that grieves the Spirit of the Lord. Those genuinely called to the office of the prophet, depending on their grace and position on the prophetic spectrum, may indeed be required by the Lord to declare the accurate truth of a matter—popular or not! True prophets do what the Spirit says regardless of the outcome.

Prophets who are loved by all resemble the status of false prophets whom Jesus referred to in Luke 6. If a prophet desires to be spoken well of over being obedient to the Voice of God and shrinks back as a result, it is wrong. I do not believe shrinking back makes them a false prophet. They may be a disobedient prophet in need of repentance and a change of heart with a side of courage added, but shrinking back doesn't mean false. However, prophets who only do what is popular and only do what causes others to speak well of them are seriously in danger of becoming a false prophet if they are not already.

FALSE PROPHETS OPERATE IN SELF-WILLED PREDICTIONS

There is nothing wrong with searching the mind of God through His Word. There is certainly nothing wrong with searching out the will of God and being open to sensing what the future holds. But those who would venture into a place regarding the prediction that the Spirit has not given them are heading for error.

Nowhere in Scripture did a prophet voluntarily have a vision of the future. They could see and say, in a word-of-knowledge fashion, but you never see a prophet leaning into the future at will and telling you what is happening. Can there be those who have many more moments of seeing the future than others? Yes, but never all the time and simply at will.

FALSE PROPHETS DON'T LET THE BIBLE GET IN THE WAY

In some of these areas of false prophecy, the followers don't bother letting the Bible get in the way of what they believe! Meaning, when they prefer to have a sensational story over a biblical foundation, they move Scripture to the side and embrace the story. If someone would dare question the validity of the revelation or bring biblical order to it, false prophets will stand opposed and let everyone know they are not to be corrected.

> *Knowing this first, that no prophecy of Scripture is of any private interpretation,* ²¹ *for prophecy never came by the will of man, but holy men of God spoke as they were moved by the Holy Spirit.*
>
> —**2 Peter 1:20-21**

FALSE PROPHETS CAUSE LISTENERS TO WANDER

> *And many false prophets will appear and will deceive many people.*
>
> —**Matthew 24:11 NIV**

One definition of the word "deceive" in Greek is *to cause to wander.* Maybe a false prophet will not completely deceive a person or a group, but they will induce a cycle of wandering in the life of the listeners.

> *Having a form of godliness but denying its power. And from such people turn away!* ⁶ *For this sort are those who creep into households and make captives of gullible women loaded down with sins, led away by various lusts,* ⁷ *always learning and never able to come to the knowledge of the truth.*
>
> —**2 Timothy 3:5-7**

False prophets fit the description of this type of activity within the Church, and as they induce a variety of misguided issues, they will cause those impacted to wander. As verse 7 states, there is a kind of individual who is impacted by those with a form of godliness who deny its power, and the end result is they are always learning. New fantastic knowledge and unique revelation seems to always be with them, yet they never arrive. It would seem these ones are never able to come to the simple knowledge of the truth of Jesus Christ, His lordship, and the foundations of the gospel. Rather they are in a perpetual loop of learning. Sadly, false prophets thrive on this type of individual and induce it within the Church.

To break free of the perpetual wandering, there must be a steadfast love of the truth both preached and taught. Without a foundation in the Word, wandering is inevitable for the susceptible.

PATTERN-BASED IMMORAL BEHAVIOR

For of this sort are those who creep into households and make captives of gullible women loaded down with sins, led away by various lusts.

—2 Timothy 3:6

False prophets will often function with a very immoral side, most often kept secret and not seen by the public; there's typically a hidden side to their life.

It should be said clearly that this is not a reference to leaders and ministers who have made mistakes or even walked into sin willingly at one time in their life. Many ministers and even prophetic voices have fallen and stumbled at various times, but that doesn't make them false!

It is what they do about it. Do they conceal or decide to repent to the appropriate people and walk in submission following their bad behavior? Or will they choose to carry on with a pattern-based lifestyle that causes them to venture into the arena of a false prophet? Only one avenue is possible for the restoration of anyone who fails, a season of measurable results through accountability.

Galatians 6 deals with how to restore or help a brother caught in such a trespass. However, those who are unwilling to repent or continuously cover over their hidden life, or even worse, attempt to teach that it is okay for them to walk in such a way—are false.

Never throw stones at anyone who has failed and then came under the conviction of the Holy Spirit, repented, and corrected their life. Heather's father, Harold, said, "Never kick a good man when he's down, because one day he will get up again—especially if his sleeves are rolled up."

I always liked that saying because there are so many good men and women out there who have been hurt or have failed and simply need someone to believe in them for a time, and they will make it back to the calling God gave them. The good ones, if they make it, are some of the most humble and easy to work with people because they know only the goodness of God keeps them going.

FALSE PROPHETS KNOW WHAT THEY ARE DOING

This is not so with false prophets with false intentions. One major and defining factor with false prophets is they know what they are doing!

Insights into False Prophets and False Prophecy

And the word of the Lord came to me, saying, ² *"Son of man, prophesy against the prophets of Israel who prophesy, and say to those who prophesy out of their own heart, 'Hear the word of the Lord!'"* ³ *Thus says the Lord God: "Woe to the foolish prophets, who follow their own spirit and have seen nothing!* ⁴ *O Israel, your prophets are like foxes in the deserts.* ⁵ *You have not gone up into the gaps to build a wall for the house of Israel to stand in battle on the day of the Lord.* ⁶ *They have envisioned futility and false divination, saying, 'Thus says the Lord!' But the Lord has not sent them; yet they hope that the word may be confirmed.* ⁷ *Have you not seen a futile vision, and have you not spoken false divination? You say, 'The Lord says,' but I have not spoken."* ⁸ *Therefore thus says the Lord God: "Because you have spoken nonsense and envisioned lies, therefore I am indeed against you," says the Lord God.* ⁹ *"My hand will be against the prophets who envision futility and who divine lies; they shall not be in the assembly of My people, nor be written in the record of the house of Israel, nor shall they enter into the land of Israel. Then you shall know that I am the Lord God.* ¹⁰ *"Because, indeed, because they have seduced My people, saying, 'Peace!' when there is no peace—and one builds a wall, and they plaster it with untempered mortar—* ¹¹ *say to those who plaster it with untempered mortar, that it will fall. There will be flooding rain, and you, O great hailstones, shall fall; and a stormy wind shall tear it down.* ¹² *Surely, when the wall has fallen, will it not be said to you, 'Where is the mortar with which you plastered it?'"* ¹³ *Therefore thus says the Lord God: "I will*

cause a stormy wind to break forth in My fury; and there
shall be a flooding rain in My anger, and great hailstones
in fury to consume it. [14] *So I will break down the wall*
you have plastered with untempered mortar, and bring it
down to the ground, so that its foundation will be uncov-
ered; it will fall, and you shall be consumed in the midst
of it. Then you shall know that I am the Lord. [15] *"Thus*
will I accomplish My wrath on the wall and on those who
have plastered it with untempered mortar; and I will say
to you, 'The wall is no more, nor those who plastered it,
[16] *that is, the prophets of Israel who prophesy concerning*
Jerusalem, and who see visions of peace for her when there
is no peace,'" says the Lord God.

—Ezekiel 13:1-16

PATTERNS DETERMINE CAPACITY

When identifying immoral false prophets, what we are looking at is
a *pattern-based* immoral individual, which is often one of the traits a
false prophet carries.

These types are often smooth with their words as well as persuasive
and seductive. Anyone feigning to be a prophet but has unrepented
recurring moral issues in their life is likely a false prophet. No believer is
comfortable living in a pattern-based sin period—much less a prophet!

Moral failures happen to leaders and believers alike, but those who
continue in pattern-based immoral lifestyles are very different. There is
no exception for such behavior, especially in the realm of the prophet.
Justifying such behavior by so-called prophets is a perversion of what
the office stands for.

Anyone justifying immoral behavior and claiming to be a prophet should be avoided at all costs. No matter how powerful and accurate their gifting is! Remember, gifting is not what makes a prophet! It is the responsibility God gives them to edify and equip the body of Christ that makes them a prophet.

What is horrifying is a prophetic leader operating in ministry yet walking in moral failure after moral failure and carries no repentance. That is wrong, and there comes a place when leadership should step in and stop them for the sake of the body of Christ and those they might infect with their sinful behavior.

QUALIFICATIONS OF A TRUE LEADER

First Timothy 1 deals with the qualifications for bishops and overseers in the Church. However, these should certainly apply to those in five-fold ministry offices including the office of the prophet:

> *This is a faithful saying: If a man desires the position of a bishop, he desires a good work.* [2] *A bishop then must be blameless, the husband of one wife, temperate, sober-minded, of good behavior, hospitable, able to teach;* [3] *not given to wine, not violent, not greedy for money, but gentle, not quarrelsome, not covetous;* [4] *one who rules his own house well, having his children in submission with all reverence* [5] *(for if a man does not know how to rule his own house, how will he take care of the church of God?);* [6] *not a novice, lest being puffed up with pride he fall into the same condemnation as the devil.* [7] *Moreover he must have a good testimony among those who are outside, lest he fall into reproach and the snare of the devil.* [8] *Likewise*

deacons must be reverent, not double-tongued, not given too much wine, not greedy for money, ⁹ holding the mystery of the faith with a pure conscience. ¹⁰ But let these also first be tested; then let them serve as deacons, being found blameless. ¹¹ Likewise, their wives must be reverent, not slanderers, temperate, faithful in all things. ¹² Let deacons be the husbands of one wife, ruling their children and their own houses well. ¹³ For those who have served well as deacons obtain for themselves a good standing and great boldness in the faith which is in Christ Jesus.

—1 Timothy 3:1-13

THE WICKED SONS OF ELI

Now the sons of Eli were corrupt; they did not know the Lord.

—1 Samuel 2:12

These two reprobate sons of Eli (Hophni and Phineas) were corrupt to the core. In complete rebellion, they misappropriated the sacrifices, keeping the best for themselves. They were fiscally corrupt and sexually abusive, taking advantage of women who had likely dedicated themselves in service at the Tabernacle (1 Samuel 2:22). Sadly, these women had likely dedicated themselves to serve in the Tabernacle of meeting. It is detestable to God when young people give themselves in service unto God with a pure heart only to have that act of worship be used against them by a perverse leader. It was possible these young ladies did whatever the two filthy sons required as they believed they were doing it unto the Lord. What pure evil to see young worshipers used in this fashion.

It would be better for him if a millstone were hung around his neck, and he were thrown into the sea, than that he should offend one of these little ones.

—Luke 17:2

ELYMAS THE FALSE PROPHET

Now when they had gone through the island to Paphos, they found a certain sorcerer, a false prophet, a Jew whose name was Bar-Jesus, [7] *who was with the proconsul, Sergius Paulus, an intelligent man. This man called for Barnabas and Saul and sought to hear the word of God.* [8] *But Elymas the sorcerer (for so his name is translated) withstood them, seeking to turn the proconsul away from the faith.* [9] *Then Saul, who also is called Paul, filled with the Holy Spirit, looked intently at him* [10] *and said, "O full of all deceit and all fraud, you son of the devil, you enemy of all righteousness, will you not cease perverting the straight ways of the Lord?* [11] *And now, indeed, the hand of the Lord is upon you, and you shall be blind, not seeing the sun for a time." And immediately a dark mist fell on him, and he went around seeking someone to lead him by the hand.*

—Acts 13:6-11

False prophets can masquerade in the Church and certainly outside of it. An interesting observation is that Elymas was a sorcerer who influenced government officials—something we see in various parts of Scripture. According to 2 Timothy 3:8, two false prophets, by the names of Jannes and Jambres, resisted Moses. That verse says other false prophets also resist the truth. Further insight reveals that these false ones are "men of corrupt minds, disapproved concerning the faith."

COUNTERFEIT SPIRITUAL INFLUENCE ON GOVERNMENTAL LEADERS

This was true in Daniel's time and other instances throughout Bible history where an imposter to the office of a prophet had the ear of a city leader or governmental official. The kingdom of darkness sends counterfeits to pervert the purpose of the Lord.

Real prophets are meant to not only speak to the Church, but there are statesmen prophets anointed and called, such as Daniel was to speak to kings. Joseph, while in Egypt, fulfilled a similar role.

Tragically, similar narratives are seen throughout recent history as well. A character such as Grigori Rasputin was the equivalent of a false prophet to Russian royalty in the early 1900s.

LYING TALES AND SUPERNATURAL TRICKERY

> Also, from among yourselves men will rise up, **speaking perverse things**, to draw away the disciples after themselves.
>
> —Acts 20:30

Speaking: The Greek word *laleō* means *to use words in order to declare one's mind and disclose one's thoughts.*

Perverse things: means they intentionally misinterpret what the Scripture is saying. To draw away disciples after them.

> *For false Christs and false prophets shall rise, and shall shew signs and wonders, to **seduce**, if it were possible, even the elect.*
>
> **—Mark 13:22 KJV**

Seduce: the Greek word *apoplanaō* meaning *to cause to wander; to deceive, pervert, seduce, to swerve from, apostatize.*

> *And through covetousness shall they with **feigned words** make merchandise of you...*
>
> **—2 Peter 2:3 KJV**

Feigned: is the Greek word *plastós;* (where we get our word for *plastic*) meaning *to mold, artificial, false, hypocritical, deceitful,* or words easily shaped as desired.

Feigned words: mean these ones tell fantastic stories and outlandish teaching—molded and fashioned just the way the speaker wants it to be.

False prophets mold and fashion their words, or stories, making them so believable it might even convince tenured believers. This includes outlandish supernatural stories taking the listener into the most colorful tales and experiences which appeal to their senses. Ultimately it is for the benefit of the false prophet to gather followers and influence.

SPECIAL OR UNCONVENTIONAL
REVELATORY TRAINING

But I fear, lest somehow, as the serpent deceived Eve by his craftiness, so your minds may be corrupted from the simplicity that is in Christ.

—2 Corinthians 11:3

Normal, conventional doctrine is never enough for false prophets, and they must come up with something special or unique. They do so to stand out from the rest and have a special insight or way of operating only known to them. But they will reveal it to their followers. A move straight out of the false prophet playbook!

*I know your works, your labor, your patience, and that you cannot bear those who are evil. And you **have tested those who say they are apostles and are not, and have found them liars;** [3] and you have persevered and have patience, and have labored for My name's sake and have not become weary.*

—Revelation 2:2-3

Tested: in the Greek means to put them through the fire again and again with no determined amount of time—until they manifest the truth of who they are or they manifest Christ in these circumstances.

The church of Ephesus had the issue of individuals wanting recognition so they would stand up and publicly declare they were part of the fivefold ministry. These would say, "I am an apostle," or "I am a prophet!" Rough estimates say the church in Ephesus had up to 100,000 members! To gain any attention as someone special, individuals would stand up and say they were a special office gift in the church for the purpose of gaining a following. Leadership in the Ephesus church resorted to test them vigorously through fiery trials and intense scrutiny until they were found to be false or true.

These likely claimed to have special abilities and may have even offered their followers the opportunity to be trained by them. We see this today. Among the many special insights so-called prophetic voices train people to experience are gifts to see angels on demand, taking trips to heaven again and on demand, or teaching people how to move in the prophetic in a unique and heightened way. So heightened it is not even in the Bible! With the new insights comes pointing at all the others and conveying to the followers they don't want you to know about this! Or they don't believe in what I'm about to tell you etc. from here, and they go on to explain what the secret sauce is.

Nothing is new about the misappropriation of supernatural abilities or the teaching of extra-special supernatural abilities. What some of them teach is just a technical way to describe witchcraft in one various form or another.

THIRD EYE TRASH

There are several topics like this out there. One that made the rounds a while back and is coming back around is the teaching called "Opening your third eye."

Since when did Hindu ideology and terminology using the language of the third eye become okay by any means? An example of this type of deception is using scriptures such as Matthew 6:22 which says, "The lamp of the body is the eye. If therefore your eye is good, your whole body will be full of light," and other twisted takes on Scripture. There are teachers who tell people how to open their third eye. As they do so, they will demonstrate with a shocking word of knowledge. Street names, home addresses, and way more detail than that.

Here is what it is when false teachers or false prophets move in a shocking ability.

1. *They are circus performers*, no different from going to the carnival. They use trickery and showmanship to wow the listener. A game that involves someone being planted in the crowd or gathering data on people before they attend a meeting and a variety of ways in which a con artist would be willing to operate for the desired effect. As horrible as this is, remember, false prophets will do anything to get power, influence, and money to name a few things.

2. *The gifting and ability might be real*—but it is without the unction and wind of the Holy Spirit. What do I mean? Psychic abilities can be developed to see things without the Holy Spirit, which can involve mentalism, the practice of reading thoughts or injecting thoughts into a person's mind.

Much of the latter may involve soul-astral projection, which means they have denied the flesh and natural distractions so much and have focused so intensely on seeing into the spirit realm that they can actually cross from the gray area into the dark realm—suddenly able to see and perceive things that they are not permitted by God to access.

Sweat lodges and various other self-deprecating disciplines function along these same lines. It is like taking a narcotic that can open the unseen realm for the purpose of sight. These types of false prophets might ask you to do a disciplined regimen, denying yourself food, sex, and media, allowing for no distractions.

Intense fasting and discipline for days on end might seem like a holy thing to do, but 2 Timothy 3:5 describes it as, "Having a form of godliness but denying its power." Why? Because it is all about seeking an ability rather than following the Holy Spirit. The Word of God tells us in 1 Corinthians 14 we are to *eagerly desire the gifts*, but this doesn't mean we go into a crazy cult-like regimen to open up a third eye!

FALSE PROPHETS OFFER DEMONSTRATION RATHER THAN TRANSFORMATION

There is a place for prophetic training and wild encounters. I am a major proponent of such things. However, adding Hindu mysticism or any other foreign unbiblical concepts into the prophetic is a doctrine of demons—opening an avenue for the demonic to operate. This is much like the Tower of Babel in Genesis 11, where they began to venture into rebellion against God by building a tower that would access heaven, or the spirit realm without His approval. False prophets offer doors and avenues to the unseen realms outside the will of God.

All of these are humanistic non-Holy Spirit-induced access points into the realm of the spirit, going to places the practitioner has not been invited to nor given permission by God. This is rebellion and is unauthorized access to the realm of the spirit—also known as witchcraft!

DANGER FOR THE NAÏVE

Upon taking the steps that these third-eye teachers or any other strange "prophetic sailor" would guide them into, they are allowing foreign spiritual engagement access into their life. If you venture into realms you are not invited to by the legitimate Holy Spirit and grounded in the Word of God, you are granting access to all kinds of wickedness into your mind, soul, family, and destiny!

> But **these speak evil of whatever they do not know;** and whatever they know naturally, like brute beasts, in these things they corrupt themselves. [11] Woe to them! For they have gone in the **way of Cain,** have run greedily in the **error of Balaam** for profit, and perished in the **rebellion**

of Korah. [12] *These are spots in your love feasts, while they feast with you without fear,* **serving only themselves.** *They are clouds without water, carried about by the winds; late autumn trees without fruit, twice dead, pulled up by the roots;* [13] *raging waves of the sea, foaming up their own shame; wandering stars for whom is reserved the blackness of darkness forever.* [14] *Now Enoch, the seventh from Adam, prophesied about these men also, saying, "Behold, the Lord comes with ten thousands of His saints,* [15] *to execute judgment on all, to convict all who are ungodly among them of all their ungodly deeds which they have committed in an ungodly way, and of all the harsh things which ungodly sinners have spoken against Him."* [16] *These are* **grumblers, complainers, walking according to their own lusts; and they mouth great swelling words, flattering people to gain advantage.**

—Jude 1:10-16

But there were also **false prophets** *among the people, even as there will be* **false teachers** *among you, who will secretly bring in destructive heresies, even denying the Lord who bought them, and bring on themselves swift destruction.* [2] *And many will follow their destructive ways, because of whom the way of truth will be blasphemed.* [3] *By* **covetousness they will exploit you with deceptive words;** *for a long time their judgment has not been idle, and their destruction does not slumber.*

[4] *For if God did not spare the angels who sinned, but cast them down to hell and delivered them into chains of darkness, to be reserved for judgment;* [5] *and did not spare the ancient world, but saved Noah, one of eight people, a preacher of righteousness, bringing in the flood on the*

world of the ungodly; [6] and turning the cities of Sodom and Gomorrah into ashes, condemned them to destruction, making them an example to those who afterward would live ungodly; [7] and delivered righteous Lot, who was oppressed by the filthy conduct of the wicked [8] (for that righteous man, dwelling among them, tormented his righteous soul from day to day by seeing and hearing their lawless deeds)— [9] then the Lord knows how to deliver the godly out of temptations and to reserve the unjust under punishment for the day of judgment, [10] and especially those who **walk according to the flesh** in the **lust of uncleanness** and **despise authority**. They are **presumptuous, self-willed.** They are **not afraid to speak evil of dignitaries,** [11] whereas angels, who are greater in power and might, do not bring a reviling accusation against them before the Lord. [12] But these, like natural brute beasts made to be caught and destroyed, speak evil of the things they do not understand, and will utterly perish in their own corruption, [13] and will receive the wages of unrighteousness, as those who count it pleasure to carouse in the daytime. They are spots and blemishes, carousing in their own deceptions while they feast with you, [14] having eyes full of adultery and that cannot cease from sin, enticing unstable souls. They have a heart trained in covetous practices, and are accursed children. [15] They have forsaken the right way and gone astray, following the way of Balaam the son of Beor, who loved the wages of unrighteousness; [16] but he was rebuked for his iniquity: a dumb donkey speaking with a man's voice restrained **the madness of the prophet.** [17] These are wells without water, clouds carried by a tempest, for whom is reserved the blackness of darkness forever. [18] For when they speak *great swelling words of emptiness, they allure through the lusts of the flesh, through lewdness, the ones who have actually escaped from those who live in error. [19] While they promise them liberty, they themselves are slaves of corruption; for by whom a person is overcome, by him also he is brought into bondage. [20] For if, after they have escaped the pollutions of the world through the knowledge of the Lord and Savior Jesus Christ, they are again entangled in them and overcome, the latter end is worse for them than the beginning. [21] For it would have been better for them not to have known the way of righteousness, than having known it, to turn from the holy commandment delivered to them. [22] But it has happened to them according to the true proverb: "A dog returns to his own vomit," and, "a sow, having washed, to her wallowing in the mire."*

—**2 Peter 2:1-22**

DRAWING PEOPLE AWAY

False prophets will say statements such as, "No one else wants this taught because it is so important." Or, "The devil fights this deep revelation."

Ultimately, what they teach and reveal draws people away from the true purpose of prophecy, which is to bring about the testimony of Jesus.

FALSE PROPHETS TALK ABOUT JESUS

As interesting as this will sound, false prophets can talk about Jesus all the time. Much like the fortune teller girl in Acts 16 who followed Paul around saying, "Listen to these men!" She was pointing at the truth but by a demon of divination!

Again, the way to avoid such a disaster is by training your five senses by the Word of God! Hebrews 5:14 says, "By reason of use have their senses exercised to discern both good and evil." Never develop gifts that the Bible does not clearly teach.

Ultimately the goal of a false prophet is to gain control, followers, access, power, money, all of these and more.

In their heart they are not dying to themselves and following Jesus as servants to the Most High Living God—rather, they are serving themselves and need followers ignorant enough and immature enough to run after them.

The Word of God admonishes us to be not deceived! It is our individual responsibility to stay close to the Lord on a personal level by His Word and in relationship to the Holy Spirit—you will avoid false prophets this way.

HOW APOSTLES DEAL WITH FALSE PROPHETS

This charge I commit to you, son Timothy, according to the prophecies previously made concerning you, that by them you may wage the good warfare, [19] having faith and a good conscience, which some having rejected, concerning the faith have suffered shipwreck, [20] of whom are

Hymenaeus and Alexander, whom I delivered to Satan that they may learn not to blaspheme.

—1 Timothy 1:18-20

Paul turned over those who were destroying the faith of believers to Satan so that they might be taught not to blaspheme. A surprising scripture for certain, yet there is a place in true apostolic authority where false prophets or those who are bringing destruction to the Church fall under the governmental jurisdiction of the apostle. By which the apostle, under the guidance of the Holy Spirit, may do what Paul did in 1 Timothy 1:18.

JUST BECAUSE SOMEONE HAS THE THOUSAND-YARD PROPHETIC STARE DOESN'T MEAN THEY ARE OF GOD.

Jesus is Lord, and by following His Holy Spirit, being rooted and grounded in His Word, deception will never take hold of you! I pray protection and discernment over you right now in Jesus' name!

…Worship God! For the testimony of Jesus is the spirit of prophecy.

—Revelation 19:10

AGENTS OF GOD

There was a man sent from God, whose name was John. This man came for a witness, to bear witness of the Light, that all through him might believe.

—John 1:6-7

CHAPTER EIGHTEEN

ENCOUNTERING PROPHETS

Early on in my life, there were many unique encounters with prophets. A prophetic thread has been with me since I was very young. Many experiences have followed me and continue to this day. Some, early on as well as throughout my journey, have been profoundly life-changing!

I WANT TO MEET A REAL PROPHET

In my early teen years, I did not properly understand what an actual prophet was, so the term intrigued me. One day I said to the Lord, "If there are any real prophets today, I want to meet one." This was a very interesting prayer that must have come from the unction of the Holy Spirit.

Over the course of those early years, that prayer began to be answered as I met various people who claimed to be prophets and others who undeniably moved in prophecy.

That season of my life was amplified by a habit of devouring the Word of God. I would read entire books of the Bible in short periods. It became highly important to me that God's Word was inside me.

MY GRANDPARENTS
AND MOM KIDNAPPED US

My grandpa, grandma, and mom had all conspired to kidnap my siblings and I to take us to a family camp. True story! Their purpose in being so secretive was to avoid my dad and grandfather finding out because they would protest and take legal action, given the occasion. My grandparents were wonderful people who sincerely loved the Lord and believed they had a word from God to get us to this camp to hear a particular speaker. Grandpa and Grandma were right in this action as far as it concerned me.

Their efforts that summer became the turning point into a series of events that set my life on a collision course with the living God. It still makes me laugh, thinking about my grandmother and grandfather—a mother of ten and prayer warrior and a successful businessman highly dedicated to the Lord—crafting this master plan together. Whatever the strategy was, they had heard God and obeyed, and I am forever grateful.

Little did I know, a wild man named Dave Duell was ministering that week. Dave had a unique ministry filled with humor and amazing demonstrations of Holy Spirit power. He told captivating stories that were often hilarious, but it was his relationship with God that fascinated me most.

One of his many powerful stories was of the time he was invited to minister to Yasser Arafat and his staff. He also expounded upon the many times he had seen blind eyes open and deaf ears healed. He went on with volumes of testimonies about the supernatural things God had done for him. Up to that point, his message was the greatest thing I had ever heard.

When he finished speaking, he said, "Well, that's enough talking. It's time for some demonstration!"

I thought, Demonstration? He isn't going to try to do the stuff he talked about, is he? The stories were great, but surely that kind of thing won't happen here!

Dave spoke again, "Does anyone here have asthma?" I looked around the room, thinking, *Who would answer a question like that?* Suddenly, a person raised their hand.

"Get up here," Dave yelled. This person quickly came to the front, and my full attention was fastened on them. As soon as he reached the front, Dave said, "I'm going to chop that thing off!" He took his hand and, like an axe, ran it over his head and down the guy's back, making a "Cha" sound with the movement. My eyes widened as this person fell on the floor as though he had been shot dead! I gazed at him on the floor as Dave laughed in response to the asthma the person "used to have!"

The place became electric over the man falling under the power of God. Before I knew it, many more people came forward and received the same touch of power. They were experiencing legitimate miraculous healing in their bodies! It was the most beautiful thing I had ever seen.

What sealed the whole experience for me was when my nine-year-old brother went forward because he had a turned ankle that was causing him to have difficulty walking. It wasn't just a temporary condition, as he had been going to specialists to help him correct it.

Dave sat him down on the stage, my brother's legs dangling over the edge. Dave got down on one knee, picked up my brother's ankle, and commanded it to be straight. To my shock, it straightened out—I watched it straighten out! Then his leg grew until it was even in length with the other.

Seeing this gave me the nerve to ask for prayer regarding a horrible allergy to bee stings that had caused me some awful experiences. Dave prayed for me, and the last thing I recall was coming back to my senses and looking at the ceiling because I had been knocked out by the power of God!

During one of those services, a person practicing witchcraft came to the front and screamed. Dave cast a demon out of her. When it came out, it sounded like something was roaring. It was that spirit shouting as it left the woman. It was scary, yet so powerful to see that woman free of the torment inside of her. She left the meeting that night entirely free!

A CUP OF COLD WATER

This created a hunger in me for the Holy Spirit. At the end of that meeting, people in the parking lot needing prayer surrounded Dave. He prayed and kept ministering for hours! This made a great impression on me. So, I ran to the kitchen area and got a cup of water. I made my way through the compressed crowd and got in front of Dave and offered it to him. He took it with appreciation and drank it.

Then Dave asked me, "What do you want?"

Without knowing where it came from or why I said it, I eagerly replied, "Boldness!"

Dave responded with, "You got it!" He prayed over me and released the power of God for boldness into my life, and it still works today! When the Spirit of God comes on me to do something, that supernatural boldness rises.

One of the best parts about this meeting was that, not long after, I was stung by a bee on both my throat and face. Typically, it would have caused significant swelling and put me down for days. Yet this time, nothing happened!

After encountering Jesus and the Holy Spirit through the ministry of Dave Duell, my life changed. There was no going back. Everything I witnessed and received at this family camp was enough for me to go all in and give my life to Jesus. I told God that whatever He had, I wanted it! Even if it cost me my life, there was now no other way I could live other than entirely for Jesus.

THE GORBACHEV PROPHECY

During that following summer, in August of 1991, we went back to camp for a week to see Dave Duell again.

As the week progressed, the meetings grew so large they had to be taken outside due to a lack of seating. As a result, chairs were set up in the parking lot and all the way up the opposing hill. Dave found himself preaching and ministering on the front steps of the building. It was thrilling for me to see people with such a hunger for God. I thought, *They are even willing to sit outside at night!*

A dramatic thing happened to me on one of the final nights. Dave said something that piqued my attention. A coup had occurred in the now-former Soviet Union, and their leader, Mikhail Gorbachev, was placed under house arrest.

In the context of these events with Gorbachev, Dave stood up under the power of the Holy Spirit and said, "I just heard the Holy Spirit say that this situation in Russia will be over shortly, and Gorbachev will be set free."

It was a simple but unambiguous word from God. As I heard it, the power of the Holy Spirit overwhelmed me. It was the first time I had ever experienced a prophetic word that boldly predicted the outcome of a current event.

It was astonishing to me, and my heart burned for more. History shows that it wasn't but a few days after the coup that the word Dave released came true, and Gorbachev was free. This most recent encounter with the Voice of God woke up something inside me. It was as if God said, "That's right, Joseph. I want to speak to you."

This was one of my first encounters with a real prophetic voice!

PROPHETIC WORD FROM JOHN PAUL JACKSON

Once while attending a youth conference in Minneapolis, Minnesota, a particular encounter took place that dramatically impacted me. The keynote speaker was a man named John Paul Jackson. He was known as a prophet who knew the Voice of God. His name was new to me, but later I found out he was a seer prophet who could see things about people's current lives or potential future events.

During this conference, speakers talked, one session after another, with prayer times. It wasn't until I heard John Paul speak and minister that something significant happened. He was different from the others, and what I felt when he shared was different.

He shared a message in the same format as the other speakers, but following his message, he did something none of the others did. At the closing of his message, he took a moment, became still, and slowly surveyed the audience. He looked around the room up into the stadium seating, panning his eyes left and right as if looking for something.

This continued for a brief time until he rested his eyes on an individual and calmly pointed out the person. He spoke what he was seeing and then moved on to another person. He continued in this fashion for several minutes.

The arrangement of the meeting space was stadium-style seating, as there were several hundred people in attendance. The audience ascended upward with each subsequent row from the stage. He continued pointing out different people in this sizable audience, telling them precise details no one could know about their lives.

As this happened, Dave Duell's prediction about Mikhail Gorbachev came to mind. John Paul's ministry to the crowd felt the same: it was thrilling to experience so many people being impacted in such a unique way.

PUBLIC WORD OF KNOWLEDGE

Suddenly, to my surprise, John Paul looked at me. My heart pounded as he paused, gazing at me as if looking through me. His eyes were steely, which made me think, *Please don't say anything!* My seat was on the front row of this packed-out college gymnasium, one of the best places to see from any angle, so there was nowhere to hide.

I was wearing a metal cross around my neck—a gift from my mother. It had distinct metallic colors, mostly charcoal, bright with worn silver on its high points. He identified me by referring to it.

I gulped hard when he pointed at me, "Young man wearing the iron cross." John Paul described many things about me and my future and declared I had a mighty calling. He also went into great detail about a woman God had set apart for me, and even went into detail about her life: how she was and the current challenges she was experiencing. He said that she would come through those things and was being prepared for me.

Man, did I feel put on the spot! He charged me by saying I was to bring protection over her life and that God would use me as a covering that would save her life. He shared many more details, all of which impacted me greatly.

After the service, I was invited to speak with him. I can vividly recall his strong eyes. I was surprised when standing with him that he was a lot taller than me. He was happy to speak with me about what he had told me and helped me understand anything I had questions about. I was thankful for the opportunity to talk with him.

This moment made me think, *Wow, God answered me; I finally met a prophet!* Little did I know, this moment was only a tiny fraction of God's answer to my prayer. Every time I met someone prophetic, they would prophesy many powerful things over me. They nearly always revolved around two recurring themes: my future wife and my future wealth. He was preparing me for a coming day when He would place excessive amounts of resources into my hands, to manage and distribute wealth for the Kingdom.

A DEFINING PROPHETIC ENCOUNTER

A defining encounter occurred on my 20th birthday. It was a Sunday morning, and my pastor was hosting a guest speaker. This meeting was in a school gymnasium that our church was renting at the time.

This guest speaker also happened to be a prophet. I thought, *Well, I've seen some of this ministry before.* However, there was such a stirring inside me before he got up to minister; I wasn't sure why it was happening, but the presence and power of the Holy Spirit was nearly palpable. There was a deep sense of something powerful and significant, as though God would appear or something. I hadn't felt this sensation since I first saw Dave Duell.

After the pastor introduced the guest speaker, he walked to the front of the meeting and began to speak. I don't remember his message topic, but I will never forget the ministry time.

After a lengthy message, he stopped preaching and stood directly before me like a general. As he did so, the Word of the Lord came to him, and he boldly spoke words over me.

He told me about the call of God on my life and how I would reach many lives around the world. He said that when my time was done, those whom I disciple would do even more than I had on a global scale. At one point, he talked about my future wife and how the Lord had preserved her for me—again, that word came.

He ministered over me with such accuracy and clarity that I was floored and in awe of the Holy Spirit. I will never forget the main point he drove home: "The Lord requires you to step into a long season of much learning. You need much training, much learning, and much being teachable! You have the heart, but you must acquire knowledge."

It was so good for me to hear that. Those words lit a fire in me to learn and become better equipped. Many more powerful words were spoken by that man to me. I felt the significance of the Holy Spirit's calling over me burning deep.

FORTY-FIVE MINUTES OF FIRE ALARMS

As he finished saying these things and much more, I sensed the Holy Spirit say, "Happy Birthday." No sooner had this come through my heart than the prophet stepped into a middle aisle and ministered to a woman halfway back in the meeting. As he told her that God wanted to touch her life, she jumped to her feet and screamed. She shouted in a grisly voice, "I will kill this woman before I let her free! She is mine!

You cannot have her—I will kill you!" At precisely that moment, the fire alarms in the gymnasium sounded.

The demon inside this woman screamed threats through her as the fire alarms blared. The prophet's response was surprising. He assured the crowd, "Nobody worry; this is normal."

Normal?! I thought. *How could this be normal?* Though a jarring sense of panic had been present in the beginning, now—amid almost deafening sirens and a screaming demon—an unexplainable peace flooded the gym.

It was a miracle that we could still hear the speaker through the sound system. He took authority over the demon and told the woman to sit down. She did and remained quiet.

However, the alarms didn't stop! They continued for 30-45 minutes—no exaggeration, they just kept going! The entire time, no one moved, and the prophet went throughout the room with authority and power, sharing astonishing details with many people.

When the alarms finally stopped, he continued ministering—no one left for hours. What started as a typical Sunday morning ministry went into the night and carried on into several weeks of meetings.

FIRST TIME VISITORS

An interesting side note about that Sunday meeting: We later discovered that a couple decided to try something different for church this particular Sunday. They said to one another, "Let's try one of those charismatic churches." So they looked up our church in the directory and came for the first time that morning. Wouldn't you know, they chose seats directly in front of the woman who stood up with a demon speaking through her!

When this happened, the woman was leaning over this couple, grabbing the back of their chairs while screaming. They had never been to a Spirit-filled service before! It makes me laugh a little, imagining what their conversation might have been like on the way home. They must have thought all charismatic meetings are like that all the time!

That Sunday turned into about three years of doing periodic weeks of meetings that would often last all night and drew large crowds. The city's mayor attended, and the whole occasion made the newspapers. Many thrilling and extraordinary things happened during this season.

My life became engaged with the Voice of God in a way I had never known, even when I was younger. After being exposed to this type of setting, the gifting in my life was stirred, and I became more active than ever before. My dreams became prevalent and filled with details of events, people, places, and scenery that I had never seen in person. These dreams always came a day or two before walking into that exact place, meeting those very people. It was a wild ride!

The encounters with this prophetic ministry greatly impacted my life. One word that was given to me was in a private leadership meeting. The prophet pulled me aside, and he declared over my future. Calmly and with authority, he told me the Lord called me to a higher walk of purity. If I kept myself pure and waited, I would receive the absolute best, and as I waited, she would be an amazing woman. He closed the word he spoke over me by saying, "As you wait, it will be a sign to you at seven o'clock in the evening. It will be raining on that day. You will know that God has been with you every step of the way."

The leadership chuckled a little as the word was given. As colorful as that statement sounded, it was very powerful, and I took it very seriously. It had always been imperative to me that I waited for my wife, but this word from the man of God caused me to walk the line!

THE PROPHET'S DAUGHTER BECAME MY WIFE

It was nearly two years later that this prophetic word was fulfilled. It was 7 p.m., and it began to rain as I asked Heather to marry me. Her father was the man who gave me the prophetic word and he became my father-in-law!

MY FIRST TRANCE

There was a season in the mid-1990s when there were worldwide meetings where the power of God was on display. These meetings drew huge crowds, which made them stand out. Two of the most well-known were in Toronto, Canada, and Brownsville, Florida.

Shortly after the meeting on my birthday, I was invited to go to the Brownsville Revival. It took more than 30 hours by bus to get from Minnesota to Florida—that was a miserable ride.

When we arrived at our destination, the line of people camping out to get into the meetings was quite a sight! It was several blocks long. Everyone was outside in lawn chairs, talking with one another about where they were from and what Jesus had done for them. People from all around the world were there; it was amazing!

We walked into the meeting shortly before the service began, and the presence of God in that place was powerful. Many people were getting healed, delivered, and saved. We attended those meetings for days.

On the final day, after being in that environment, rich in faith and power, we boarded the bus home.

While making it to my seat, suddenly a profound and supernatural moment was unveiled to me. Occurrences with the supernatural were not entirely new to me. As a very young boy, they happened in highly unique ways, but this was different. It was all-encompassing and unavoidable. It was, to me, a reaction by the Spirit for spending so much time in His presence.

In short, somewhere between stepping onto that bus and sitting down, I was suddenly and supernaturally taken to another place—I was no longer on the bus; everything around me was different.

While I approached my seat, something was measurably different in my being. Clarity in my mind and a heightened sense of perception reached beyond my natural surroundings. My cousin Jordan was with me. He and I sat by each other on the bus, and that's when an encounter happened that greatly impacted me. Sitting there, I was, in one moment, completely aware of my surroundings. Suddenly—as if I were waking up from a dream or sleep, I opened my eyes and was physically standing somewhere completely different!

My senses were no longer aware of the bus or Jordan sitting right next to me. It wasn't clear to me if I was in or out of my body. What I do know is everything was photo-real. I could empirically observe my surroundings; it seemed corporeal and tangible—no different from any real setting I've ever stood in.

CONCRETE LANDSCAPE

Once my bearings equalized, I began noticing where my feet were standing—stony ground but smooth. Everything under my feet was concrete, and all the surrounding terrain was solid concrete. My eyes went up from my feet and looked out in front, and as far as I could see, the buildings and even the trees seemed to be concrete. Everything was concrete!

SEED IN MY HAND

At this moment, I had a sense of something in my hand. Upon looking down at my right hand, I identified a seed in my palm. It was a tiny seed. I didn't identify what kind of seed it was specifically, but I have often referred to it as a *mustard seed; however*, it was simply a small, white seed.

Upon seeing this seed in my right hand, a Voice prompted me to throw the seed. The little seed violently slammed into the concrete as if a two-ton wrecking ball had been dropped from 300 feet. Its impact made an explosion, producing a barbaric crunching sound like a meteor strike—it hit the ground with such force that I jumped back in shock!

As the seed punched through that thick concrete, the ground bounced into broken pieces as it sought the soil beneath.

The violent breakthrough revealed a large crater with broken concrete slabs standing on end and sideways, the way broken ice would sit if something broke the surface of a frozen lake. Only these concrete remnants were lying in broken pieces inside the slope of this crater, which had a diameter of at least 20 feet.

SO SHALL YOUR WORDS BE TO THE HEARTS OF MEN

It was astonishing as dirt flew from under the broken thick concrete slab. Suddenly, as that dramatic scene had taken place, a Voice spoke to me, saying, *"So shall your words be to the hearts of men!"* Those words dramatically altered my heart at that moment. However, the words were sealed up for a future day when the Lord determined.

After coming out of the trance and/or vision, I was still seated on the bus, and Jordan was there next to me. Whatever I mentioned of that encounter was very little. To everyone around me, nothing out of the ordinary had happened. I, however, was profoundly impacted by that revelatory moment.

> *Sow for yourselves righteousness; reap in mercy; break up your fallow ground, for it is time to seek the Lord, till He comes and rains righteousness on you.*
>
> —Hosea 10:12

Twenty-five years later, my family and I drove into that same parking lot where the bus was parked at the Brownsville Revival Church. I stood in the exact spot where the Spirit of the Lord caught me up and showed me that vast landscape made of concrete. What was shown to me that day was a snapshot of the culture and what the world would develop into—today's world. Very hard or fallow ground requires a special word from the Lord, carried by His messengers.

Looking back on that moment, I now know the Lord had called me on that day as a voice to speak His Word. However, as stated earlier, this was not the first time an encounter with the prophetic had occurred in my life. Ever since I was young, the supernatural realm and communication seemed to be a large part of everything, so much so that I thought everyone had that same experience.

VISION ABOUT MARRIAGE

I had a prophetic encounter that settled the decision to marry Heather. This took place during a time of questioning if it was God's will for us to get married. While driving alone, the Holy Spirit flooded my vehicle one day. It was so powerful—palpable.

It was as if the Lord Himself had sat in the passenger seat, and had I reached over, I could have physically touched Him!

However, an intense reverence and fear made it difficult to look, much less reach over, to the passenger seat. So with eyes straight ahead and two hands on the wheel, time seemed to slow down. I felt like I was no longer driving but floating. Everything became silent, including the sounds of the road, wind, and motor. It was like being in a vacuum.

A vision of Heather appeared. She was standing in a shaft of light. The Lord showed me that she would accomplish great things for the Kingdom with me as her protector.

At the end of the vision, God asked, "Do you want Heather as your wife?"

Speechless for a moment and unsure if this was some kind of test, my answer was, "Please, Sir, You decide."

It went quiet, but the intense presence was still very apparent. After an awkward silence, I spoke again, "You decide, but I sure do love Heather."

Suddenly, the presence lifted, and time and space returned to normal. Now completely aware of my surroundings and curious how the van was still on the road, these words came out, "Did I do something wrong? Was that pleasing to You?"

Silence.

The next day was my birthday, so Heather came to where I was staying.

She said, "I've been thinking. Why are we wasting time trying to figure out if this is the right thing or not? I have an overwhelming sense that we should go forward!"

I responded, "Me too!"

There was never a question again. It was long before I told Heather about my encounter with God while driving down the highway.

VISION IN THE DIALYSIS UNIT PARKING LOT

During a challenging time in our lives, the Lord met me while in the parking lot at the dialysis center. This was from Heather having double kidney failure due to a hereditary condition. The day she developed serious symptoms, she was preaching on stage. Right at the end of the meeting, I had to rush her to the hospital as she was about to collapse; shortly after, she was placed on dialysis, a season that lasted two and a half years.

One day, while she was in the dialysis unit, I was sitting in the truck outside, working and speaking out against the constant thoughts that Heather may die.

The doctors had consistently been telling us to prepare for the worst, as she had various challenges throughout the process. Yet she was a star patient due to overcoming unbelievable odds. Each time she received terrible news, we would stand in faith, and it was overturned with a miracle!

The Holy Spirit sustained her due to her intense daily routine of mixing her faith with the Word of God. She would spend hours every day listening to the teaching that God wanted her healed, and she relentlessly meditated on the scriptures. It got to the point that we would start laughing in faith in front of the doctors whenever we received bad news. They didn't know what to do with that. It wasn't meant to be disrespectful, but we knew we had to be in faith, or she wouldn't make it. We would thank them and say, "It's not you. We just are expecting something far better than these continuous bad reports!"

Even with these victories, the journey was still very taxing. Combating thoughts of her not making it, and having to raise our children without her, was a daily fight of faith. Yet we knew that we were going to push forward.

I returned to the parking lot where I was parked outside on this particular day; it was cold. The heater was on, and I was deep into my routine of answering emails, scheduling events, writing, media work, etc. Suddenly, the atmosphere in the vehicle began to change, and that familiar, intense presence began to fill the truck.

Again, I was afraid to look at the passenger seat due to the intense, palpable sensation engulfing me. This time, although the hair on my neck and arms was standing up, the presence of God wasn't there to present me with a choice. It was different. I felt a merciful and deeply loving sensation at the deepest level, beyond anything I had ever experienced before.

At first, silence was His vocabulary. I don't know how long the complete stillness lingered. I couldn't say anything, as the presence was overwhelming. Eventually, the Voice of God spoke clearly. It is difficult to say whether it was audible, but one thing was sure—God spoke.

His Voice said, "I just want to look at you for a moment."

Now bursting with tears and unable to speak, I could only listen intently. His unmistakable Voice spoke again, "You're doing a good job." A long pause followed until He said, "You are going to be okay."

Tears were still rolling down my face as His presence lifted. It was a powerful moment, a direct promise from the Voice of God that everything would be okay and that we were following the right path.

As I came out of this moment, time and space once again returned to normal. Suddenly, I realized that lights were flashing behind me in front of the dialysis building. Quickly pulling myself together, I exited the truck and ran to the entrance to discover what was happening. My only thought was, *All that matters is that Heather is safe!*

A man seated not far from Heather in the unit decided he no longer wanted to live. He began shouting, "I can't take this anymore!" and pulled the dialysis tubes out of his arm.

These tubes were connected to the main arteries that go to the heart, so when he ripped them out, his blood began spraying in every direction and onto the floor. It was horrible, as the power of his heart pumped his blood out without any blockage.

The courageous nurses fought to rescue this man. Heather witnessed this nearby and was praying out loud while also shouting along with the nurses, "Please stop! We don't want you to die!"

She had great compassion for him and the hopelessness he must have felt. The fire department and ambulance arrived with emergency lights and sirens blaring in an attempt to save this man's life. We don't know if he lived or died, as he was rushed out of the facility, and we never saw him again.

I still find it interesting that this encounter of the Lord's reassurance occurred outside, just as this drama unfolded inside. Heather's powerful prayers and faith must have been a factor in this moment. Not long after, an impossible miracle happened, a donor came forward that was a match for Heather, and she received a miracle kidney! We rejoiced because we were told she would never qualify to receive a new kidney due to complications. Jesus knew better!

POST OFFICE PROPHECY

There have been many prophetic moments that would often find me in unique places.

One day I was at the post office to get the ministry mail and open a new post office box. While walking to the new box to test the keys, someone shouted at me, "Is your name Joseph?"

There were a good amount of people checking their mail also. After closing the box and turning toward the voice, I responded, "Yes!" The person calling my name was about 60 feet away, with several people between us.

The others quickly parted to the sides and exited the building. The man prophesied loudly, saying, "The Lord would say to you, you are called to a new land and will go there. In this place, you will establish and build beyond those who trained you. The Lord needs your voice and influence on a large scale, and you will leave many behind. This will be difficult for you but necessary."

I thanked this post office prophet and, out of honor to the word of the Lord spoken through him, gave him all the cash in my wallet. We ended up moving to Colorado a season after that word.

A POT BLESSING PROPHECY

At the end of one of our meetings, we had a dinner gathering. It was in typical church fashion, boasting paper plates and an assortment of veggies with dip, chips, coffee, and chili. It was an intense season of our life. I was tired, Heather was tired, and I had begun to make internal plans to pull back and fade out of the ministry picture, partly because of Heather being sick and partly because of our intense schedule. There was no one to talk to about this without discouraging those around me. I was trying to figure out how to do it in a good way for everyone.

At this meeting, one of my associate leaders was speaking. When finished, we gathered downstairs. An African man abruptly walked up to us, within an arm's reach of me. I had never seen him before and haven't seen him since. There I was, stuck in a corner with a paper plate in hand, and there was no escape route. It all seemed very unusual.

He said, "The Lord sent me here to tell you something! You cannot quit now! The Lord needs you and your written words! You have a message the Lord has given you that must go across America!

"You have thought about slowing down and stepping out of sight, and you must not! God has called you and not another! Are you not His prophet? You are called to prophesy the Word of God! Bless you, man of God."

Then he left just as abruptly as he had come. No one knew who he was.

POLICE OFFICER PROPHECY

Years ago, we were staying at our friends' home way up in the cold reaches of northern Minnesota. The Holy Spirit told me to go to a certain man's house because he had a prophetic word for me. It was not far away; it was within walking distance. After walking and praying about what the Holy Spirit had spoken, my feet found the front door-step of this man's home. After sheepishly knocking on the door with no answer, I decided that he was most likely not home.

As I left the porch, there was a sense of leaving something uncompleted; I had no feeling of closure. I didn't understand why the Holy Spirit would speak to me about receiving a word from a specific person, and the person was not home.

After returning to our friend's house, we embarked on the three-hour journey back to Minneapolis. It was a long drive home that evening. That experience caused an unresolved question mark for many years.

FIFTEEN YEARS LATER

Fast-forward 15 years: I was speaking at a church in that same area. The meetings were good, and people were blessed. The last night, as we were returning to the hotel, my friend Jason was driving, and Heather was in the back seat, making us all laugh. This was a typical scenario while driving after a meeting. Suddenly, lights flashed behind us; a squad car was pulling us over!

The officer came to the window and explained that although we were slightly speeding, he mostly pulled us over because he hadn't seen anyone on the road all night.

The officer was kind and humorous. During our conversation, we told him we had been speaking at a local church. This is where it gets interesting. Accompanying the officer was a chaplain. As we continued talking, the officer was abruptly moved out of the way by this chaplain!

All at once, he leaned through the window across Jason, grabbed me by the arm, and declared, "The Lord says to you." I thought, *Whoa, what's happening?* But this chaplain prophesied over me!

Shockingly, he prophesied in detail about specifics regarding the last season of our journey. He spoke about our challenges and how we had survived and overcome them. Then he went on to declare what was coming next.

He said, "There is a *shift happening right now for you*, and more will come out of you than ever! You are not done with the areas you minister in, and there will be more fruit than ever! There is a new city God is calling you to, and there will be a type of center, or meeting hub, that will begin to train and produce leaders and prophetic voices. Music will come out of it as well." Many more accurate and powerful things were spoken over us.

Tears gushed down my face, knowing the Lord was powerfully speaking to me.

Part of the overflow of emotion was the sudden realization that this chaplain was the same man whose house the Holy Spirit had sent me to for a word 15 years before.

The Voice of God whispered to me, "Delay is not denial." The word meant so much more following a 15-year wait. It made the whole process special and showed me that the Lord knew what we would go through 15 years beforehand!

GOD IS ALWAYS SPEAKING

The Spirit of the Lord is always speaking—this has become clear for many years; and through many different encounters, I know God speaks through His prophetic voices. God wants to speak to you more than you want to hear Him!

CHAPTER NINETEEN

OFFICE OF THE PROPHET

And He Himself gave some as apostles, some prophets, some evangelists, and some as pastors and teachers.

—Ephesians 4:11

After all the years of experiencing many good and negative things involving the office of the prophet, it has become clear to me that the best way to avoid a foundation of dysfunction is to define biblically what the office of the prophet is!

A short and working definition of a prophet is a governmental office gift functioning by revelation and responsibility to a segment of the body of Christ.

CONSTRUCTED IMAGE

An image may be created in your mind whenever you hear the word "prophet." Of course, this is based on the reference point you are coming from.

Prophets, as depicted in the Bible and how they are perceived, are likely the most controversial governmental gift in the Church today. I desire to offer a biblical definition for the right expectation of the office it stands in and its operation.

PROPHET JESUS

Our very best example of a prophet is Jesus. He demonstrated the office of the prophet in the highest sense. Jesus says in John 14:24 (NIV), "These words you hear are not my own; they belong to the Father who sent me."

During the closing months of His public ministry, Jesus taught about the last days. Entire chapters in the Gospels, such as Matthew 24, have futuristic and predictive prophecies told by Jesus. Not to mention the word of knowledge He spoke to Nathaniel.

Another form of the prophetic through Jesus was that He was able to know the thoughts of the Pharisees and many other revelatory traits. Further, at the very beginning of His ministry, Jesus proclaimed what the Old Testament prophets had prophetically spoken regarding what was being fulfilled in Him!

> He [Jesus] *went to Nazareth, where he had been brought up, and on the Sabbath day he went into the synagogue, as was his custom. He stood up to read,* [17] *and the scroll of the prophet Isaiah was handed to him. Unrolling it, he found the place where it is written:* [18] *"The Spirit of the Lord is on me, because he has anointed me to proclaim good news to the poor. He has sent me to proclaim freedom for the prisoners and recovery of sight for the blind, to set the oppressed free,* [19] *to proclaim the year of the Lord's favor."* [20] *Then he rolled up the scroll, gave it back to the attendant and sat down. The eyes of everyone in the synagogue were fastened on him.* [21] *He began by saying to them, "Today this scripture is fulfilled in your hearing."*
>
> **—Luke 4:16-21 NIV**

It is evident that Jesus walked in the office of the prophet along with moving in every gift of the Spirit.

RESPONSIBILITY OVER GIFTING

Many believe that a prophet is one who can prophesy to others, tell them the future or see into the realm of the spirit. Although this point of view is correct—it is incomplete. Prophets prophesy; they definitely see into the spirit realm. However, that is not what defines a prophet.

In the Old Testament, the name *seer* was converted into *prophet*. Those days under the Old Covenant required a prophet to see or directly speak for God without any variance to the direct message.

> *Formerly in Israel, when a man went to inquire of God, he spoke thus: "Come, let us go to the seer"; for he who is now called a prophet was formerly called a seer.*
> **—1 Samuel 9:9**

Seers are, simply put, prophets whose gifting operates in visions, dreams, and experiencing the future. Depending on the type of prophet, their scope of operation will do more than see. They can also speak, cast vision, teach, lead, and more.

POWER-STEERING VERSUS SPIRIT-FILLED

As you just read, the gifts *to see* and *say* are not limited to that part of the scope but have more attributes. These gifts have a different function, especially now that we are in a New Testament era. "Why?"

someone might ask. To answer, we must again consider that the covenant has changed. In the Old Covenant, God's Spirit would descend upon an individual; it was a "power-steering" type of relationship! God would glaringly tell the prophet what to say, and it would be relayed word for word.

God took it seriously if a prophet presumed to speak for Him or made an uninspired prediction that did not come to pass.

> *"But the prophet who presumes to speak a word in My name, which I have not commanded him to speak, or who speaks in the name of other gods, that prophet shall die."* [21] *And if you say in your heart, "How shall we know the word which the Lord has not spoken?"—* [22] *when a prophet speaks in the name of the Lord, if the thing does not happen or come to pass, that is the thing which the Lord has not spoken; the prophet has spoken it presumptuously; you shall not be afraid of him.*
>
> **—Deuteronomy 18:20-22**

New Testament-era prophets and the office of the prophet have a different connection to God, the Father, through Christ Jesus, the Son. His Spirit lives *within* us and not *upon* us! This affects how we hear and how those who hear relay what they hear to others. Today prophets know in part and prophesy in part.

INTERPRETATION, NOT TRANSLATION

Old Testament prophets were allowed zero failure, while New Testament prophets, although called to accuracy, are under the new covenant when the Lord is constantly speaking to all of His people—His sheep hear His Voice. The point is the office of the prophet and prophecy itself is today an interpretation. No longer is it a direct word-for-word translation. Rather it is an interpretation by those who know in part and prophesy in part.

JESUS TURNED ON THE LIGHTS

"Spirit-filled life" is an interpretation of the Spirit, not a direct translation. Why mention this? To point out that our relationship with the Voice of God has changed since Jesus turned the lights back on within those who receive Him and are filled with His Spirit. A better way to understand this would be to say that the ability to hear with their spirit or inner self in the Old Testament was next to impossible. However, in the New Testament, believers in Jesus can hear because their spirit is directly connected to God the Father through Christ the Son.

NEW TESTAMENT PROPHECY IS NOT PAINT BY NUMBERS

Today, prophecy is a powerful interpretation of what the Spirit is saying. It is not a painting by numbers, relaying what they heard. It is instead a soulish expression of imagery induced by the Spirit and laid out on the canvas by interpretation.

A PROPHET BY DEFINITION

And He Himself gave some to be apostles, some prophets, some evangelists, and some pastors and teachers, [12] *for the equipping of the saints for the work of ministry, for the edifying of the body of Christ.*

—**Ephesians 4:11-12**

The governmental office of the prophet is a responsibility. Much like a public servant in politics, a prophet is a servant to the body of Christ. This governing office equips and edifies the body of Christ through the four operations on the prophetic spectrum. Prophets are also called to a segment of the body of Christ or a specific territory.

Let's review the four operations on the prophetic spectrum.

ROEH

Visionary. Seer

NABI

Mouthpiece—Proclaimer; Declarer. Forth teller; Herald. Nabi literally means "to bubble up."

CHAZAH

To gaze at, mentally perceive, or supernatural sight by visions and dreams.

CHOZEH

A Beholder: one who leans forward

peering into the distance.

Prophets have jurisdiction, much like apostles.

If I am not an apostle to others, yet doubtless I am to you.
For you are the seal of my apostleship in the Lord.

—1 Corinthians 9:2

In the 1 Corinthians 9:2 scripture, we see that the apostles have assigned people. They are not apostles to others, but they are to the ones they are assigned to and are responsible for. This is a form of jurisdiction. With apostles and prophets working so closely together, it is reasonable to consider that prophets also have a jurisdiction or an assigned people, place, or arena they are anointed to speak.

Allow me to reference additional insight into the office of the prophet by my friend and trusted Bible scholar, Rick Renner. Rick gives excellent insight into the word "prophet" from his masterpiece book, *Apostles and Prophets*. He not only defines the word but adds mighty insight into how a prophet should operate—like a ship that is completely dependent on the wind to hit its sail!

> The word "prophet" that is used in the Septuagint Greek version of the Old Testament and in the New Testament is a translation of the Greek word *prophetes*, which is a compound of *pro* and *phemi*, which is the preposition *pro* that is compounded with the word *phemi*. The word *pro* carries a wide range of meaning, which you will see in the following paragraphs, but the second part of the word, *phemi*, explicitly means to say, to speak, or to communicate. The word *phemi* can also signify the shedding of light on a subject.
>
> Thus, this word tells us that when a prophet delivers a prophetic message, he gives light on the message God wishes to communicate. The use of the word *phemi* immediately lets us know that a prophet is a speaking or saying ministry or one who is intended to communicate.

As noted, the preposition *pro*—the first part of the word "prophet"—adds a wide range of meanings that are all critical to understanding the meaning of the word "prophet," which we will study in the following pages. There are four primary pictures conveyed to us in the Greek word *prophetes*. All four of the following points are true about all prophets in the Old Testament, early New Testament, current times, and in the days to come.

The following are four variations of how the word *prophemi* applies:

1. Prophemi: *Speaking before the Lord.* Or a prophet's position before God, listening to what God would say to them. Then speaks first *to* God, then *for* God. God may speak through a vision or a different mode involving the four New Testament themes or types of prophecy. Prophets are to linger in the presence of God. To deliver the emotion of God. Making sure to really understand God's message. Most prophets spend a lot of time in the presence of God until they get a message.

2. Prophemi: *In front of.* When a prophet has a message from the Lord, they *stand in front of people* giving a message from the Lord. Be a clear channel. When speaking prophetically in front of people, you are not to add your own commentary. A prophet is to accurately represent God's message.

3. Prophemi: *They speak on behalf of.* Agabus 2 times Acts 11:27, 28 prophets from Antioch.

4. Prophemi: *In advance: with a certain predictive ability.* Talk about things in advance. Acts 21:10-11 took Paul's belt. Thus, saith the Holy Ghost.[12]

SAILS CANNOT OPERATE WITHOUT THE WIND

Although prophets can develop in the word of knowledge and operate by the gift God placed within them, they cannot induce the unction of the Holy Spirit!

Just because a prophet can, doesn't mean they should. They must wait as they put up their spiritual sails and allow the wind of the Spirit to blow, guiding them, directing them, and giving them the unction to engage.

A real prophet cannot have an unction on his own! He must spend actual time with God. When God decides to say something, the prophet is surrendered in the presence of God and has his sails set open. The wind of God comes and blows, moving the prophet to do whatever the Lord wants.

> And when the ship was caught, and could not bear up into the wind, we let her drive. [16] And running under a certain island which is called Clauda, we had much work to come by the boat: [17] Which when they had taken up, they used helps, undergirding the ship; and, fearing lest they should fall into the quicksands, strake sail, and so were driven.
>
> —**Acts 27:15-17 KJV**

The Acts 27:15-17 scripture reference carries the same understanding for *move*. To move the ship was completely dependent on the wind! The sails had to be put in place. The ship workers could not produce the wind! They could only catch the wind.

ALWAYS HAVE THE SAILS PREPARED!

To be moved along by God is always to have your sails prepared! This comes mainly from surrendering your gift and experiences to the Word of God.

DIFFERENT TYPES OF PROPHETS

One type is the community church prophet who the pastor and leadership recognize as a trusted voice. These often operate in words of knowledge and discernment and offer spiritual guidance and encouragement to the leader.

Another type is the John the Baptist-type of prophets who are anointed to call out seats of authority and do so demonstratively! John the Baptist did this toward Herod, ultimately costing him his life. However, he spoke to the institution of his day.

DIFFERING ASSIGNMENTS, SAME HOLY SPIRIT

Different categories of gifting and operation may bleed over into one another. Still, you can see a general theme and distinction in the various New Testament prophetic characters who shared similar traits with Old Testament characters and their contemporaries alike.

Agabus

Predicted a famine in Acts 11:28. He worked in the word of knowledge with a corresponding prophetic act when he used Paul's belt to bind his hands and feet, saying, "Thus says the Holy Spirit, 'So shall the Jews at Jerusalem bind the man who owns this belt, and deliver him into the hands of the Gentiles'" (Acts 21:11). Agabus is a representative of what a regional or even national prophet looks like as a voice to the church's senior leaders.

Philip's Daughters

Prophesied and were another representative of what it looks like to have a company of prophetic voices in a local setting. Agabus joined them, having a clear word for Paul (*see* Acts 21:9-11).

John the Revelator

A mighty example of a New Testament prophet who operated in *chozeh*. He beheld the future and was peering into the distance with the guidance of the Holy Spirit. A series of encounters that resulted in the penning of the *Revelation of Jesus Christ!*

Daniel the Prophet and John the Revelator

Saw in similar ways and displayed similar attributes of excellence, kindness, and love. They also each lived long lives. Daniel was a statesman prophet who powerfully was shown the future. John's revelation equally was shown the future. John, in many ways, complements what Daniel saw, even bringing about greater clarity.

Gad the Prophet and other seers

Served as King David's seer and did not hesitate to declare the words the Lord gave him for the king (2 Samuel 24:11). David had more than one seer (1 Chronicles 25:5; 2 Chronicles 29:25). The functions of a seer as indicated by this term included, besides receiving and reporting the word of the Lord, writing about David's reign (1 Chronicles 29:29); receiving and writing down visions (2 Chronicles 9:29); writing genealogical records under Rehoboam's reign (2 Chronicles 12:15).

It was not uncommon for kings to have groups of prophets around them. (1 Kings 22:22; 2 Chronicles 18:21-22). Prophets were designated from Israel (Ezekiel 13:2,4), Samaria (Jeremiah 23:13), and Jerusalem (Zephaniah 3:4).

Further, in an unusual development, David set aside some of the sons of Asaph, Heman, and Jeduthun to serve as prophets. Their prophesying was accompanied by musical instruments and possibly brought on and aided by them. This phenomenon is described mainly in 2 Chronicles (*see* 2 Chronicles 29:30).

Barnabas

A prophet. Imagine that the son of encouragement was also a prophet! Acts 13 gives us insight into this understanding.

MULTIFACETED PROPHETS

Now in the church that was at Antioch there were certain prophets and teachers: Barnabas, Simeon who was called Niger, Lucius of Cyrene, Manaen who had been brought up with Herod the tetrarch, and Saul.

—**Acts 13:1**

A point of interest is the phrase "certain prophets and teachers." Some commentators suggest it is probable that these were not distinct offices; both might be vested in the same persons—these were likely a group of teaching prophets!

WIDER SCOPE

Understanding that the office of the prophet carries a wider scope than simply prophesying is an important realization. It may surprise some that the primary role of prophets is not giving out prophetic words but involves so much more! In Acts 13, we see the example of teaching prophets.

Although revelation and speaking under the unction of the Holy Spirit is undoubtedly a distinct part of the office of the prophet, prophets move in more than one operation and gifting.

JUDAS AND SILAS

> *Then it pleased the apostles and elders, with the whole church, to send chosen men of their own company to Antioch with Paul and Barnabas, namely, Judas who was also named Barsabas, and Silas, leading men among the brethren.*
>
> —**Acts 15:22**

The interesting point is to see the way apostolic teams were sent out. Paul and Barnabas were apostles, yet we know from Acts 13 that Barnabas was a teaching prophet. It could be said that Barnabas operated with a major as a prophet who taught, and a minor in apostolic ministry. We will also see in a moment that Paul, being an apostle, was accompanied by prophets! Barnabas, Judas and Silas. The latter two had a unique ministry in the prophetic.

> We have therefore sent Judas and Silas, who will also report the same things by word of mouth.
>
> —Acts 15:27

Judas and Silas were prophets who would go out as messengers to make announcements or report on happenings.

> Now Judas and Silas, themselves being prophets also, exhorted and strengthened the brethren with many words.
>
> —Acts 15:32

The Acts 15:32 scripture also confirms these two are prophets, offering a glimpse of their ministry. They exhorted and strengthened the brethren with many words. Being that they were prophets lets us know that although they were saying encouraging words such as stories, testimonies, and direct personal encouragement to those listening, the word of knowledge is likely what is also meant here when it states *with many words*. These words were delivered in various ways. They were prophesying publicly to those who attended the church.

MAJORS AND MINORS

Understanding that no two gifts or operations are alike is essential, as God works through people in distinct and often unique manners. For example, a prophet may operate in *nabi*, or what some would call extemporaneous preaching. But they may also operate at times in *chazah*, or word of knowledge. One is a major based on them having an unction to work in one of the operations more frequently than any other. However, they may have a secondary operation, even a third and a fourth. Meaning, at the will of the Holy Spirit, any prophet can be used in all four of the operations.

PROPHETS CANNOT SEE THE FUTURE AT WILL

A point should be made that revelatory gifts involving the future are not something you can simply turn on. Allow me to explain a little further. A prophet cannot turn on visions, trances, or apocalyptic insights into the future. They must be shown. A point of danger is present when prophets attempt to see the future and venture where the Holy Spirit does not invite them.

SEEING AND SAYING

Having said that, there is a place where the prophetic can be turned on, similar to speaking in tongues. This is what I refer to as "seeing and saying." Much like extemporaneous preaching with *nabi* or the vision casting of *roeh*, *chazah* can be activated by faith on purpose. This is what word of knowledge looks like in operation.

ACCESSED BY FAITH

Over the many years of ministering prophetically to individuals, I have learned much, like speaking in tongues or praying for healing. The word of knowledge can be accessed by faith for whoever is standing in front of you.

Sometimes the information is profound, other times it is simple; nonetheless, word of knowledge can be used on demand. First Corinthians 14 deals with a whole congregation that prophesied. The gift they are operating in was the word of knowledge, and it was a prophetic operation that caused convincing and conviction due to the clarity and secrets of the heart that was revealed. Uniquely enough, it was all who were able to do this!

PROPHETS HEED ONE ANOTHER'S WORDS

In the first year of his reign I, Daniel, understood by the books the number of the years specified by the word of the Lord through Jeremiah the prophet, that He would accomplish seventy years in the desolations of Jerusalem.
—Daniel 9:2

Daniel was one of the greatest prophets of God in Scripture, and his life is an excellent example for all prophets. Daniel did the basics by looking into the Word of God and spending time in prayer. This combination keeps prophets on track!

A point of interest and importance is that Daniel took Jeremiah's prophecies literally! Not figuratively like so many cessationists or as preterism[13] teaches. Daniel was considering prophecies from the prophet Jeremiah. In Daniel 9, he references Jeremiah 25:12 as well as Jeremiah 29:10.

Mature prophetic figures should base everything on what the Word of God confirms and what the other prophets say. Prophets should never violate what the Spirit has shown them unless it violates the Bible. Yet humility is found in those who consider other voices for God!

WHAT PROPHETS DO

See, I have this day set you over the nations and over the kingdoms, to root out and to pull down, to destroy and to throw down, to build and to plant

—Jeremiah 1:10

Prophets build up, tear down, and call churches into action. They are anointed to speak to current and cultural issues in real time. The prophets are vital to a generation. They are anointed to do impossible missions.

Inasmuch as an excellent spirit, knowledge, understanding, interpreting dreams, solving riddles, and explaining enigmas were found in this Daniel, whom the king named Belteshazzar, now let Daniel be called, and he will give the interpretation.

—Daniel 5:12

Prophets solve enigmas like Daniel was gifted to accomplish.

*And He Himself gave some to be apostles, some prophets, some evangelists, and some pastors and teachers, [12] for the **equipping of the saints** for the work of ministry, for the **edifying of the body** of Christ.*

—Ephesians 4:11-12

A New Testament prophet will ultimately equip and edify the body of Christ. It is what they are called to do as a governing office. They, alongside the other fivefold ministry offices, are anointed to make the body of believers better!

APOSTLES ARE CHOSEN, PROPHETS ARE GROWN

This letter is from Paul, chosen by the will of God to be an apostle of Christ Jesus. I am writing to God's holy people in Ephesus, who are faithful followers of Christ Jesus.
—Ephesians 1:1 NLT

Anyone truly called to ministry is called; upon answering that call, they become chosen. However, when considering the offices of apostles and prophets, there seems to be a theme that apostles are chosen for work and set on a unique path toward it. Prophets are grown. It is as if they are called to a course of buffeting and hammering to get the desired result from them when they arrive at their destination. Similar things can be stated for anyone in ministry or following the call of God.

THE SECRET TO THE LIFE OF JOHN

However, there is a difference throughout the Old Testament in the way God dealt with the prophets and the way He waited until the end of John's life to unveil the revelation to him. What a profound thought that is. John was in his late 90s when the revelation was revealed to him. For many years, I have taught a message regarding the life of John called "The Secret to the Life of John." In this teaching, I cover the unique story arc of John in his mid-teen years when he followed Jesus. I address how John and his brother James went from being the sons of thunder, who said to Jesus, in Mark 10:37, "Grant us that we may sit, one on Your right hand and the other on Your left, in Your glory." Following this, Jesus replied by saying, "You do not know what you ask. Are you able to drink the cup that I drink, and be baptized with the baptism that I am baptized with?' They said to Him, 'We are able'" (*see* Mark 10:28-39). The other disciples were irritated by those brothers for having the gall to ask such a question!

John and James were the ones who requested Jesus to call fire down on the Samaritans and were rebuked by Jesus for thinking that way (*see* Luke 9:54).

Several decades later, James did drink the cup Jesus prophetically mentioned to them, and it killed James. Not John, however; he lived! Even when boiled in oil (which was his version of drinking the cup) at Emperor Domitian's command.

It is my firm belief that it was John's revelation of God's love for him that caused him to live long. He outlived the rest, he survived certain death, and he stepped into the highest prophetic experience in the Bible! All because of a revelation—he was the disciple whom the Lord loved!

John reached his late 90s, possibly beyond, and it was at this time that the office of the prophet came into full force in his life. He penned Revelation! Arguably the most prophetic book of the Bible!

It isn't a doctrinal finality, but prophets are developed. Some possibly for one defining moment. The moment they were born for. Everything else in the journey was used as a fine-tuning for the one defining moment when they would hit a target ordained by God at the foundation of the world.

THE HOLY SPIRIT CALLED ME TO THE OFFICE

I remember the day so clearly when the Holy Spirit flooded my truck—seasonally, it was a long time in the wilderness, both figuratively and literally. We were in the high Rockies of Colorado at the time. I will never forget the words He said to me that day, "You know what I've called you to do." Not very profound when you read a simple sentence like that, but it was a roar of the Spirit to me!

The office of the prophet was a label I had little to no desire for. It wasn't appealing to me. After seeing the prophetic and what the popular idea of a prophet was in the Church—my interest was at an all-time low. It seemed better to me to go into business and really show the Church what giving looked like. However, once again, the Lord manifested Himself to me, and my journey culminated in a palpable moment of choice.

"You are called to be a prophet, Joseph"—is, in essence, what the Lord was saying to me. Every encounter leading to this moment was training. All the preceding challenges and victories developed under-standing. It became clear the Lord had placed a deposit in my life, and it was His appointed time to make a withdrawal—if I was willing.

At 18, a word was spoken over me about my calling into ministry. My journey was to be filled with preparation for leadership and, "To whom much was given, much would be required" (*see* Luke 12:48). Those words still impact me deeply.

Of course, I answered the Lord, *yes*. Then was overtaken by the Holy Spirit, and I screamed for about an hour under the power of God. It was unbelievable. I realized that was the small beginning of what I was to do. Many years have passed since then; and in my life, every day still points to destiny by His construct. Many challenges and hardships have helped me to stay on the path of developing, much like John the Son of Thunder, into John the Apostle of Love, and finally, John the Revelator. I greatly resonate with John.

PROPHETS ARE DIFFERENT

One day a dear friend and mentor told me, "You know, Joseph, you're different. Prophets are different." It was affectionate, but it still let me know that prophets sometimes do things in unique ways. In the following scripture passages, you will see how a prophet prophesied in a unique way and got himself in front of King Ahab. It resembles the way Nathan, the prophet, confronted David. Look at this story with me.

> *Meanwhile, the Lord instructed one of the group of prophets to say to another man, "Hit me!" But the man refused to hit the prophet. 36 Then the prophet told him, "Because you have not obeyed the voice of the Lord, a lion will kill you as soon as you leave me." And when he had gone, a lion did attack and kill him. 37 Then the prophet turned to another man and said, "Hit me!" So he struck the prophet and wounded him. 38 The prophet placed a bandage over his eyes to disguise himself and then waited beside the road for the king.*
>
> —1 Kings 20:35-38 NLT

Here we see one of the sons of the prophets asking his neighbor to strike him. The neighbor refused. In response, the prophet then predicted that a lion would kill him for disobeying the voice of the Lord—and a lion did kill the man!

The prophet then commanded another man to strike him, and he did. The wounded prophet then went to Ahab in disguise and, not unlike Nathan, who, although was not in disguise, met with David under a hidden pretense (*see* 2 Samuel 12:1-31). This prophet met with King Ahab and told a story of a man he was obligated to keep or forfeit his life. He told the story that he'd let the man escape. As a result, Ahab judged him accordingly.

The prophet removed his disguise and predicted that Ahab would be punished for not executing Ben-Hadad (see 1 Kings 20:39-43). Uniquely, Ahab thus passed the sentence on himself as David did.

This is one isolated example from Scripture showing that prophets are unique creatures! In the New Covenant, without a proper hermeneutic or healthy explanation of both apostles and prophets, they can easily be misunderstood or, even worse, misidentified.

Misidentification is tragic on a few fronts. One is that the body is missing out on some of the most excellent ministry offices due to a lack of teaching or simply an insufficient understanding of the topic. Additionally, the other fivefold ministry will miss out on the highest and best Jesus provided for His Church when He ascended.

PASTORS DON'T MAKE PROPHETS

As we say, prophets don't make teachers; and pastors and teachers don't make prophets. Instead, teachers make teachers, and prophets make prophets. The difficulty we have had often is that pastors and teachers have tried to raise office gifts unlike themselves without the experience, authority, or Holy Ghost unction to do so.

This creates a dysfunctional government in the body. For example, pastors and teachers automatically assume and call someone a prophet because someone moves in a prophetic word of knowledge—this is an error. Why? Because when we mislabel office gifts in the body, it brings dilution and confusion to the real thing.

HIERARCHY IS NOT GOD'S PLAN

We then end up with a dysfunctional governmental structure. Another side to this that is very unhealthy is creating a hierarchy out of the offices; this also should not be!

Someone might say, "Oh brother, this is not a big deal if we rightly identify these offices! Who cares? It's not a big deal." Well, it was a big deal to the early Church.

APOSTLES AUTHORITY

The only governmental gift that has real authority to raise up the other four gifts is the apostle. The highest form of raising up the governmental church structure is through the teamwork of the apostle and the prophet. Why? Because the Bible says so!

> *Having been built on the foundation of the apostles and prophets, Jesus Christ Himself being the chief cornerstone.*
> **—Ephesians 2:20**

This references the first 12 gifts and then onward and speaks of the foundation that the Church is built on.

My journey has been one of riding the roller coaster of extremes and imbalances only to arrive at the destination, which states God's system is best!

What we see in our church structure today is primarily made up of traditionalism. Meaning pastors are the highest authority in the body, and this has been a result of not handling the Word of God rightly. I believe God honors faith, and pastors have had the intense job of making up for nearly all the other office gifts in the body. Pastors should be *celebrated* more than any government gift because of their strength and faithfulness.

However, if we were building the Church the way the New Testament prescribes, we would have things more functional and in better order.

HOW PROPHETS ARE CALLED—
FOUR WITNESSES

I can do nothing on my own. I judge as God tells me. Therefore, my judgment is just, because I carry out the will of the one who sent me, not my own will. [31] *If I were to testify on my own behalf, my testimony would not be valid.* [32] *But someone else is also testifying about me, and I assure you that everything he says about me is true.* [33] *In fact, you sent investigators to listen to John the Baptist, and his testimony about me was true.* [34] *Of course, I have no need of human witnesses, but I say these things so you might be saved.* [35] *John was like a burning and shining lamp, and you were excited for a while about his message.* [36] *But I have a greater witness than John—my teachings and my miracles. The Father gave me these works to accomplish, and they prove that he sent me.* [37] *And the Father who sent me has testified about me himself. You have never heard his voice or seen him face to face,* [38] *and you do not have his message in your hearts, because you do not believe me—the one he sent to you.* [39] *You search the Scriptures because you think they give you eternal life. But the Scriptures point to me!*

—John 5:30-39 NLT

FOUR QUALIFICATIONS OF BEING CALLED BY GOD

These qualifications can be applied to any fivefold calling. The prophet is very important as the call can be subjective. These four points (taken from John 5:31-39) to the calling of Jesus serve as a good standard and qualification for a calling:

1. *Know* that God has called you. No one can take this from you unless you willingly surrender it!

2. *Voice of authority* bears witness that you are called. A proven leader to confirm the call.

3. *Works*—a specific function in the body. You carry yoke-breaking power in your gift!

4. *Word of God*—You possess the Word of God in you, bearing witness to your calling. No Word, no lasting results!

SPIRITUAL SONS OF THE PROPHETS

Prophets ultimately are to develop a fathering anointing and will often attract sons and daughters. This is displayed in the spirit of Elijah.

> *Look, I am sending you the prophet Elijah before the great and dreadful day of the Lord arrives.* [6] *His preaching will turn the hearts of fathers to their children, and the hearts of children to their fathers. Otherwise, I will come and strike the land with a curse.*
>
> **—Malachi 4:5-6 NLT**

In the Old Testament, there are several references to the *"sons of the prophets,"* a phrase indicating bands or companies of prophets, *"son"* in this case meaning a member. Another term for this was the "school of the prophets."

Prophets have a distinct calling from God for the body of Christ and the world. However, Moses made a statement that shows the heart of God:

> *Two men, Eldad and Medad, had stayed behind in the camp. They were listed among the elders, but they had not gone out to the Tabernacle. Yet the Spirit rested upon them as well, so they prophesied there in the camp.* [27] *A young man ran and reported to Moses, "Eldad and Medad are prophesying in the camp!"* [28] *Joshua son of Nun, who had been Moses' assistant since his youth, protested, "Moses, my master, make them stop!"* [29] *But Moses replied, "Are you jealous for my sake? I wish that all the Lord's people were prophets and that the Lord would put his Spirit upon them all!"*
>
> **— Numbers 11:26-29 NLT**

Today we are the body of Christ, and you can prophesy to the level of any prophet. The difference is a prophet has a responsibility to fulfill, as Ephesians 4:11-12 says, *to edify, equip,* and *father* believers in the body!

CHAPTER TWENTY

A PROPHET'S REWARD

He who receives a prophet in the name of a prophet shall receive a prophet's reward....

—**Matthew 10:41**

The days are approaching when God's people will need a revelation of His supernatural provision, unlike any time in modern history. Woven throughout the biblical narrative are moments in time of great difficulty and significant intervention. God has used prophets to create an avenue of supernatural provision, protection, and guidance, which interrupted dark agendas being marshaled against His people.

EZEKIEL AND THE VALLEY OF DRY BONES

God will speak through His prophets to release His word, for His Voice is a multiplier. Ezekiel 37 speaks of the valley of dry bones. God asked Ezekiel what he saw, then commanded him to prophesy to the bones as He commanded.

With each prophetic command, an advancement of life transpired. Finally, an exceedingly great army stood before the prophet.

A MAN OR WOMAN WITH A REVELATION FROM GOD IS NEVER AT THE MERCY OF A CULTURE GONE MAD!

Prophets in the right place, at the right time, and under the instruction of God will cause life and stand against darkness, death, and destruction. Power takes place when the Voice of God comes through the office gift to declare a way where it all seems impossible.

Prophets walk in revelation; and remember, a man or woman with a revelation from God is never at the mercy of a culture gone mad!

Being aligned with a legitimate prophet will cause an increase. For the Voice of God is a multiplier and *calls those things which be not as though they are* (*see* Romans 4:17). Prophets walk in an office that demonstrates this.

THE PROPHET'S REWARD

The "prophet's reward" can be a number of things. Some commentators suggest it is a teacher giving a lesson or a preacher giving out a great sermon. Although the commentators may be partially correct, they are incomplete as in context; Matthew 10:41 doesn't only say prophets, it also speaks of a righteous man's reward.

> He who receives you receives Me, and he who receives Me
> receives Him who sent Me. [41] He who receives a prophet
> in the name of a prophet shall receive a prophet's reward.
> And he who receives a righteous man in the name of a
> righteous man shall receive a righteous man's reward. [42]
> And whoever gives one of these little ones only a cup of

cold water in the name of a disciple, assuredly, I say to
you, he shall by no means lose his reward.

—Matthew 10:40-42

REWARDS ASSOCIATED WITH SPECIFIC INDIVIDUALS

There are more than one classification of a reward as it relates to a specific individual. When the text is specific to a certain individual, it is pointing to a reward based on who that individual is and the honor they receive. When it says prophet, it means prophet. When it says righteous man, it means righteous man. When the text says in the name of a disciple, that is what it means.

We will focus on the prophet *in the name of a prophet*. In other words, for the prophet's reward to engage, they must first be honored and received as a legitimate prophet.

HONOR ENGAGES THE PROPHET'S REWARD

It should be said honor is what engages the prophet's reward. To the *level* honor is given to the office will likely be the same *level* of reward that will come through the office in return.

And he said to him, "Look now, there is in this city a
man of God, and **he is an honorable man;** *all that he*
says surely comes to pass. So let us go there; perhaps he
can show us the way that we should go." [7] Then Saul said
to his servant, "But look, if we go, what shall we bring the

man? For the bread in our vessels is all gone, and there is no present to bring to the man of God. What do we have?"

⁸ And the servant answered Saul again and said, "Look, I have here at hand one-fourth of a shekel of silver. I will give that to the man of God, to tell us our way." ⁹ (Formerly in Israel, when a man went to inquire of God, he spoke thus: "Come, let us go to the seer"; for he who is now called a prophet was formerly called a seer.) ¹⁰ Then Saul said to his servant, "Well said; come, let us go." So, they went to the city where the man of God was.

—1 Samuel 9:6-10

Saul heard of a seer who could tell what he needed to know about his lost donkeys. The seer prophet that Saul went to find was Samuel. Notice how they brought a gift with them. It was what they had. Not to buy a prophecy, as that is always wrong, and anyone who teaches you must give to receive a prophetic word is also wrong.

SAMUEL'S OBEDIENCE SAVES ISRAEL

Earlier, Samuel's obedience radically saved Israel from a military take-over! It is an interesting discovery that only a few chapters before this moment shows Samuel giving sacrifices to the Lord as the Philistines were preparing to invade the land! A major but often overlooked point is that as the Philistines began to move in—God interrupted their army!

Now when the Philistines heard that the children of Israel had gathered together at Mizpah, the lords of the Philistines went up against Israel. And when the children of

Israel heard of it, they were afraid of the Philistines. ⁸ So the children of Israel said to Samuel, "Do not cease to cry out to the Lord our God for us, that He may save us from the hand of the Philistines." ⁹ And Samuel took a suckling lamb and offered it as a whole burnt offering to the Lord. Then Samuel cried out to the Lord for Israel, and the Lord answered him. ¹⁰ Now as Samuel was offering up the burnt offering, the Philistines drew near to battle against Israel. But the Lord thundered with a loud thunder upon the Philistines that day, and so confused them that they were overcome before Israel.

—**1 Samuel 7:7-10**

THE LORD THUNDERED ON THE PHILISTINES

This fulfilled a prophecy spoken by Samuel's mother, Hannah, in 1 Samuel 2:10, saying, "The adversaries of the Lord shall be broken in pieces; from heaven He will thunder against them."

Historian Josephus said God responded to the Philistines with lightning, which flashed in their faces, and shook their weapons out of their hands so that they fled disarmed, and with an earthquake that caused gaps in the earth, into which they fell. The Philistines were disturbed, frightened, and thrown into confusion and disorder. Many of them were destroyed by this thundering of God against them.

The Philistines were smitten before Israel, meaning even though the Philistines fled before Israel, it was not Israel who killed them! Before Israel could even come out against them to fight with them, the Philistines were smitten and destroyed, many of them by the thunder and lightning and by the earth opening upon them and devouring them![14]

When God thundered, I can only imagine the enemy's face being lit up with flashes of lighting, and when God roared at them, it sounded like thunder, much like Sinai. Can you imagine it? If there was lightning and the ground was opening to swallow the enemies each time He thundered, I imagine every time He spoke—boulders and rocks must have exploded at His thunderous roar! It must have been terrifying for anyone near this display of God's jealousy over His people!

Again, this is part of the prophet's reward—intense levels of protection.

GOD'S BEST WAS TO RULE THROUGH SAMUEL

God was the overseer of Israel, and working with His prophet Samuel the foreign enemies didn't stand a chance! As shocking as this might be, it was God's best and highest desire to work with the prophet and His nation directly. God didn't want to put a king over the nation. He wanted to be their God and lead the people through His prophet!

Sadly, it was the nation and the people who cried out for a king. They wanted kingly representation like the other heathen nations, to have a king go to battle on their behalf.

Amazing and tragic that God offered His best and was their greatest Defender, yet the human heart desires to trust in their own mechanisms. Even more astonishing is that God told Samuel to tell the people what it would cost them to have a king rather than to have Him rule with a prophet, and they still chose to go the way of the heathen nations.

A GLIMPSE OF THE PROPHET'S REWARD

A glimpse of the prophet's reward is in this narrative. God working through the office of the prophet caused national protection and provision. The people honored Samuel, and Samuel honored God. Resulting in God Himself thundering against the enemy of His people!

Think what could have been if the people had continued with God ruling the nation with the prophet and the reward working for them? It is likely they would have been an unstoppable force of protection and provision, unlike anything in Scripture. The prophet's reward would have been immense protection and provision over the nation. Receiving Samuel as a prophet whom God ordained would have continued the intense protection by God Himself, just as when He stopped the Philistines by thunder!

After the events of God and the prophet stopping the invasion of Israel, the people requested a king—God gave them what they wanted. A powerful lesson can be learned here. That God sometimes will answer the requests of His people even if it is not entirely what He wants. What an amazing God we serve.

PRAYER

Dear reader, let's pray right now that our desires line up with His desires!

> *Lord, I pray that You would reveal to us more and more what Your desires are for us as Your Church and for our nation. Open the Scripture to us in a new way. We ask for a heightened sensitivity to Your Spirit regarding such matters. We ask this right now in Jesus' name.*

SOWING WITH PROPER MOTIVE INDUCES REWARD

Sowing has to do with the heart, not the amounts given. Honor when it comes to sowing always has to do with motive and what the gift means to the one giving it.

IF IT DOESN'T MEAN MUCH TO THE GIVER, IT MIGHT NOT HAVE MUCH IMPACT WITH GOD.

However, if what you give gets your attention, you are more likely to engage the reward. Why is that? Because what you sow has to do with the heart. If your heart is moved, you will know it! You will also know when you have been truly generous, as you will not forget the offering you gave for some time! It will stick with you in your heart!

RADICAL GIVING

Many times, Heather and I have emptied our entire bank accounts to give to a man or woman of God in this manner, specifically into the office of the prophet, which has induced tremendous results over the years. We had sown when there was zero backup and no promise of anything coming in after we gave it all away.

SOWING ACTIVATES GOD'S ECONOMY

Once when we were in a meeting where we received a prophetic impartation, we gave the last of what we had and even added to it when we had more finances come into our hands following the meeting. It was at that same time we gave our car away! We were giving so much during those days that we received ridicule for doing so. We had an awakening to giving, and it was vital to us that we acted on it. God's economy is activated by sowing.

YOU CANNOT OUTGIVE GOD

We were broke during those days but had a revelation of honor through giving and would always hear, "You can't outgive God!" I said, "True, but it seems most people never try." We weren't being impulsive or reckless; we legitimately had meditated on giving with honor so much that it changed our lives!

On one occasion, we had one hundred dollars to our name. We made the agreement that if either of us decided to give, we wouldn't even check with the other. In this particular meeting, with hundreds of people in attendance, I was overcome with the desire to sow everything we had. I looked to my right to see if Heather was in agreement, and when I did, she wasn't there! She was already walking with a check!

This was one of those churches with security that looks like the secret service, which I am very appreciative for because they keep us safe at times today!

HEATHER'S RISKY OFFERING

As Heather was walking up the middle aisle with the check in her hand, I remember thinking to myself, *You're too far, too close to the front!* I looked down from the balcony I was seated in when the thought came to me, *Oh wow, babe. They're going to take you down. You're going down, yup, they're going to put you on the floor.* There was no way for me to get to her in time to stop her from walking all the way up on stage! So, my little fiery wife boldly walked to the front in this huge meeting, ascended the platform stairs, and slapped our check on the podium!

No one took her down! She sowed our last hundred dollars; and following that, a person came up to us and gave us a few hundred dollars. In the same period, we found ourselves down to our last dollar and 50 cents. So we decided to sow it into the wealthiest people we knew in the prophetic and who supported the prophetic! We did so, and it was a powerful moment.

SOWING AND REWARD

Not long after that season, we began to have resources and cars. The time came when we graduated from giving one hundred dollars—which was a lot of money—to regularly give one thousand dollars, which was an unbelievable stretch of faith in those days.

I remember giving a prophet a good portion of money for a motorcycle that he really wanted during that time. It blessed me to do it, and seeing the joy come to his face when he realized he would be able to attain that bike was priceless.

We kept giving from what we didn't have until we arrived at a place of being able to give much larger amounts. We came to the place of being able to give tens of thousands of dollars when we didn't have it to give. We bought new cars for people even when it was hard to do so because money was tight. However, we would do anything the Lord prompted us to do.

We graduated into sowing far more than we could have ever imagined, and we have done it over and over again with honor. We know it has been through radical giving that meant something to us, each time, to such a level that we would sweat from concern and yet rejoice at the same time!

GOD, YOU HAVE A PROBLEM!

We came to the place in our giving journey that if the Lord tells us to give, we don't flinch. When we have issues, we give or tithe against the value of the issue, and say, "Wow, looks like You have a problem, God!" Often saying, "If that were my problem, I'm not sure what I would do, but thankfully it's Yours!"

We mean it when we say that. When we sow in the middle of difficulty, we are intentionally making God responsible for the problem we are facing.

PROPHETS CARRY INCREASE

We learned that certain ministries have much more increase on them than others, especially the office of the prophet. It might shock you to realize that prophetic ministry isn't just those who stand up and make predictions about what is to come. It isn't always about those who can prophesy to people on an individual level.

Sometimes the office of the prophet is a ministry that broadcasts or has a voice and a special message for this season. Prophets may have pastored, they may even pastor today, but they are typically ones who do the impossible after intense seasons of persecution. Prophets mobilize the troops and give marching orders. They deliver notably powerful teaching as well as revelatory insights.

Sowing into a fully operational prophetic office with honor and joy, will cause the prophet's reward to engage. We learned this, and it has been life changing.

ALL SOIL IS NOT THE SAME

All the giving is from a heart of honor and a desire to sow into God's economy. The most potent seed we have ever sowed was into the legitimate office of the prophet, working in faith and flowing in the legitimate power of God. Giving to prophets who have a revelation about increase and are massive givers themselves. Remember, all soil is not the same. When we have given under the leading of the Spirit into the right kind of soil, with our hearts in the right place, there has been explosive results in our lives and ministry!

Through our radical giving, we have had two vehicles given to us on the same day. Property and houses paid for, monetary miracles with buildings, and open doors of opportunity.

Supernatural resources have arrived repeatedly right when we needed them for what God has called us to do. When you give in an unbridled way, you will see unbridled response and blessing overtake you.

A giving heart toward the right soil, such as true prophetic ministry, can open a reward of the prophet's word to you, as well as other miraculous provisions!

THE ANOINTING TO MULTIPLY

Prophets are representatives of the Voice of God. They carry a unique anointing to do the impossible. When you sow into it with honor, impossible breakthroughs can happen in your life. Prophets carry an anointing for supernatural multiplication.

> *Then a man came from Baal Shalisha, and brought the man of God bread of the firstfruits, twenty loaves of barley bread, and newly ripened grain in his knapsack. And he said, "Give it to the people, that they may eat."* [43] *But his servant said, "What? Shall I set this before one hundred men?" He said again, "Give it to the people, that they may eat; for thus says the Lord: 'They shall eat and have some left over.'* [44] *"So he set it before them; and they ate and had some left over, according to the word of the Lord.*
>
> —2 Kings 4:42-44

One of the supernatural gifts God placed on the prophet is the anointing to multiply! When operated with purity, this is a potent force for the Kingdom of God. We see this in 2 Kings 4:42, as the man from Baal Shalisha, which was an area known for crops and having its harvest arrive before other areas.

WHAT BAAL SHALISHA REPRESENTS

Baal Shalisha represents:

1. Baal Shalisha represents a firstfruit offering placed at the feet of the prophet.

2. Baal was the god of selfish prosperity and mammon of the Old Testament. This offering was exchanging the wealth of the wicked to provide a miracle for the righteous.

The conduit was the prophet. When laid at his feet, the reward kicked in, and a miracle of multiplication transpired!

Jesus basically performed the same miracle when feeding the five thousand (*see* Matthew 14:13-21).

THE PROPHET'S REWARD IS A PROPHET'S RESPONSIBILITY

The prophet should have a mindset of *detachment* from offerings and personal monetary gain. Prophets must see themselves as a conduit, a servant by which God's people can benefit and receive the reward that comes through their vessel.

TRUE PROPHETS SOMETIMES SAY NO

At times, the prophet will need to say no to gifts and special favors. The prophet must also purpose in his own heart to be the most generous person people know. Extravagant generosity is the best way to stay clean in the area of monetary gain.

A prophet who gives aggressively is a prophet who will *break the demon of mammon* off of themselves and their ministry. This is also rich soil to sow into as it will produce a reward.

PERVERSION OF THE PROPHET'S REWARD

The desire for personal gain by Balaam is what the Bible refers to as the *error of Balaam*, who wasn't a true prophet of God. He was into occultic practices, as no true prophet would dare curse the children of God or teach others how to defeat them.

Some believe Balaam was related to or was connected to Jannes and Jambres, the two diviner false prophets who resisted Moses.

BALAAM LOVED MONEY

Balaam's twistedness was driven by the love of money. Loving money is one of the biggest downfalls for any minister, or person for that matter.

When ministries use gimmicks for giving, such as a vial of water from some river, for sowing, etc., that is not the prophet's reward in action. As said earlier, if any supposed prophet says send X amount of money and you will get a prophecy in return, they are a false prophet.

How a prophet handles the blessing of the reward on their life is a serious matter. False prophets sensationalize and merchandise on the prophet's reward. That is a very dangerous place to be.

MONEY ALONE IS A TOOL—MAMMON IS THE LOVE OF MONEY

No one can serve two masters; for either he will hate the one and love the other, or else he will be loyal to the one and despise the other. You cannot serve God and mammon.

—Matthew 6:24

THE DEVIL DOESN'T HAVE THE ANOINTING, SO HE USES MONEY

In my book *Breaking Hell's Economy*, I deal extensively with the topic of mammon:

> Mammon is a spirit, and it is the love of money. It takes hold of people and causes them to do whatever they must to get money. Mammon is evil, and it is the currency of hell's economy. It is a powerful revelation once you understand that the devil cannot operate under the anointing or through God's supernatural power of the Holy Spirit. He cannot function in the blessing; therefore, his substitute is mammon! He has enticed mankind to fall in love with money, which is a simple definition of mammon. Mammon creates a self-reliance that cuts God out of the picture and places self on the throne of your provision. This is the foundation of hell's economy.

The prophet's reward is a potent force used by the Holy Spirit to destroy the bondage to mammon. Prophets have a hatred for the love of money! By revelation, the spirit of faith will rise up through legitimate prophets (who live what they preach) and teach on supernatural provision—and a breakthrough of resources will happen.

Real prophets understand the difference between the blessing and mammon. Proverbs 10:22 says, "The blessing of the Lord makes one rich, and He adds no sorrow with it." Preaching and radical giving induced by the prophet will break people into God's economy!

TAX MIRACLE

Jesus was more than a prophet; but when He spoke instruction like a prophet and those around Him listened to Him and responded, there was a reward. Taxes were paid by a prophetic miracle!

> *Nevertheless, lest we offend them, go to the sea, cast in a hook, and take the fish that comes up first. And when you have opened its mouth, you will find a piece of money; take that and give it to them for Me and you.*
>
> —Matthew 17:27

DEBT FREEDOM

> *But as one was cutting down a tree, the iron ax head fell into the water; and he cried out and said, "Alas, master! For it was borrowed.* [6] *So the man of God said, "Where did it fall?" And he showed him the place. So he cut off a stick, and threw it in there; and he made the iron float.*
>
> —2 Kings 6:5-6

One day a worker was cutting down a tree, and the iron head of his ax fell into the water. The man had a borrowed ax! He was in debt to the lender with potentially serious ramifications. Elisha did a prophetic act of faith and supernaturally resolved the man's debt! The prophet's reward has a debt-release ability!

SOWING IS BEST RESPONSE TO TROUBLE OR CRISIS

The prophet's reward is to be delivered supernaturally from lack in the middle of hardship or famine.

> So he arose and went to Zarephath. And when he came to the gate of the city, indeed a widow was there gathering sticks. And he called to her and said, "Please bring me a little water in a cup, that I may drink." [11] And as she was going to get it, he called to her and said, "Please bring me a morsel of bread in your hand." [12] So she said, "As the Lord your God lives, **I do not have bread, only a handful of flour in a bin, and a little oil in a jar; and see, I am gathering a couple of sticks that I may go in and prepare it for myself and my son, that we may eat it, and die.**" [13] And Elijah said to her, "Do not fear; go and do as you have said, but **make me a small cake from it first**, and bring it to me; and afterward make some for yourself and your son. [14] For thus says the Lord God of Israel: '**The bin of flour shall not be used up, nor shall the jar of oil run dry, until the day the Lord sends rain on the earth.**'" [15] So she went away and did according to the word of Elijah; and she and he and her household ate for many days. [16] **The bin of**

flour was not used up, nor did the jar of oil run dry, according to the word of the Lord which He spoke by Elijah. ¹⁷ *Now it happened after these things that **the son of the woman who owned the house became sick.** And his sickness was so serious that there was no breath left in him.* ¹⁸ *So she said to Elijah, "What have I to do with you, O man of God? Have you come to me to bring my sin to remembrance, and to kill my son?"* ¹⁹ *And he said to her, "Give me your son." So he took him out of her arms and carried him to the upper room where he was staying, and laid him on his own bed.* ²⁰ *Then he cried out to the Lord and said, "O Lord my God, have You also brought tragedy on the widow with whom I lodge, by killing her son?"* ²¹ *And he stretched himself out on the child three times, and cried out to the Lord and said, "O Lord my God, I pray, let this child's soul come back to him."* ²² *Then the Lord heard the voice of Elijah; and **the soul of the child came back to him, and he revived. And Elijah took the child and brought him down from the upper room into the house and gave him to his mother.*** ²³ *And Elijah said, "See, your son lives!"* ²⁴ *Then the woman said to Elijah, "Now by this I know that you are a man of God, and that the word of the Lord in your mouth is the truth."*

—1 Kings 17:10-24

Such a powerful example of the prophet's reward. Elijah requested that the woman give him the last of her food in the middle of a famine! It was her act of obedience that engaged the prophet's reward causing miracle provision for both her and her son!

Additionally, we see that a second reward came through the prophet when the widow's son died, and the prophet brought him back to life.

All of this was due to the widow of Zarephath giving a sacrificial offering to the prophet! The reward kept coming.

ELISHA AND THE PROPHET'S REWARD

This is mirrored in the story of Elisha in 2 Kings 4 with another widow who was in debt, and the creditor was coming to take away her two sons. Interestingly, in the story, there was a miracle where oil continued to flow from as many jars as the woman brought. The moment she stopped with the jars was the moment the oil stopped flowing. There is a word in this somewhere that suggests to us the prophet's reward will continue operating according to what you bring and by your faith. Had she kept bringing jars, the oil would have likely continued filling them!

Elisha also brought back the life of the Shulamite woman's son. Again mirroring what Elijah did years beforehand.

THE PROPHET'S REWARD
FOREWARNS CALAMITY

And in these days prophets came from Jerusalem to Antioch. ²⁸ Then one of them, named Agabus, stood up and showed by the Spirit that there was going to be a great famine throughout all the world, which also happened in the days of Claudius Caesar. ²⁹ Then the disciples, each according to his ability, determined to send relief to the brethren dwelling in Judea. ³⁰ This they also did, and sent it to the elders by the hands of Barnabas and Saul.

—Acts 11:27-30

Part of the prophet's reward is to see evil coming and prepare for it. In the case of Agabus, the people heard the word he shared and made provision for the coming famine! They didn't tremble. Rather they acted.

> *A prudent man foresees evil and hides himself, but the simple pass on and are punished.*
>
> **—Proverbs 22:3**

When you release what you possess into the Kingdom, the possibilities for what God can do become limitless. It takes supernatural empowerment to accomplish everything you are purposed to do in God's design. This does not happen by chance. We all have an active part in causing our lives to move forward.

In the areas of increase, it takes place through our giving, seeking first the Kingdom with what we possess. Hebrews 7:8 says, "Here mortal men receive tithes, but there he receives them, of whom it is witnessed that he lives." This means we first give in the natural, but in the supernatural, there is a corresponding action. When we choose to make it a priority to be a consistent giver, that corresponding action in the supernatural begins to spill over into our natural world.

IF YOU ENGAGE THE PROPHET'S REWARD, YOU ARE ENGAGING IN A SUPERNATURAL REACTION!

The prophet's reward is only one part of God's provision plan, much like a miracle worker who releases healing or a miraculous event in your life. The prophet's reward is supplemental to walking in the blessing of the Lord through sowing.

So they rose early in the morning and went out into the Wilderness of Tekoa; and as they went out, Jehoshaphat stood and said, "Hear me, O Judah and you inhabitants of Jerusalem: **Believe in the Lord your God, and you shall be established; believe His prophets, and you shall prosper."**

—2 Chronicles 20:20

DE-INSTITUTIONALIZING A REVELATION

For thus says the Lord to the men of Judah and Jerusalem: "Break up your fallow ground, and do not sow among thorns."

—Jeremiah 4:3

Prophetic voices and prophets are called to remind the institutions of their first love. There are those of an older wineskin who cannot discover their generation's present truth. These are bound by institutionalism—prophets are called to break them out!

If the cause is too small, men will fight.
If the cause is big enough, men will unite.

Breathing life into institutions is one of the things prophets are called to do. Leaders and those looking for a word from God are the primary assignments of prophets! They do this by whatever gift God has assigned them to function in. Each generation needs to be reminded of their destiny and the end game. Prophets have an anointing to rally the troops. This can be done by the influence of the leaders they speak to, and it may be accomplished by the platform they stand on. However, they know, like William Wallace or other cultural icons, that *if it's too small, men will fight. If it's big enough, men will unite!*

TRIBES THAT LEAD TO MOVEMENTS

Then the Lord put forth His hand and touched my mouth, and the Lord said to me: "Behold, I have put My words in your mouth. [10] *See, I have this day set you over the nations and over the kingdoms, to root out and to pull down, to destroy and to throw down, to build and to plant."*

—**Jeremiah 1:9-10**

The office of the prophet is anointed to step in by the word of the Lord, and depending on the station given them, may be set over nations and kingdoms. The office of the prophet has an anointing *to root out and to pull down, to destroy and to throw down, to build and to plant,* which involves speaking and arranging things by the word of the Lord.

Identifying those in tribes and certain circles with a prophetic unction to build activates a catalyst for merging tribes into movements. *Roeh* prophets do this, and in each generation present, truth is brought forward by appointed voices to cause a generational movement. This generation is no different!

BREAKING UP FALLOW GROUND

Prophets expose things, sometimes by simply being present. It is part of the anointing God placed on them. Certain ones don't like prophets as they are repulsed by the sense of exposure they carry. Many times, in my experience, when people have hidden agendas or rebellion in their hearts, they can do and say all the right things to everyone, it seems, but the prophetic flushes out what is inside them. Often, they don't even know why they are acting in a certain manner. They might have a sense of anger or dread being around a prophetic person. This is something I have encountered many times with hidden agendas people carry. It doesn't matter how nice or kind you are to them. They will have an issue with the true prophetic anointing.

In order to break up hard *ground* and see a move of God, the prophet will sometimes be in the midst of those who are gatekeepers to allow the Spirit to move or quench that move. Through the words they give or by the anointing, they move in. What begins to happen is the fallow ground becomes challenged. It will either persecute the prophet or reformer, or the ground will yield, repent, and begin walking in humility.

Going back to the trance I had in 1997, which I shared in Chapter 18, when taken to the landscape covered in concrete, it was the seed that broke up the concrete or fallow ground. The seed is both the Word of God mixed with faith and the prophetic word I was to say by the unction of the Holy Spirit. Much like Ezekiel 37, who prophesied as he was commanded and dry bones came to life, my trance was a Holy Spirit command to break up the stony hearts of men. That is what fallow ground represents, the non-fertile and hardened ground. A word spoken in due season through teaching, prophecy, or correction breaks up the fallow ground.

Rebellion or other hidden issues will not be comfortable with true prophetic anointing. Why? Because the spirit of prophecy is the testimony of Jesus and will oppose anything that is not of the Spirit of God.

DE-INSTITUTIONALIZING THE FIRST LOVE

Nevertheless I have this against you, that you have left your first love.

—Revelation 2:4

It begins with those in places of authority getting a now word. Prophets help with this. The devil knew he could not beat the Church, so he did the next best thing—he joined it! One of the tactics he implemented was that he denominated the nation—he persuaded the one body of Christ to split apart into denominations. Again, *if it is too small, men fight*. Denominations were created based on what we all disagree about. Rather than uniting over what we agree on.

TIMES OF REFRESHING

Repent therefore and be converted, that your sins may be blotted out, so that times of refreshing may come from the presence of the Lord.

—**Acts 3:19**

As prophetic people, we are called to bring times of refreshing from the Spirit to institutions and those in them, which have become dry and fallow. These have married a method, yet the Holy Spirit will bring new wine in and disrupt the method with the present truth or now word He wants to be manifested.

Those who deeply value and understand times of refreshing from the Lord are those who have walked through the most difficult times. Rejection and betrayal, having every reason to act out in the flesh, yet choose not to out of reverence for God and His Word.

This is the way God put it: "They found grace out in the desert, these people who survived the killing. Israel, out looking for a place to rest, met God out looking for them!" God told them, "I've never quit loving you and never will. Expect love, love, and more love! And so now I'll start over with you and build you up again, dear virgin Israel. You'll resume your singing, grabbing tambourines and joining the dance. You'll go back to your old work of planting vineyards on the Samaritan hillsides, and sit back and enjoy the fruit—oh, how you'll enjoy those harvests! The time's coming when watchmen will call out from the hilltops of Ephraim: 'On your feet! Let's go to Zion, go to meet our God!'"

—Jeremiah 31:2-6
The Message

The Lord appeared to him from afar, saying, "I have loved you with an everlasting love; Therefore I have drawn you with lovingkindness. ⁴ Again I will build you and you will be rebuilt, O virgin of Israel! Again you will take up your tambourines, and go forth to the dances of the merrymakers. ⁵ Again you will plant vineyards on the hills of Samaria; the planters will plant and will enjoy them. ⁶ For there will be a day when watchmen on the hills of Ephraim call out, 'Arise, and let us go up to Zion, to the Lord our God.'"

—Jeremiah 31:3-6
NASB1977

OUTCASTS TURNED INTO BROADCASTS

Regardless of where you are in your journey, what you have survived, or how you are searching for the significance God has called you to, remember, wherever you are—God is out searching for you! He wants you to hear His Voice even more than you want to. The scriptures from Jeremiah 31 have given me great hope over the years that God was looking for me to complete the assignment no matter where I was in the journey. He is always speaking, but the question is, are we listening?

> *For I know the thoughts that I think toward you, says the Lord, thoughts of peace and not of evil, to give you a future and a hope.*
>
> **—Jeremiah 29:11**

You have a design, purpose, and prophetic plan God has marked in you since the foundation of the world. Your life is not an accident! He assigned you to be here. Right now is the most crucial time of your life! What is God saying to you? Where are you headed? Who do you belong with? These questions are all vital to understand and resolve.

> *So Jesus answered and said, "Assuredly, I say to you, there is no one who has left house or brothers or sisters or father or mother or wife or children or lands, for My sake and the gospel's, [30] who shall not receive a hundredfold now in this time—houses and brothers and sisters and mothers and children and lands, with persecutions—and in the age to come, eternal life."*
>
> **—Mark 10:29-30**

When you specifically give it all up for the Kingdom, He will make your life increase, and the anointing to take territory will follow you all the days of your life. Persecution may come, but it is only practice for the assignment God gave you to accomplish. As you give up, to go up, remember you are developing your expression of faith!

DEVELOPING THE EXPRESSION OF YOUR FAITH

> *But without faith it is impossible to please Him, for he who comes to God must believe that He is, and that He is a rewarder of those who diligently seek Him.*
>
> **—Hebrews 11:6**

Grasping your expression of faith will empower you to know the will of God and continue taking territory by His leading. Your expression of faith is what God has called you to do. Much of it doesn't come by head knowledge and mental ascent. Instead, it comes by hearing the Word of God until it begins speaking back to you on the inside.

WHAT IS AN EXPRESSION OF FAITH?

Consider all the heroes of faith who went before us. Each expressed their faith in response to what God called them to do. Let's look at a few of these heroes straight out of Hebrews 11, which has been affectionately called the "Hebrews Hall of Faith."

+ *If you asked Abel what faith is, he would say to offer God an excellent sacrifice.*

+ *If you asked Enoch what faith is, he would say to walk so close with God that He will take you away!*

+ *If you asked Noah what faith is, he would say to build an ark!*

+ *If you asked Abraham what faith is, he would say to leave home, go to a land you yet know about, and be the father of many nations!*

+ *If you asked Sarah what faith is, it would be to have a child when you are way too old to have a child!*

+ *If you asked Joseph what faith is, it would be to give instruction about his bones, knowing they were all leaving bondage one day! (See Genesis 50:25.)*

+ *Joshua would tell you it is a wall falling!*

+ *Moses would say it is forsaking the system of Egypt for a better promise!*

+ *Others would say it is to be cut in half, not denying their God!*

We could talk exhaustively about what faith is to individuals in the Bible.

PICKING UP THE ASSIGNMENT OF ANOTHER

I'm reminded of historical figures in the Bible who did not finish their assignment. One powerful character is Moses. He left an unfinished assignment for the next in line. His successor was Joshua. Moses didn't finish—Joshua had to.

MOSES CAUSED A 30-YEAR PROPHETIC DISCREPANCY

It is interesting to consider that Moses added about 30 years to the plan of God because he took matters into his own hands when he killed the Egyptian man. Often we think God is all controlling and whatever happens must be His will. Well, Moses messed up God's prophetic timeline for the children of Israel by trying to accomplish things in his power and outside the will of God.

I am thankful to Andrew Wommack who brought this thought to my attention. After considering the notion of Moses altering the timeline of the Exodus, it dawned on me that Moses was altering prophecy! It's remarkable that God still worked through Moses like no other in the Old Testament.

Let us look at this deeper for a moment. Acts 7:25 reveals that Moses supposed that the Jews would recognize him as God's deliverer, but they didn't. Moses knew he was a Jew and was called to lead the Jews out of Egypt. But his actions added time to the prophetic word, which declared when the Exodus would happen—Moses' actions altered the 400-year prophecy given to Abraham by 30 years!

> Then He said to Abram: "Know certainly that your descendants will be strangers in a land that is not theirs, and will serve them, and they will afflict them **four hundred years**. [14] And also the nation whom they serve I will judge; afterward they shall come out with great possessions."
>
> **—Genesis 15:13-14**

You can see in Genesis 15:13 that the Lord told Abram that his descendants would be servants in a strange land (Egypt) for 400 years. Then Exodus 12:40-41 (KJV) says, "Now the sojourning of the children of Israel, who dwelt in Egypt, was 430 years. And it came to pass at the end of the 430 years, even the selfsame day it came to pass, that all the hosts of the Lord went out from the land of Egypt."

After the prophetic declaration of 400 years was given, the actual and exact number of years was 430 to the day when the children of Israel came out of Egypt! How is it that there was a 30-year discrepancy between what the Lord spoke prophetically to Abram and what Exodus states?

MOSES WAS TEN YEARS PREMATURE

On God's timeline, Moses was ten years premature. Andrew Wommack says it best:

> If you subtract the 40 years that Moses spent in the wilderness (Acts 7:30) from the 430 years, you will find that Moses killed the Egyptian man and tried to free the Israelites in the 390th year of their captivity. He was ten years premature in trying to fulfill God's will for his life. Moses altered the prophecy by his impulsive behavior, believing he would fulfill what God called him to do.

The problem was that Moses was fulfilling it his way, not God's way or timing! There is a strong word in this scenario, and it might be shocking for many to realize Moses wasn't ready to lead the children of Israel out just yet.

Someone might say that if God wasn't ready for Moses to bring the Israelites out of Egypt then, why didn't He wait to reveal His will to Moses? There could be many reasons, but one main reason is that it would take at least ten years for the Lord to get Moses ready for the job. We wrongly assume that when the Lord puts a vision in our hearts, He is ready to bring it to pass right then.

This is a point to consider when looking at times and seasons. We must surrender to the call of God and allow Him to work it all out in front of us. So many ministers and ambitious people, in general, would save themselves a great deal of pain by heeding and surrendering to God.

There was another occasion in which Moses frustrated the will of God. When the Lord asked him to speak to the rock, causing water to flow in the wilderness, what happened? Moses struck the rock!

> *"Behold, I will stand before you there on the rock in Horeb; and you **shall strike the rock**, and water will come out of it, that the people may drink." And Moses did so in the sight of the elders of Israel.*
>
> —**Exodus 17:6**

> *"Take the rod; you and your brother Aaron gather the congregation together. **Speak to the rock** before their eyes, and it will yield its water; thus you shall bring water for them out of the rock, and give drink to the congregation and their animals." [9] So Moses took the rod from before the Lord as He commanded him. [10] And Moses and Aaron gathered the assembly together before the rock; and he said to them, **"Hear now, you rebels! Must we bring water for you out of this rock?"** [11] Then **Moses lifted his hand and struck the rock twice with his rod; and water came out abundantly**, and the congregation and their animals drank. [12] Then the Lord spoke to Moses and Aaron, **"Because you did not believe Me, to hallow Me in the eyes of the children of Israel, therefore you shall not bring this assembly into the land which I have given them."***
>
> —**Numbers 20:8-12**

Moses was told in the second passage to speak to the rock. Instead, he lifted his staff and struck the rock twice! Resulting in Moses not being allowed to lead the children of Israel into the land of promise. He could not enter.

An interesting point to consider is that those who feel called, do not feel qualified. Rather it is often just the opposite. Many who are called are shocked that God would use them at all! When you think about this, it is good news; meaning if God can use some of these crazy individuals who also didn't feel worthy, He can use you! *Feeling* called has nothing to do with it. What the Bible says is the only thing that matters.

Fulfilling your prophetic destiny requires a discovery of your expression of faith. You just read a few examples from Hebrews 11. Using Jesus as our basis to understand our calling shows us a measurable way to identify our calling.

Remember, God will bless you in your doing. When you get really busy serving and actively participating in the body of Christ through your church or ministry you are aligned with, your calling will manifest itself. Say your prayers, read your Bible, and work diligently and faithfully. This is the fast track to unite with your calling.

INSTITUTIONALIZING A REVELATION

Institutionalizing a revelation means tradition is placed above what God is doing:

> *Making the word of God of no effect through your tradition which you have handed down. And many such things you do.*
>
> **—Mark 7:13**

Systems are necessary when you achieve what the Lord has called you to do. However, those very systems may hinder future generations from taking hold of what God is calling them to do.

Traditions can make the Word of no effect when placed above the Word of God and the wind of the Spirit. Consider the Sanhedrin as an example. An institution started as a blessing and a benefit to Moses for great assistance in governing the people of God.

> Moreover you shall select from all the people able men, such as fear God, men of truth, hating covetousness; and place such over them to be rulers of thousands, rulers of hundreds, rulers of fifties, and rulers of tens. 22 And let them judge the people at all times. Then it will be that every great matter they shall bring to you, but every small matter they themselves shall judge. So it will be easier for you, for they will bear the burden with you.
>
> **—Exodus 18:21-22**

Moses' appointment of this group developed into an assembly of 23 or 71 elders, also known as rabbis, appointed to sit as a tribunal in every city in the ancient land of Israel. A group created for good eventually became institutionalized, holding their own religious traditions above the Word of God. Eventually, what began as a blessing ultimately persecuted Jesus and the early Church. A lesson for us all is that as we develop, we must constantly be sensitive to that fresh word from God so as not to persecute the arriving generation sent by the Holy Spirit.

FULFILLING YOUR PROPHETIC ASSIGNMENT

Can you mess up the plan of God? Well, not entirely, but you can mess up the timing and even disqualify yourself to the point that He is forced to find another to finish the assignment.

Take heart, though, and keep walking with Him! God gives more grace to the humble, and God desires that you win even more than you desire it!

> *Being confident of this very thing, that He who has begun a good work in you will complete it until the day of Jesus Christ.*
>
> —Philippians 1:6

God has a specific assignment for you. This is why you need to hear and discern His Voice as He is always navigating you by the Holy Spirit.

CLOSING THOUGHTS

Here is your takeaway—do whatever God places in front of you with all your heart, cheerfully and with enthusiasm. So that neither you nor I miss what He has purposed through us for our generation in these times and seasons. Watch what He can do through a completely yielded vessel—you!

With everything you have walked through and will experience, settle it in your heart that you will never give up. Keep fine-tuning your spiritual ear to hear His Voice. Keep listening for His highest and best purpose for your life. God wants you to live, move, and have your being in Him. He deeply desires for you to hear Him, communicate with Him, and walk in what He says.

I know for me, this life of following the Spirit has been the most rewarding and crushing venture I could have been part of. Much like you, dear reader, my journey feels as if it is just beginning, and should Jesus tarry, we have a very significant job to accomplish. Think of it, it is much sooner than we all realize when we will be standing before Him in eternity. All the doctrinal issues won't be the focus. All the things we held to so tightly will not carry the substance there as they now do here. You will realize the pain and cost of what you walked through here was nothing compared to the weight of glory and future responsibility there.

Go for it, develop, and obey the Spirit! Read your Bible until it starts talking back to you in your soulish decisions and activities. Jesus wants you to win more than you do; He wants you to hear His Voice more than you want to hear it! This is it, right here, right now—the first moment of the rest of your life.

The day when Jesus returns is getting closer every moment, and you have nothing to lose. Take your calling seriously, take the Voice of God seriously, and you will find yourself on a journey that you were made for. Start living, and dig in. I encourage you to do it now! While it is still daylight, while we still can do things that apply to eternity.

Hearing His Voice will show you that your life matters; your voice filled with His Voice greatly matters. So many are dying to hear one word from God. You can give that to them. Jesus is Lord—He loves you, and there is nothing you can do to stop His love for you! You might as well get to really know Him and the Voice of His Holy Spirit.

Walking in the prophetic is a wonderful journey; and on a bad day, prophetic people are anointed to be the best there is! Remember, this generation needs you—God needs you!

DEAR READER

Dear reader, you mean more to the Kingdom of God than you might realize. Brand this into your heart. A man or woman of God with a revelation is never at the mercy of a culture gone mad! This is you, the one whom God wants to give revelation. He desires that you receive His impartation of clarity and direction. You are, after all, part of His Ekklesia—His only plan to change the world!

Thank you for joining me as we walked through this book together. Prophecy is a vast subject; it has been my desire to share it in a fresh and very grounded manner and in a way that caused it to be understandable and yet retain its power. God led you to this book, don't forget that. Take what you can and use it to serve your generation.

Dear reader, I love you, and as I write this, I'm praying for you. God knows you, God sees you, and He will finish what He started in you.

For Jesus,
Joseph Z

NOTES

1. Chuck Missler, *Learn the Bible in 24 Hours* (Nashville, TN: Thomas Nelson, 2011), 17-18.

2. Zodhiates Hebrew Word Study and Strong's Concordance.

3. M. Kendig, ed., *Alfred Korzybski Collected Writings, 1920-1950* (Forest Hills, NY: Institute of General Semantics, reprint edition, 1990).

4. *Treasury of Scripture Knowledge Commentary*, Ezekiel 12:3.

5. Flavius Josephus, *The Antiquities of the Jews*, translated by William Whiston (1737), 20:9.

6. Ibid., 10.106.

7. Samson H. Levey, *The Messiah: An Aramaic Interpretation: the Messianic Exegesis of the Targum* (Cincinnati, OH: Hebrew Union College-Jewish Institute of Religion, 1974).

8. Daniel 9:24-27; see also "Daniel's 70 Weeks" by Chuck Missler, *Koinonia House*, November 1, 2004; https://www.khouse.org/articles/2004/552/; accessed September 11, 2023.

9. Jordan Gaines Lewis, PhD, "The Neuroscience of Déjà vu," *PsychologyToday.com*, August 14, 2012; https://www.psychologytoday.com/us/blog/brain-babble/201208/the-neuroscience-d-j-vu; accessed September 11, 2023.

10. F. Bartolomei, et.al., "Cortical stimulation study of the role of rhinal cortex in déjà vu and reminiscence of memories," *NIH, Neurology*, September 14, 2004; https://pubmed.ncbi.nlm.nih.gov/15365137/; accessed September 11, 2023. Also, Fabrice Bartolomei, et.al., "Rhinal-hippocampal interactions during déjà vu; https://www.researchgate.net/publication/51649111_Rhinal-hippocampal_interactions_during_deja_vu; accessed September 11, 2023.

11 The Oxford Dictionary of the Christian Church (OUP Oxford), 5330.

12. Rick Renner, *Apostles and Prophets: Their Roles in the Past, Present, and Last-Days Church* (Shippensburg, PA: Harrison House Publishers, 2023).

13. "Preterism" means holding that the prophecies in the Bible about the end times have already been fulfilled, according to Merriam-Webster Dictionary.

14. Josephus, *The Antiquities of the Jews*, l. 6. c. 2. sect. 2.

ABOUT JOSEPH Z

Joseph Z is a Bible teacher, author, broadcaster, and international prophetic voice. Before the age of nine, he began encountering the voice of God through dreams and visions. This resulted in a journey that has led him to dedicate his life to the preaching of the gospel and the teaching of the Bible, often followed by prophetic ministry.

For nearly three decades, Joseph planted churches, founded Bible schools, preached stadium events, and held schools of the prophets around the world. Joseph and his wife Heather ministered together for 15 years and made the decision in 2012 to start Z Ministries, a media and conference-based ministry. During this time, they traveled the United States, taking along with them a traveling studio team live broadcasting from a new location several times a week. A season came when Heather became very ill due to hereditary kidney failure. After three years of dialysis and several miracles, she received a miracle kidney transplant. Joseph and Heather decided to stop everything, they laid everything down and ministered to their family for nearly three years.

In 2017 Joseph had an encounter with the Lord and received the word to "go live every weekday morning"—Monday through Friday. What started with him, Heather, and a small group of viewers, has turned into a large and faithful online broadcast family. Today, his live broadcasts are reaching millions every month with the gospel and current events—which he has labeled "prophetic journalism." He additionally interviews some of the leading voices in the Church, government, and the culture.

He and his wife, Heather, have two adult children who faithfully work alongside them. Joseph's favorite saying when ending letters, books, or written articles is, "for Jesus." As, "for the testimony of Jesus is the spirit of prophecy." —Revelation 19:10

Joseph spends his time with his family, writing books, broadcasting, and training others in the Word of God.

From
JOSEPH Z

Thriving in God's Supernatural Economy

There's a war being fought over you! The Kingdom of God offers you divine provision while the Kingdom of Hell fights for territory in your life as a crisis looms on the world's horizon.

Will you break free of Hell's economy? International prophet and Bible teacher Joseph Z say it's urgent to break free now as we rapidly plunge into global difficulties involving worldwide market collapse, bank closures, a digital one-world currency, power grids failing, cyber war, medical deception, natural catastrophes, and unprecedented international conflict.

In *Breaking Hell's Economy*, Joseph makes it clear that we're at a destination in history that requires a revelation of God's supernatural economy—your ultimate defense against rising darkness.

Lay hold of this revelation, defy Hell, and live your life knowing you are destined to thrive in the last days!

Purchase your copy wherever books are sold

Joseph and Heather have ministered together for over 20 years; with a passion to see others be all they are called to be. For many years, Joseph & Heather have had the heart to offer life-changing materials and teaching at no cost to the body of Christ. Today, they have made that a reality by offering various media resources and biblical training free of charge. Joseph and Heather currently reside in Colorado Springs, CO with their two children, Alison and Daniel.

Learn more at
www.josephz.com

For Further Information

If you would like prayer or for further information about Joseph Z Ministries, please call our offices at

(719) 257-8050
or visit **josephz.com/contact**

Visit JosephZ.Com for additional materials